Guerrilla Marketing

GUERRILLA MARKETING

VOLUME THREE

Advertising and Marketing Definitions, Ideas, Tactics, Examples, and Campaigns to Inspire Your Business Success

**JASON MYERS
MERRILEE KIMBLE
JAY CONRAD LEVINSON**

NEW YORK

LONDON • NASHVILLE • MELBOURNE • VANCOUVER

GUERRILLA MARKETING

Advertising and Marketing Definitions, Ideas, Tactics, Examples, and Campaigns to Inspire Your Business Success, Volume 3

© 2023 Jason Myers, Jay Conrad Levinson, Merrilee Kimble

All rights reserved. No portion of this book may be reproduced, stored in a retrieval system, or transmitted in any form or by any means—electronic, mechanical, photocopy, recording, scanning, or other—except for brief quotations in critical reviews or articles, without the prior written permission of the publisher.

Published in New York, New York, by Morgan James Publishing. Morgan James is a trademark of Morgan James, LLC. www.MorganJamesPublishing.com

Proudly distributed by Ingram Publisher Services.

ISBN 9781631958274 paperback
ISBN 9781631958281 ebook
Library of Congress Control Number: 2021950223

Cover Design by:
Rachel Lopez
www.r2cdesign.com

Interior Design by:
Chris Treccani
www.3dogcreative.net

Morgan James is a proud partner of Habitat for Humanity Peninsula and Greater Williamsburg. Partners in building since 2006.

Get involved today! Visit MorganJamesPublishing.com/giving-back

We dedicate this book to the memory of Jay Conrad Levinson who began a global movement and has inspired us to continue his legacy of helping businesses grow and thrive.

CONTENTS

Acknowledgments xi
Preface xii
Welcome To Volume Three xiii
What Makes This Volume of Books Unique? xiv
Introduction xvi

SECTION I   The Strong Foundation of Guerrilla Marketing Success   1
Overview 2
1.11 | Intelligent Guerrilla Marketing 6
1.12 | Endurance 10
1.13 | Consumer Decision-Making 12
1.14 | Business Foundation 14
1.15 | Implementation 17
1.16 | Brand Marketing 19
1.17 | Alignment 21

SECTION II   Guerrilla Maximedia Marketing   25
2.16 | Testing 27
2.17 | Attribution 30
2.18 | Optimization 34
2.19 | Alternate Out-of-Home (OOH and DOOH) Advertising 37

SECTION III   Guerrilla Minimedia Marketing   41
3.30 | Shop the Block 43
3.31 | Pop-Up 46
3.32 | Experiential Marketing 48
3.33 | Proof 51

SECTION IV   Guerrilla E-Media Marketing   53
4.57 | Marketing and Sales Funnels 56
4.58 | Opt-In Forms 60
4.59 | Social Selling 62
4.60 | Social Commerce 65

4.61 | Customer Relationship Management Platforms (CRMs) — 66
4.62 | Digital Attribution — 68
4.63 | Online B2B Networking — 70
4.64 | Social Linking — 73
4.65 | Artificial Intelligence (AI) Overview — 74
4.66 | AI Marketing Copy and Content — 77
4.67 | AI Audio and Video — 79
4.68 | AI and Marketing Performance — 80
4.69 | AI Creativity — 82
4.70 | Nimble — 83
4.71 | Timing — 84
4.72 | Unsubscribe — 88
4.73 | Responsive Search Ads — 89

SECTION V   Guerrilla Info-Media Marketing — 91
5.19 | Creating Sharable Content — 93
5.20 | Creating Personalized Content — 98
5.21 | Creating Sellable Content — 101
5.22 | Advertorials and Magalogs — 103
5.23 | Creating Social Desire — 105

SECTION VI   Guerrilla Human-Media Marketing — 107
6.23 | Appealing to Emotions — 109
6.24 | Business Personality — 112
6.25 | Appealing to Needs — 114
6.26 | Conversation Starters — 115
6.27 | Calibration — 118
6.28 | Inside Out — 121
6.29 | Motivate — 122
6.30 | Consumer Intentions — 124

SECTION VII   Guerrilla Non-Media Marketing — 127
7.24 | Exclusive Experiences — 129
7.25 | Unlimited — 131
7.26 | Unexpected — 133
7.27 | Customer Spotlight — 134

7.28 | Cycling — 136
7.29 | Blockchain Solutions — 137
7.30 | Irresistible — 140

SECTION VIII Guerrilla Company Attributes — 143
8.43 | Being Memorable — 146
8.44 | Customer Lifetime Value (CLV or LTV) — 149
8.45 | The Power of Color — 153
8.46 | Appeal to the Senses — 155
8.47 | AI Business Optimization — 157
8.48 | Balancing Act — 160
8.49 | Perception and Reality — 161
8.50 | Ideal Customers — 162
8.51 | International Expansion — 165
8.52 | International Fulfillment and Shipping — 168
8.53 | Longevity — 170
8.54 | Customer Segmentation — 172
8.55 | Lead Scoring — 174
8.56 | Ideal Employees — 176
8.57 | Disruption — 178

SECTION IX Guerrilla Company Attitudes — 181
9.27 | Unconventional — 184
9.28 | Skilled Thinking — 186
9.29 | Relationship Builder — 191
9.30 | A Superb Listener — 192
9.31 | Focused on Success — 194
9.32 | Mystery Shopping — 195
9.33 | Thirst for Knowledge — 197
9.34 | Right People, Right Places — 198
9.35 | Customer First — 199

SECTION X Guerrilla Marketing Case Studies — 201
Introduction — 202
Guerrilla Marketing Case Study 9 — 203
Guerrilla Marketing Case Study 10 — 207

| Guerrilla Marketing Case Study 11 | 212 |
| Guerrilla Marketing Case Study 12 | 216 |

SECTION XI   125+ Free Tools — 221
125+ Free Tools to Propel Your Guerrilla Marketing Success into Profits — 222

SECTION XII   Guerrilla Marketing Definitions — 253
The Definitions — 254

Authors Note	275
Guerrilla Club	277
What the Guerrilla Marketing Book Series Will Do for You and Your Business	278
About the Authors	280
Endnotes	284
Index	296

ACKNOWLEDGMENTS

We want to extend our appreciation to:

David Hancock and the Morgan James Publishing family. They share our gratitude for what Guerrilla Marketing has done to help businesses succeed for several decades. They also share our passion for how Guerrilla Marketing will continue to help businesses everywhere to understand what marketing really is and how it works for their success.

Cortney Donelson of vocem, LLC, whose ease, skill, and dedication make book editing a delight.

All the successful Guerrilla marketers that have proven, over the last several decades, that intelligent Guerrilla Marketing is supported with knowledge, low-cost, unconventional, and creative tactics that convey and promote their compelling product(s), service(s), and ideas to drive limitless profits.

Lastly, and very importantly, we want to extend our appreciation for all the people whose dream is to take their idea and create, grow, and eventually sell or hand off their profitable business. To turn that dream into a successful business requires seizing proven techniques, such as Guerrilla Marketing, which uniquely set their business apart from the competition.

PREFACE

When Jay Conrad Levinson wrote *Guerrilla Marketing*, he stated his vision:

> *Guerrilla Marketing simplifies the complexities and explains how entrepreneurs can use marketing to generate maximum profits from minimum investments. Put another way, this book can help make a small business big. This book can help an individual entrepreneur make a lot of money as painlessly as possible. Often, the only factor that determines success or failure is the way in which a product or service is marketed. The information in these pages will arm you for success and alert you to the shortcomings that lead to failure.*

We're proud to have been selected to carry the torch forward with Guerrilla Marketing and to continue to level the playing field for entrepreneurs. Guerrilla Marketing shows entrepreneurs, businesses, and people with a burning idea they want to turn into a business all the ways they can be intelligent and successful marketers. In doing so, they lead their businesses to growth, impact, and profitability for the benefit of themselves and their families, employees, customers, community, as well as the world at large.

WELCOME TO VOLUME THREE

We're thrilled you have selected to add Volume Three to your collection of the all-new series of *Guerrilla Marketing* books. This volume is packed with more tools, tips, and examples to grow your success.

Guerrilla Marketing is a 360-degree, consistent methodology that weaves through every aspect of your business. Each of your marketing tactics is woven together with others. Therefore, in each volume, we refer you to other related sections and tactics, within this book and other volumes, to help your business weave your marketing together for 360 degrees of powerful and consistent Guerrilla Marketing.

Guerrilla Marketing is intelligent marketing that utilizes knowledge, strategy, and a plan supported with a toolbox of tactics. With the all-new series of *Guerrilla Marketing* books, you have a toolbox of low-cost, unconventional, and creative tactics to choose from to convey and promote your compelling product(s) or service(s) and drive your competition mad.

WHAT MAKES THIS VOLUME OF BOOKS UNIQUE?

Guerrilla marketers are unique, and they know it and promote it. Therefore, we had to ask ourselves: "How can we make this all-new series of books unique?" After all, Guerrilla Marketing, since the original Guerrilla Marketing book was introduced in 1984, has supported and empowered entrepreneurs, small and medium-sized businesses, solopreneurs, and people with ideas they want to turn into a business to:

- Start and/or build successful Guerrilla businesses
- Understand why and how marketing works, why Guerrilla Marketing is intelligent marketing, and your toolbox of options
- Weave the consistent methodology of Guerrilla Marketing through every aspect of their business
- Create profits for the benefit of themselves, their families, their employees, their community, and the world at large
- Tap into their Guerrilla Creativity to create highly profitable marketing
- Utilize Guerrilla Creative strategies to ensure that their Guerrilla Marketing tactics hit the target
- Create and execute their Guerrilla Marketing plan and Guerrilla Creative and Advertising strategy
- Utilize consistency in their marketing to build familiarity which, in turn, builds trust; and that trust creates sales, repeat purchases, and precious referrals from their customers
- Define the authentic attitudes of their business and use the power of authenticity in their marketing
- Identify their company attributes and consistently make their prospects and customers aware of them in their marketing and advertising
- Track their marketing to build on their successes and remove their unsuccessful efforts
- Make the truth fascinating
- Thrive with low-cost tactics
- Thrive with unconventional tactics
- Deliver their marketing tactics with creative, low-cost, and unconventional methods

- Upend their competition, big and small
- Sell their successful businesses and start all over again or perfect their favorite pastime as their full-time endeavor
- Win, on purpose

Where does it all begin? That's a simple answer: with a strong foundation of Guerrilla Marketing. In Volume 1, we reviewed the strong foundational elements of Guerrilla Marketing. We'll also provide a summary in this book, in Section I, called "The Strong Foundation of Guerrilla Marketing Success." It will be a great refresher for those who are currently using Guerrilla Marketing tactics in their business and a good overview for those who are new to Guerrilla Marketing.

For those who are new to Guerrilla Marketing (or those who want to learn more), we'll take it online with a FREE companion course (visit gMarketing.com/Club) to help you build your rock-solid Guerrilla Marketing foundation. In the companion course, we'll dive deeper with video tutorials, exercises, and the tools you'll need to build that crucial foundation from which your Guerrilla Marketing success will be born. Please know this: Businesses that fail have a poor foundation. If you build your castle on a poor foundation, don't be surprised when it collapses into rubble.

We'll spend the remaining sections of the book building on the tactics, tools, tips, and examples from Volume 1 and Volume 2 as we continue to share more of today's Guerrilla Marketing tactics, tools, and tips (many of which are free). In Volume 3, we have numerous new Guerrilla Marketing tools, tactics, and tips to give you even more options to choose from.

These Guerrilla Marketing tactics, tools, and tips are options that every business needs to succeed and generate profits. With the addition of each volume in your collection, you have a toolbox packed full of information and resources to choose from to build a strong Guerrilla business and drive your competition mad.

In our FREE companion course, you'll also find a growing list of tools and resources to help you going forward. In addition, you'll find many examples at gMarketing.com/Club to give you a head start. We are thrilled to continue Jay Conrad Levison's vision, and we're thrilled for the profits you'll generate in the pages that follow.

INTRODUCTION

Whether you realize it or not, you're marketing with every interaction you and everyone in your business have, inside and outside of your business. Therefore, be intentional about it and reap the rewards.

Guerrilla Marketing is intelligent marketing that utilizes knowledge, strategy, and a plan that is supported with a toolbox of low-cost, unconventional, and creative tactics to choose from to convey and promote a compelling product or service. Guerrilla Marketing makes the truth fascinating. Guerrilla Marketing turns knowledge, time, energy, imagination, and information into profits.

Guerrilla Marketing was introduced to the world in a self-titled book in 1984, by Jay Conrad Levinson, as an unconventional system of marketing that relies on knowledge, time, energy, and imagination rather than a big marketing budget.

We are continuing Jay Conrad Levison's unconventional system of marketing. By revealing not only what marketing is but why it works, we give small and medium-sized businesses (SMBs) the opportunity to think and grow big. When you understand the power of your SMB and what you can do with Guerrilla Marketing, it not only levels the playing field with your competition but also tilts the playing field to your advantage.

The pillars of Guerrilla Marketing are as strong today as they were decades ago when it was introduced to the world. The tactics, tools, and tips are continually evolving, and our desire is to keep you at the forefront of Guerrilla Marketing.

Whether you're an entrepreneur, SMB, or solopreneur, we understand that your business (or your idea that you want to turn into a business) is your dream, and you will never settle. What do you plan to do with your precious opportunity? Will you succeed beyond your wildest expectations? Will you give in to doubt and fold?

Guerrilla Marketing exists to give you a toolbox of tactics, tools, and tips to choose from to succeed beyond your wildest expectations. Your marketing options are growing faster than ever, and we are committed to keeping your toolbox full with this new volume in our new series of Guerrilla Marketing books. If you haven't already done so, we encourage you to pick up a copy of Volume 1 and Volume 2, which are packed with tactics, tools, tips, and examples. If you've already done so, we want to extend our heartfelt gratitude.

To implement Guerrilla Marketing is to challenge yourself and/or your business to learn and implement intelligent marketing. You can stick to what you're doing now with your marketing. You can stick with what others are telling you to do with your marketing. Or you can challenge yourself to understand Guerrilla Marketing and implement it to your full advantage.

The simple question is: Will you act and succeed, or will you fold? We think you're ready to act and claim your success, so let's get to it.

Many business owners think marketing is a light switch that you turn on and off. Therefore, they conduct their marketing activities as if they are turning the switch on and off. As an SMB, you can perform excellent marketing as easily as you can perform poor marketing.

Fortunately, for those who wisely choose to understand and implement Guerrilla Marketing in their business, they understand that the light switch is always on, and the lights are always shining brightly. With the bright lights on, Guerrilla marketers are intentional with their marketing efforts, and precious profits are their rewards.

Many businesses fail to utilize Guerrilla Marketing to its fullest benefit. They do so by failing to execute the Guerrilla Marketing fundamentals, which guide your marketing and allow you to perform 360 degrees of intelligent, impactful, and consistent marketing that drives profits for your business. Instead of mastering the fundamentals, they jump right to the tactics and implement them like light switches—turning them on and off and flipping from one to another without a plan, strategy, consistency, repetition, or an understanding of who their prospects and customers are or who their business is and how it's seen in the marketplace.

Why? Many think it's not exciting or necessary to build a strong marketing foundation for their business. However, Guerrilla marketers understand that their strong marketing foundation is where their Guerrilla Marketing success is born.

Guerrilla Marketing isn't simply about implementing tactics that appeal to customers and prospects. It's a 360-degree, consistent methodology that weaves through every aspect of your business. A strong, successful Guerrilla business is built on a Guerrilla Marketing foundation that keeps you focused on, in part:

- Why marketing works

- Who your prospects and customers are, the problems you want to solve, and the way you want those problems solved
- Being clear as you tell your prospects and customers what you can do for them
- Caring about and knowing who your customers are, why they make additional purchases, and why they refer friends, family, and associates
- The input and opinions of your prospects, customers, employees, vendors, and community that can lead to long-term satisfaction, success, and profits
- Why ongoing relationships build your business
- What makes your business unique and fascinating and how to make sure everyone knows about it
- Why you're better than the competition and making sure everyone knows your advantages
- Why measuring your marketing and measuring your creativity turns into profits
- Understanding that you're marketing with every interaction, so you're intentional about it
- The power of consistency and repetition

As an entrepreneur, SMB, or solopreneur, you need Guerrilla Marketing more than ever because the competition is smarter, more sophisticated, and even more aggressive than ever before. Fortunately, that is not a problem for successful Guerrilla marketers.

If your competition is a large business, you may find that they employ some Guerrilla Marketing tactics, but they don't have the advantages that you do as a smaller business. As a smaller business, you are nimble, engaged, and focused, which is the rich fertilizer that your Guerrilla Marketing needs to bloom.

More than ever before, consumers receive "vanilla" or "one-size-fits-all" service from large companies. That creates the perfect opportunity for you to utilize Guerrilla Marketing to make your business shine.

Guerrilla Marketing takes a quality product or service and sets it apart from the competition. How?

We'd venture a bold guess that fewer than ten percent of the new and existing small-business owners have a plan or strategy. Additionally, they have likely explored less than a dozen of the marketing tools and tactics available to them. Guerrilla marketers, on the other hand, recognize that the more they understand how and why marketing works, combined with their plan, strategy, Guerrilla Creativity, and a toolbox of options, the better they will be able to take the right action that creates the right results.

Businesses that implement Guerrilla Marketing have a tremendous advantage over businesses that don't. The business that implements Guerrilla Marketing is ridiculously hard to replicate, and that makes their business unique.

That uniqueness makes their business more valuable. That increased value means that as the business grows, larger businesses are more likely to want to partner with or acquire the business. Without the unique advantages of that business, due to their successful Guerrilla Marketing efforts, the larger business wouldn't see their value. They would just replicate the business model and dominate the smaller business by competing with them.

If you're not where you want to be, it's a good indicator that there is more you can do. Guerrilla Marketing helps you to realize every facet of marketing—and the more you know, the more you can achieve.

In the wise words of Jay Conrad Levinson in the book Guerrilla Marketing:

> *Guerrilla Marketing is always intentional. It pays close attention to all the details of contact with the outside world, ignoring nothing, and realizing the stunning importance of those tiny but supercharged details.*

Guerrilla Marketing is about getting all of the details right so that when you deploy an attention-getting Guerrilla Marketing tactic, it works. Why does that make sense?

As an answer, let's look at an example If you drive by a business and see a street team or group of picketers, you're likely to look. Then you notice they are holding clever signs that promote the business and ask you to honk because you love this business. If you find it clever, amusing, or intriguing, your reaction will likely be to inquire via word of mouth (e.g., ask a friend) or look the business up (e.g., search engines, social media), whatever you prefer.

Street teams and friendly picketers are versatile (handing out samples, directing people to their location, working a booth at an event, etc.), and they can garner attention and pique the interest of your prospects and customers. However, it's what happens next that determines if that piqued interest will be turned into profits. Now is the time when your attention to the details (great reviews, a clear and compelling description of the business and what makes it unique, easy-to-access hours, and contact information) will make that attention turn prospects into customers.

If the business gets people's attention, but then it's hard to find in an online search or its marketing is disconnected, its prospects:
- Aren't sure about the business and become skeptical
- See that its social media looks different than its website, which makes them more skeptical
- Can't understand the copy because the fonts are hard to read, and they find the graphics unappealing
- Find its hours and contact information are inconvenient, incomplete, or missing

That's a business that views marketing as a series of disconnected gimmicks, or it's a business that thinks marketing is a light switch they turn on and off. That business takes action, but it doesn't understand how to set itself apart with good Guerrilla Marketing.

Energy alone is not enough. One disconnected marketing gimmick, designed to get attention, is not the way. Equally, Guerrilla Marketing always obeys the highest code of ethics and is authentic and honest. Illegal, dishonest, or unethical acts are never a part of Guerrilla Marketing.

Energy must be directed by intelligence. Successful Guerrilla businesses are intelligently designed and operated from the outside in (from the customers' point of view, needs, desires, and expectations), not the inside out. They are designed with forward and backward thinking. Equally, those businesses use intelligent marketing, which is Guerrilla Marketing.

Successful Guerrilla Marketing means prospects experience a business that's:
- Easy to find in an online search and whose social is consistent with its website
- Convenient to reach, in the way the prospects want to reach it
- Clear and appealing while it quickly explains a relatable problem and is compelling with how it solves it
- Unique and has several competitive advantages

The Guerrilla business has appealing and consistent marketing while being easy and convenient to do business with. Because the business has carefully and consistently executed its marketing, it builds familiarity with its prospects, and that familiarity allows the business's quality product(s) or service(s) to shine. Guerrilla Marketing emphasizes the truth that consistency builds familiarity;

familiarity builds trust, and trust creates sales, repeat purchases, and precious referrals, which is the fuel for long-term success.

Often, the only factor that determines the success or failure of a business is the way they market their product(s) or service(s). Businesses who are successful Guerrillas get it right because they know the secrets of intelligent Guerrilla Marketing.

Guerrilla Marketing is a 360-degree consistent methodology that weaves through every aspect of your business. If you want to succeed with Guerrilla Marketing, and we know you do and can, let's get started with building a strong marketing foundation from which your Guerrilla Marketing success will be born.

To implement Guerrilla Marketing, it's time to challenge yourself and/or your business to implement intelligent marketing and use it to your full advantage. You'll begin in "Section I" by building your strong marketing foundation by focusing your energy and underscoring your understanding of:

- Research and Knowing
- Guerrilla Creativity
- Unique Selling Proposition (USP)
- Guerrilla Marketing Ten-Word Profit Challenge
- Guerrilla Marketing Plan Challenge
- Guerrilla Creative and Advertising Strategy Challenge
- A Guerrilla Marketing Calendar

To understand the role and importance of each of these building blocks for your strong marketing foundation, we'll first provide an overview in this book.

For those of you who are new to Guerrilla Marketing (or those who want to learn more), we encourage you to next take it online for your FREE companion course (visit gMarketing.com/Club). In the companion course, we'll dive deeper with video tutorials, exercises, and the tools you'll need to build that crucial foundation for your Guerrilla Marketing success.

With your rock-solid marketing foundation established, it's time for options. The tools, tips, and tactics that begin with "Section II" are the fuel you need to create success and profits for your business. Throughout the book, we will reference correlating sections to help you build your toolbox.

We're excited to see you unleash your Guerrilla Creativity and guide your business to success beyond your wildest expectations.

Section I

The Strong Foundation of Guerrilla Marketing Success

Overview

Guerrilla Marketing is intelligent marketing that's built on knowledge and a rock-solid Guerrilla Marketing foundation. In Volume 1, we addressed those elements in detail. We encourage you, to maximize your success, to invest the time to establish your strong foundation with Volume 1.

In summary:

Research and Knowing

Effective Guerrilla Marketing starts with market research and defining your target market or prospects. Your market research time is the important time that you spend on your business, instead of in your business.

Think about marketing as a continuous and ever-growing game of darts. Your marketing is the dart, and your prospects (and customers) are the dartboard. However, both the darts and dartboard evolve and change over time.

In Volume 1, we provided the tools and resources that you need to learn about and keep up with your ever-changing prospects and customers. See Volume 1, Section 1.1, "Research and Knowing," for more information.

Guerrilla Creativity

The ability to tap into and stoke your Guerrilla Creativity isn't by chance. The more you know about marketing, and the more you know about your customers and prospects, the more creative your ideas will be.

In Volume 1, we addressed how to generate and measure your Guerrilla Creativity. See Volume 1, Section 1.2, "Guerrilla Creativity," for more information.

Unique Selling Proposition (USP)

A USP is a unique selling proposition. Your USP represents one of your greatest marketing opportunities. Most businesses neither promote nor have identified their USP. Your USP is your proprietary competitive advantage that is stated clearly and succinctly.

In Volume 1, we provided the four traits an effective USP needs. What is unique about your business is what makes it interesting and memorable, so promote it. Guerrilla marketers don't let their USP remain a secret. See Volume 1, Section 1.3, "Unique Selling Proposition (USP)," for more information.

Guerrilla Marketing Ten-Word Profit Challenge

The Guerrilla Marketing ten-word profit challenge is designed to help your business drive profits. In ten words, you'll express your core concept, make a memorable statement that will build familiarity, and compel your prospects to want to learn more.

In Volume 1, we provided exercises to help you determine the ten words that can help your marketing compel your prospects to notice your business and for your customers to want to make repeat purchases and provide precious referrals of their friends, family, and associates. See Volume 1, Section 1.4, "Guerrilla Marketing Ten-Word Profit Challenge," for more information.

Guerrilla Marketing Plan Challenge

Guerrilla Marketing is first and foremost focused on a core idea. All of your marketing must be an extension of that core idea: advertising, direct mailing, USP, sales presentations, packaging, online presence, uniforms, store design, innovation, etc.

Fortunately, Guerrilla Marketing is a 360-degree, consistent methodology that weaves through every aspect of your business. To succeed, it isn't enough to have a better idea; you need to have a focused plan and strategy.

In Volume 1, we provided a simple formula to help you develop a Guerrilla Marketing plan that you can commit to. That plan, which changes over time, will help you remain focused as you consistently market and advertise your business. See Volume 1, Section 1.5, "Guerrilla Marketing Plan Challenge," for more information.

Guerrilla Creative and Advertising Strategy Challenge

If you don't know it already, advertising and marketing are different. You're marketing with every bit of interaction you have with your business—with employees, prospects, customers, and the outside world.

Advertising, on the other hand, is a part of marketing your product(s) and/or service(s). Advertising is effective when it's done in combination with your consistent marketing.

In Volume 1, we provided clarity about your creative strategy and what you're offering (i.e., the benefits of your product or service) to your prospects and customers so you can develop a clear call to action that tells them exactly what you want them to do. See Volume 1, Section 1.6, "Guerrilla Creative and Advertising Strategy Challenge," for more information.

Guerrilla Marketing Calendar

A Guerrilla Marketing calendar enables you to take your successes and move them forward into the next year. By taking the time to document your efforts and grade their success, you focus your efforts and track your progress.

In Volume 1, we addressed the importance of tracking your results. By taking the time to analyze your results, you'll quickly be doing more of what works and less of what doesn't. See Volume 1, Section 1.7, "Guerrilla Marketing Calendar," for more information.

Your Strong Foundation

With a rock-solid Guerrilla Marketing foundation in place, you're then ready to proceed with ideas, examples, and tactics of Guerrilla Marketing. Guerrilla Marketing ideas, examples, and tactics are amazingly effective when they are utilized properly and in combination. Utilize and test as many as fit with your target audience research, customer knowledge, Guerrilla Marketing plan, and Guerrilla Creative and Advertising strategy.

With your Guerrilla Marketing calendar, you'll track your tactics and follow-up to remove what's not working. You'll then do more of what's working and add new tactics. The more you do well, the harder life is for your competition.

Many businesses, big and small, view marketing as a series of disconnected gimmicks. Different messages, different colors, different fonts, different target markets, and different tactics. Fortunately for you, you're not most businesses.

With Guerrilla Marketing, you'll benefit from the power of a combination of marketing initiatives that consistently market your business. Never forget that consistency builds familiarity; familiarity builds trust, and trust creates sales, repeat purchases, and precious referrals—and that is the path to profits.

The simple and powerful act of consistently marketing the right message to the right audience will rocket your success far above and beyond that of other businesses. While you're basking in the simplicity of your success with Guerrilla Marketing, you'll notice that other businesses (hopefully your competition) are struggling with their marketing.

Those other businesses may have success from time to time, but you'll notice they use disconnected gimmicks, and they turn their marketing on and off like a light switch. They also focus on price over value, sameness over uniqueness, and irrelevant benefits. Those businesses are constantly in pursuit of new customers because their existing customers do not make repeat purchases or recommend the business to their friends, family, co-workers, and social followers.

Our Guerrilla Marketing ideas, examples, and tactics are segmented into several categories:
- Guerrilla Maximedia Marketing
- Guerrilla Minimedia Marketing
- Guerrilla E-Media Marketing
- Guerrilla Info-Media Marketing
- Guerrilla Human-Media Marketing
- Guerrilla Non-Media Marketing
- Guerrilla Company Attributes
- Guerrilla Company Attitudes

These categories are classic to Guerrilla Marketing, but the toolbox of examples and tactics within them are ever-evolving and growing, and in each volume of this all-new Guerrilla Marketing series of books, we'll give you the latest tools and tactics to succeed right now. You'll find a broad array of tactics that will help you find the right combination for your business. Utilize them properly and test as many as fit with your target audience research, customer knowledge, Guerrilla Marketing plan, and Guerrilla Creative and Advertising strategy. Keep in mind that Guerrilla marketers don't jump straight into executing a mix of tactics without first creating a strong foundation.

Guerrilla Marketing should be thought of as a band, or even as an orchestra. The individual pieces of your marketing and advertising (i.e., the instruments)—when beautifully playing the same song in perfect harmony—contribute to an extraordinary piece of music that people enjoy hearing over and over. However, when one or more pieces are out of harmony (or playing a different song), it's the kind of music that people either never notice or, worse, they press dislike or skip or change the station.

Visit gMarketing.com/Club to access your free companion course and a simple Guerrilla Marketing calendar example.

As a reminder, in Volume 1, we addressed:
1.1   Research and Knowing
1.2   Guerrilla Creativity
1.3   Unique Selling Proposition (USP)

1.4	Guerrilla Marketing Ten-Word Profit Challenge
1.5	Guerrilla Marketing Plan Challenge
1.6	Guerrilla Creative and Advertising Strategy Challenge
1.7	Guerrilla Marketing Calendar

In Volume 2, we addressed:

1.8	Crucial Skills for Effectively Using Guerrilla Marketing
1.9	Guerrilla Marketing Consistency
1.10	Guerrilla Marketing Repetition

Now, we'll pick up where we left off. Without further ado, let's get started.

1.11 * INTELLIGENT GUERRILLA MARKETING

Now that we have reached Volume 3, it's a good time to take a moment and break down, why intelligent marketing is Guerrilla Marketing. Let's begin, as we stated in the Introduction to Volume 1, with:

> *Energy alone is not enough. Energy must be directed by intelligence. Successful Guerrilla businesses are intelligently designed and operated from the outside in (from the customers' point of view, needs, desires, and expectations), not the inside out. They are designed with forward and backward thinking. Equally, those businesses use intelligent marketing, which is Guerrilla Marketing.*

Guerrilla Marketing begins with your idea, product(s), and/or service(s) that you want to share with others while bringing revenue and profit into being. When you're getting started, you have a lot of marketing questions, and the answers are found in intelligent Guerrilla Marketing.

With your idea, product(s), and/or service(s) in mind, you first build your rock-solid Guerrilla Marketing foundation. Throughout this section (Section I in each volume), you're building that rock-solid Guerrilla Marketing foundation.

With that rock-solid foundation, you're well on your way to implementing intelligent Guerrilla Marketing.

You're continually researching and getting to know your prospects and/or customers and understanding what motivates them to take action, make purchases, and refer their friends, family, and associates to your business. To do so, these are the prior sections to which you can refer:

- Volume 1, Section 1.1, "Research and Knowing"
- Volume 1, Section 6.8, "Guerrilla Marketing Insight"
- Volume 1, Section 6.9, "Consumer Behavior"
- Volume 2, Section 6.17, "Consumer Mindset"
- Section 1.13, "Consumer Decision-Making"
- Section 6.30, "Consumer Intentions"
- Section 9.29, "Relationship Builder"

As we referenced in Volume 1, Section 6.8, "Guerrilla Marketing Insight," intelligent Guerrilla Marketing is a circular process:

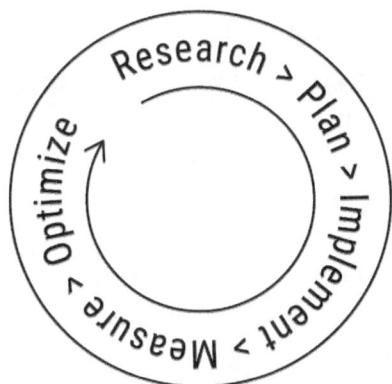

If you're just beginning, to attract customers, you may choose to broadcast your marketing message to the largest possible group of your prospects, which are the people who have certain common identifiable geographic, demographic, and/or psychographic criteria. Examples include:

- Demographics: age, education level, occupation, income, etc.
- Psychographics: activities, interests, opinions, involvement, etc.

The more you know and/or learn about your prospects, the more you can change how you market to them with your Guerrilla Maximedia Marketing (see Section II), Guerrilla Minimedia Marketing (see Section III), Guerrilla E-Media

Marketing (see Section IV), and Guerrilla Info-Media Marketing (see Section V) tactics. For example:
- Broadcast: marketing to the largest possible audience for your business to share your compelling and engaging information, products, and/or services (e.g., Advanced TV, social live broadcasts, etc.). For some specific examples, see Volume 2, Section 5.17, "Video and Audio Broadcasting," and Section 8.42, "Leveraging Social Live Broadcasting"
- Narrowcast: marketing to a smaller audience vs. broadcast, which allows your marketing message to be more focused on the pain points and pleasure points of your prospects and customers
- Nanocast: marketing to a small and precisely targeted audience that allows your marketing messages to be more personal

When you're broadcasting your marketing message, you want to target prospects with a very high propensity to want, need, and purchase what you are selling. However, since you are marketing to a larger audience, your marketing message, including your call to action, needs to be broadly appealing. By being broadly appealing, you will likely find that your marketing is attracting customers with characteristics (e.g., geographic, demographic, psychographic, etc.) that you have not previously considered.

As you study and learn from those responding to your marketing, you can narrow your audience to those that share the characteristics that make them the most likely to become your customers. In doing so, you can be more specific with your marketing message and your call to action. However, your research must be accurate for your marketing and call to action to result in sales and repeat purchases.

At the same time, you're letting your customers know they are noticed, respected, and valued. Guerrilla marketers understand the importance of their marketing efforts to their existing customers. Throughout this volume of books, you've read many tactics to appeal to your customers, and here are just a few examples:
- Volume 1, Section 6.11, "Satisfied and Delighted Customers"
- Volume 1, Section 3.6, "Personalization"
- Volume 2, Section 7.18, "Customer Loyalty"
- Volume 2, Section 7.21, "Customer Entertainment"
- Section 4.61, "Customer Relationship Management Platforms (CRMs)"
- Section 7.24, "Exclusive Experiences"
- Section 7.27, "Customer Spotlight"

- Section 8.44, "Customer Lifetime Value (CLV or LTV)"

Ongoing tracking, analysis, and measurement (see Volume 2, Section 2.12, "Measurement and Analysis") are vital to intelligent Guerrilla Marketing, and it allows you to:

- Know who your customers are (e.g., geographic, demographic, and/or psychographic characteristics) and where your customers are coming from (e.g., broadcast, narrowcast, nanocast, etc.)
- Understand what marketing messages are motivating them (e.g., pain points, pleasure points, specific call to action, etc.) to make purchases and repeat and/or additional purchases
- Discover which product(s) or service(s) are motivating them
- Know how you're delighting them (e.g., surveys, ratings, reviews, social comments, etc.) and where you can improve
- Identify your ideal customers (see Section 8.50, "Ideal Customers")
- Motivate your customers to provide precious referrals of their friends, family, and associates

With that knowledge, you can do more of what's working and less of what's not. Something that is not working, you choose to lessen while you make simple revisions to improve it, based on what you've learned from your efforts that are working. If it's still not working, it's time to eliminate it. See Section 2.18, "Optimization" for more information.

It's valuable to restate that intelligent Guerrilla Marketing is a circular process of:

Research > Plan > Implement > Measure > Optimize

By following this process, you're persistently evolving your powerful plan. Intelligent Guerrilla Marketing continually seeks to understand and appeal to the customers' ever-evolving points of view, needs, desires, and expectations.

1.12 * ENDURANCE

One of the simplest ways to make your Guerrilla Marketing successful costs you nothing. It's creating your marketing and advertising with endurance in mind. After all, impactful marketing and advertising is a marathon, not a sprint.

When you're creating your marketing, whether it's your logo, meme, or a simple online ad, think to yourself:

- How will this look ten years from now?
- How would this have looked ten years ago?

When your Guerrilla Creativity (see Volume 1, Section 1.2, "Guerrilla Creativity") is focused on endurance, your marketing and advertising are building a brand that has greater recognition. Your job is to compel your prospects to notice your business. First, they become aware of your business (i.e., brand awareness), and second, they recognize your business and the product(s) and/or service(s) associated with it (i.e., brand recognition). Once they do, your call to action must then motivate them to take a desired action (e.g., download an ebook, make a purchase, etc.).

Your existing customers also need to be motivated to make repeat purchases and provide precious referrals of their friends, family, and associates. Your marketing efforts are ideal when they appeal to each aspect (brand awareness, brand recognition, and action) at the same time.

If you're selling product(s) or service(s) that are trendy (e.g., clothing, accessories, electronics, etc.), you can still present that product or service within a framework that is created for endurance. There are many examples, such as:

- Apple: utilizes a consistent and enduring style of solid background images that makes their logo and meme highly visible. In video, they typically show their consistent logo and meme repeatedly
- Gap: allows constantly changing styles to be noticed against a simple background that also lets their logo stand out
- Target: also allows constantly changing styles and products to be noticed against a simple (typically white or red) background and that also lets their logo stand out

Take a few minutes and think of other brands in which you quickly know who is advertising, based on an enduring style that the brand consistently uses. Building your marketing and advertising with endurance in mind gives your

business significant advantages as you achieve brand awareness, brand recognition, and motivate action. Those advantages include:
- Lower marketing costs: your ability to re-use creative marketing and advertising pieces saves you time and money
- Repetition: continual use of the same or similar compelling creative marketing and advertising helps your business be top-of-mind with your prospects and customers. At the same time, repeating your logo and/or meme and tagline throughout works to your advantage. For example, your video marketing that features your logo on the uniforms, vehicles, storefront, and the product(s) or service(s) featured in the video will work to increase your brand awareness and recognition while you're motivating them to take action (see Volume 2, Section 1.10, "Guerrilla Marketing Repetition" for more information)
- Consistency: just as repetition builds familiarity, so does consistency throughout every bit of your marketing. The consistent use of your logo, meme, tagline, and business name works to your advantage (see Volume 2, Section 1.9, "Guerrilla Marketing Consistency" for more information)

When your business is creating your marketing and advertising with endurance in mind, your prospects and customers will find your business as compelling now as they did ten years ago and as they will ten years from now. There are several considerations when you're building your marketing and advertising with endurance in mind, such as:
- Images: choose clear, compelling, and timeless images
- Backgrounds: simple and uncomplicated backgrounds let your business, product(s), and service(s) stand out. Using a green screen background (for chroma keying) allows you to change out your background with minimal cost. Complicated backgrounds create noise that your business, product(s), and service(s) have to compete with for your customers' attention
- Music: choose enduring sounds instead of music that is tied to a certain time or trend
- Trends: hairstyles, clothing, etc. are always changing. Choosing enduring styles is an advantage

When you build your marketing and advertising with endurance in mind, you are also building your business with endurance in mind.

1.13 * CONSUMER DECISION-MAKING

Guerrilla marketers are wise to understand how decisions are made by consumers. For the sake of clarity, people are consumers, whether they are buying for themselves or buying for their business (i.e., B2B).

In Volume 1, Section 6.9, "Consumer Behavior," we addressed various essential behavioral factors such as:
- Apathy and Repetition
- Conscious and Subconscious or Unconscious Mind
- Know, Like, and Trust
- Left Brain and Right Brain Tendencies
- Pain Points and Pleasure Points of Prospects and Customers
- Generation
- Cultural Influence

In this section, we'll build on that information and connect it to other important sections to better understand how consumers make decisions. Why is it valuable to understand the consumer decision-making process? Simply put, the more you understand, the easier it is to be creative and effective with your marketing.

There are several important pieces of information to be aware of to help your creativity and marketing effectiveness, such as:
- According to Harvard Business School professor Gerald Zaltman, 95 percent of purchase decisions are made in the subconscious mind. Fortunately, Guerrilla marketers know that repetition is a great way to access and make an impression in the subconscious mind
- People with left-brain tendencies are motivated by logical and sequential reasoning. People with right-brain tendencies are motivated by emotional and aesthetic appeal. When your marketing appeals to both, you have the greatest effectiveness
- The consumer mind relies on and trusts images. According to PsychMechanics, "Your subconscious mind stores all your memories and experiences in the form of images and symbols." Additionally, "Everything that you see, in real life or on a screen, imagine or dream is considered real by the subconscious mind."
- "Emotions are the language of the subconscious mind. When you are awake, you can consciously notice the emotional changes that you expe-

rience and hence understand what the subconscious mind is trying to tell you," according to PsychMechanics
- When you tell your prospects and customers not to do something (e.g., don't think about a salad), their subconscious mind will conjure up that image (i.e., a salad). According to PsychMechanics, "Negative commands like 'don't' are not processed by the subconscious mind." Therefore, by carefully choosing your words, you help conjure up the right images with your prospects and customers
- The consumer mind has dual functions. According to *Psychology Today*, consumers are of two minds, the "doer" and the "purchaser." Accordingly, ". . . a browser is in a planner (deliberative) mindset, weighing costs versus benefits. In contrast, a buyer is a doer, ready to purchase. The challenge for a salesperson, then, is to shift the customer's mindset from browser to buyer."
- According to Jay Conrad Levinson, consumers search for validation to finalize their purchase decisions. Testimonials, sharing, ratings, reviews, etc. serve as validation. See Volume 1, Section 8.20, "Testimonials, Reviews, and Ratings," and Section 5.6, "White Papers, Testimonials, and Sharing" for more information
- Purchase decisions are made for emotional reasons, and those decisions are justified with logical reasoning. *Psychology Today* refers to it as self-justification and provides an example, ". . . the person who has bought a luxury item but feels guilty about it may try to alleviate his guilt by coming up with additional reasons to justify his behavior, such as, 'It was on sale, I had to buy it.'"
- Consumers often rely on their gut instincts, which is the subconscious (or unconscious) mind
- What happens after the sales can be as, or more, important for customer satisfaction, relationships, repeat purchases, additional sales, and precious referrals of their friends, family, and associates to your business, which are the fuel for your long-term success
- The unconscious mind works at high speeds and can link multiple messages. By using multiple marketing messages that appeal to the needs of the unconscious mind, your prospect can more quickly reach a committed decision

- Stories appeal to emotions, and they sell products and services (see Volume 1, Section 6.5, "Stories Sell")
- Consumers learn in a variety of ways, and it's effective to appeal to as many consumers in as many ways as possible. See Volume 2, Section 5.14, "Variety and Modality," for seven important learning styles
- Beyond demographics and psychographics, understanding as much as possible about the consumer mindset will help you to better understand the behavior of your prospects and customers. (See Volume 2, Section 6.17, "Consumer Mindset")
- Mental fatigue leads to "a greater willingness to succumb to temptation and indulgence," and when consumers are overwhelmed by too many choices, it leads to "unrealistic expectations, decision-making paralysis, and unhappiness," according to *Psychology Today*
- Color elicits moods and feelings that can be persuasive (see Section 8.45, "The Power of Color")
- The senses are a Guerrilla marketers opportunity to create an enjoyable, sharable, compelling, and motivating experience that increases sales and profits (see Section 8.46, "Appeal to the Senses")

The more your know about Guerrilla Marketing, the more you understand how decisions are made by consumers and what interests, compels, and motivates them throughout the decision-making process. A Guerrilla marketer's goal is to make their business irresistible and delightful for their prospects and customers.

1.14 * BUSINESS FOUNDATION

The strong foundation of Guerrilla Marketing success relies on a strong business foundation. Therefore, it's a good idea to review your business foundation to make sure your marketing is strong. Consider the following important aspects of your business foundation.

Legal

Establishing and maintaining legal compliance is no easy task. It's certainly not a good idea to take shortcuts or make assumptions. Fortunately, there are numerous resources at your fingertips that can help reduce the complexity, such as:

- Federal Trade Commission: the FTC business center is an important resource for your business to learn about topics from advertising and marketing to protecting your business and finding legal resources
- Small Business Administration: for help with staying legally compliant with state and federal business laws, see a list of courses, and more, visit the SBA website
- Legal Zoom: offers a choice of or combination of DIY service and attorney advice from the comfort of your computer and with the ease of flat-rate fees

Beyond legal compliance, there are other issues that your business has to consider, such as filing and maintaining trademarks to protect your business identity, copyrights to protect your creative work, and patents to protect your inventions and designs.

Cybersecurity and Privacy

One of the biggest vulnerabilities of any SMB is cybersecurity and protecting your customers' information. The success of your business relies on your robust protection systems for everything from your business network to your website.

Fortunately, there are services, such as The National Cyber Security Alliance, which focus on helping SMBs conduct business safely and securely online. They offer free checkups, tools, and education to help your business be secure and manage privacy. See Volume 1, Section 4.1, "Data Privacy and Cybersecurity," for more information, resources, and details.

Continuity Plans and Corporate Governance

It's important to plan for everything to go well, and that means thinking through what could go wrong. For example, if you have partners, how will they be separated from the business upon their choosing and/or if something unexpected happens? How will your business function if something unexpected happens to you? Is the financial responsibility for each partner defined?

Relationships in business and in life evolve. Everything is great when a business starts and everyone is on the same page. Over time, those pages can change. For example,

- One person is putting in more hours than another person
- One person is putting in more money or taking on more personal debt than another person
- One person is having more successful results than another person
- One person wants to leave the business (e.g., retire or quit), and they want to be bought out
- The parties cannot agree on a decision or direction for the business

By defining and legally structuring as many scenarios as possible upfront, you can avoid discourse and disruptions later.

Systems

From your accounting/financial system to your CRM, your business operates more smoothly with as few stand-alone systems as possible. Choosing robust systems that can grow with your business and work well together will make your business easier to operate and financially efficient. That means fewer hours of employee training, greater accuracy, and effective communication tools that keep everyone in the know and on the same page.

It sounds simple enough, but it's very easy to fall into two traps that can make things complicated. The first trap is sticking with what you have and refusing to evolve and grow your capabilities. The second trap is to add too many stand-alone systems that are not integrated. Both traps are unnecessary costs for your business, both financially and in terms of resources and efficiency.

See Volume 1, Section 8.31, "Systems and Automation," for more information, resources, and details.

Financials

You can do everything well with your marketing efforts, but if you don't have a firm understanding of your financials, your business may be ready to fall off of a cliff at any moment. If financial management is not your strength, collaborating with professional talent is a must.

A successful business owner knows their financial standing in as close to real-time as possible. When your accounting system is in as close to real-time as possible (e.g., automated bank and credit card imports), you can make accurate business decisions. By utilizing the right KPIs and an effective dashboard, you're continually measuring and monitoring your performance. See Section 2.18, "Optimization," for more information regarding KPIs.

Role Dynamics

A lack of clarity regarding each person's role in the business can create wasted time, frustration, depleted morale, employee turnover, and negative reviews (e.g., Glassdoor) that impact your ability to attract the highest-quality job candidates. Guerrilla marketers, when they have carefully selected a high-quality candidate to fill a role in the business, make sure they give them the tools they need to succeed. One of those tools is clarity.

Everyone in your business needs to understand their role, the roles of others, and who the decision-makers are. They also need a clear understanding of how to effectively contribute ideas and exceed at their jobs (without stepping on other people). It may sound like an issue you'll deal with when your business gets bigger, but in reality, if you have two or more people in your business, the time is now.

When each person's role is not clearly defined and the decision-makers are not supported, it not only creates an internal conflict but may also be conflict that your prospects and customers see and often pay the price for (see Section 6.28, "Inside Out," for more information).

At the same time, those roles need to be clearly defined to all parties. By doing so, you'll maintain a healthy, competitive, and motivating relationship between groups, such as sales vs. marketing, operations vs. sales, customer service vs. sales, and customer service vs. marketing.

1.15 * IMPLEMENTATION

We hope you have read each volume in the all-new series of *Guerrilla Marketing* books, and we are grateful and excited about your success. At this point, with Volume 1, Volume 2, and now in Volume 3, you've read more than 240 Guerrilla Marketing tactics. Consciously and subconsciously, you've been ranking them. Typically, the ranking consists of:

- Simple or "I don't need to focus on that"
- Interesting or "I should do that"
- Difficult or "I have too much to do to work on that" (or the opposite: "I'm just going to focus on that")

Guerrilla Marketing gives you the knowledge you want to understand marketing and how it works to help your business connect with your prospects and customers. The difference between a Guerrilla marketer and a traditional business is the Guerrilla marketer combines knowledge and action (see Volume 1, Section 9.9, "High Energy and Take Action") and chooses and implements every applicable (based on their prospects' and customers' points of view, needs, desires, and expectations) Guerrilla Marketing tactic, regardless of whether it's simple, interesting, or difficult.

Traditional businesses either skip over or poorly implement the tactics they rank as "simple" and "interesting." They often prioritize the "complicated" tactics because they are challenging to them, and they believe those tactics will make them stand out. In doing so, they have a weak marketing foundation. As we stated earlier, "Please know this: Businesses that fail have a poor foundation. If you build your castle on a poor foundation, don't be surprised when it collapses into rubble."

Guerrilla marketers understand how intelligent Guerrilla Marketing works and that means, in part, they tend to the tiny, supercharged details that can generate big profits. Your attention to selecting the right marketing tactics that compel and motivate your prospects and customers is important. Just as important is mastering your implementation of those tactics. Why?

When you master your implementation of each marketing tactic you choose, you will set your business apart. Your excellent implementation of tactics that seem "simple" is just as important as those tactics you consider "interesting" or "difficult."

A "simple" marketing tactic that is poorly executed can make a "difficult" marketing tactic ineffective. For example, your "difficult" marketing tactic is proving effective, and it's motivating people to click on your business in Google maps. When they do, they find that you've poorly implemented the "easy" tactic of utilizing all the options available to you with Google My Business and your Google Business Profile (see Volume 1, Section 4.22, "Google My Business"). Therefore, they can't find your hours; they can't easily schedule an appointment; they don't know what products or services you offer, etc.

When it comes to Guerrilla Marketing, knowledge alone is not enough. Equally, energy alone is not enough. Energy must be directed by intelligence. Successful Guerrilla businesses combine knowledge with action and effort. Your marketing tactics work together, and many are dependent on one another. Your every marketing tactic is only working when you master the implementation and tend to the tiny, supercharged details that can generate big profits. Always remember: The more you do well, the harder life is for your competition.

1.16 * BRAND MARKETING

Guerrilla marketers understand a powerful reality of marketing. What is that powerful reality? Every marketing and advertising initiative is brand marketing. Therefore, a Guerrilla marketer knows they don't need to think of "call to action" marketing separately from "brand" marketing.

Guerrilla Marketing is a 360-degree, consistent methodology that weaves through every aspect of your business. Therefore, a Guerrilla marketer understands that each marketing effort expresses their consistent and aligned Attributes (see Section VIII, "Guerrilla Company Attributes" in each book volume) and Attitudes (see Section IX, "Guerrilla Company Attitudes") with the intention of motivating actions that turn into sales and referrals.

According to research from Hubspot, the majority of their respondents indicated that their primary marketing campaign goal was "brand awareness." Increasing sales was second, and lead generation and increased engagement followed. Increasing revenue was fifth.

Your job is to compel your prospects to notice your business. First, they become aware of your business (i.e., brand awareness), and second, they recognize your business and the product(s) and/or service(s) associated with it (i.e., brand recognition). Once they do, your call to action must then motivate them to take a desired action (e.g., download an ebook, make a purchase, etc.). Your marketing efforts are ideal when they appeal to each aspect (brand awareness, brand recognition, and action) at the same time.

If your business engages in marketing efforts that are not designed to cause an action, it's a disservice to your prospects and customers. When they give you their attention, regard that moment as precious because their time is valuable, and it's important to treat it as such.

In each tiny moment you get of their precious attention, your goal is to convey who you are and what you want them to do. Non-Guerrilla businesses utilize marketing and advertising efforts that are mostly about themselves instead of them being about their prospects and customers, and they label it *brand marketing*.

For example, they advertise their name and logo but not their product, or they feature images that are not directly tied to their product(s) or service(s) and/or their benefits. You've likely experienced an online advertisement that motivated you to click, and when you did, it wasn't what you expected. Perhaps, it was an article of clothing that motivated you to click, and the result was something else (e.g., it's not available, it's not what they sell, etc.). You likely became quickly frustrated because they wasted your time. Your time is precious, and your prospects' and customers' time is precious too.

Guerrilla businesses are focused on how precious their prospects' and customers' time is so they seek to achieve brand awareness and brand recognition and inspire action with every marketing effort. They make sure the action is well thought through with minimal steps for your prospect to receive the amount of information they want to determine what action they will take.

It's important to make a distinction between hard selling and soft selling. Hard selling is advertising that attempts to inspire immediate action. For example, including price points and a "buy now" button. Soft selling is advertising that, for example, includes your product and motivates them to go the next step to see your pricing and buying options.

Guerrilla marketers understand that both hard selling and soft selling create action. The goal is to cater your marketing to be appealing to your prospects and customers. Typically, the higher the price point, the more effective soft selling is, and conversely, the lower the price point, the more effective hard selling is. Higher price points often require more self-justification, and soft selling is your opportunity to appeal to their emotions to justify and motivate the purchase.

The purpose of your "brand" is to better the lives of your prospects and customers and to inspire action and deliver quality results. Therefore, your every marketing effort should be aligned with the purpose of promoting your business (i.e., brand) and inspiring action and delivering quality results that better the lives of your prospects and customers.

1.17 * ALIGNMENT

As we've previously stated, Guerrilla Marketing is a 360-degree, consistent methodology that weaves through every aspect of your business. That may sound difficult to achieve, but it's not. It simply takes focus and intention, neither of which costs a dime. When your business is aligned, it's quite obvious to your prospects and customers because they experience:

	Aligned	Misaligned
Employees	Helpful, available, knowledgeable, delightful, they always know just how to . . .	Slow to respond, difficult to find, not very helpful, didn't know how to . . .
Products and/or services	Consistent high quality, innovative, desirable and/or reliable, always meets or exceeds my expectations	Some products are good, and others are not; you never know what you're going to get; they're unreliable
Payment options	Easy process with a wide variety of options	Cash only or credit card only
Marketing	Easy to recognize and recall and consistent from advertising to social media, website, physical business location, uniforms, vehicles, packaging, receipts, follow-up, etc.	Can't find their business hours; can't recall the name of the business, not open when you're ready to purchase, their service vehicle was dirty and didn't have the business name, etc.
Dependable	Yes, they never let you down	You never know what you're going to get
Memorable	Yes, they are the first business that comes to mind when I think of . . .	No
Loyalty program	Yes, it's a great program and so easy to use; you can tell they really care about their customers	No
Recommendable and shareable	Yes, I gave them five stars, and every chance I get; I recommend them to my friends, family, and associates	No

The restaurant industry is a good example of an industry that relies on alignment for its success. From the friendliness of restaurant employees to the selection of food, quality of food, consistency of preparation, ease of ordering, value, ease of paying, locations, hours, etc., there's much to align.

Think about your favorite restaurant. In what ways is it aligned? Are there any ways in which it is misaligned?

Now, think about a restaurant that you went to, didn't like, never returned to, and probably told your friends about and/or reflected your dissatisfaction in a rating/review. In what ways was it aligned? In what ways was it misaligned?

While Guerrilla marketers strive to consistently over-perform against their prospects' and customers' expectations, they know that they may not always do so. The good news is, the more your business is aligned, the easier it is for your prospects and customers to overlook a misalignment.

At the same time, your prospects and customers are eager to share their opinions with you and that's a tremendous opportunity for your business because your alignment causes them to be emotionally invested in your success. You'll hear comments, such as "You do everything so well but there is this . . . and I just wanted to let you know because you're my favorite . . . I love coming to your business, and I knew you would want to know."

When your business is aligned and your delighted customers are invested in your success, they also enjoy sharing their experiences, and their five-star reviews often reference you and your employees by name. You're the first business they think of when they are ready to make a purchase. They connect and interact (e.g., social media, email opt-in, etc.). They love recommending your business to their friends, family, and associates, and they do so with glowing words and by sharing the names of people in your business.

Simply put, alignment is the difference between a transaction and a long-term, mutually delightful relationship (see Section 9.29, "Relationship Builder") with your customers that drives your business success. It's also the difference that moves your prospects from indifference, skepticism, and/or apathy to making a purchase, making repeat purchases, referring their friends, family, and associates, and being an advocate for your business.

Choosing to be intentional with your marketing makes it easy to be aligned in your every marketing effort. After all, if you're not intentional, you're likely misaligned. Therefore, a Guerrilla marketer understands each marketing effort expresses their consistent and aligned:

- Guerrilla Maximedia Marketing
- Guerrilla Minimedia Marketing
- Guerrilla E-Media Marketing
- Guerrilla Info-Media Marketing
- Guerrilla Human-Media Marketing
- Guerrilla Non-Media Marketing
- Guerrilla Company Attributes
- Guerrilla Company Attitudes

When the Attributes and Attitudes of your business are misaligned, either with each other or with any other aspect of your marketing and advertising, it shows. Guerrilla marketers avoid roadblocks that get in their way on the road to success. Therefore, they choose to be aligned in their marketing and advertising efforts as they motivate their prospects and customers to take an action that turns into sales, delighted customers, and precious referrals.

SECTION II

Guerrilla Maximedia Marketing

GUERRILLA MAXIMEDIA MARKETING

As Jay Conrad Levison stated in Guerrilla Marketing:

> *Guerrillas must use the mass media with precision, carefully measure the results, and make the media part of an overall marketing plan. When they use the media, Guerrillas must rely on know-how, intuition and business acumen. Maximedia Marketing is about two things: (1) selling and (2) creating a powerful desire to buy. Also, Maximedia Marketing enhances the success of Minimedia Marketing—response rates to simple circulars jump when radio advertising blazes the way for them, and telemarketing results improve when TV spots pre-sell the market.*

Guerrilla Maximedia Marketing is what many people think of when they talk about "traditional advertising." Guerrilla Maximedia Marketing is at its most powerful when your Guerrilla Marketing is in full congruence. Your Guerrilla Maximedia Marketing endeavors bring your business to light in front of large audiences. Additionally, your Guerrilla Maximedia Marketing and your Guerrilla E-Media Marketing (Section IV) are typically the largest advertising investments that your business will make.

Therefore, taking the time to skillfully create your Guerrilla Creative and Advertising strategy is a must. Effective Guerrilla Maximedia Marketing is creative, clear, focused, compelling, and consistent. Your Guerrilla Creative and Advertising strategy will keep you on the path to profitable advertising. As with every marketing investment you make, understanding how advertising works equips you to make wise investments that will help you sleep well at night while your business profits grow.

We'll help you maximize the low- and no-cost ways to make your Guerrilla Maximedia Marketing investments create maximum profits for your business. Those precious profits are the fuel that makes your business engine run so you can hire talented people, acquire loyal customers, improve your community, and make your dreams a reality. Let's dive in and see how you can put Guerrilla Maximedia Marketing tactics to work for your business. In Volume 1, we addressed:

2.1   Direct Mail
2.2   Newspaper Advertising
2.3   Radio Advertising

2.4   Podcast Advertising
2.5   Television Advertising and Appearances
2.6   Magazine Advertising
2.7   Billboard Advertising
2.8   Advertising Keys to Success

In Volume 2, we addressed:
2.9   Radio Presence/Influence
2.10 Bartering
2.11 Agencies
2.12 Measurement and Analysis
2.13 Response
2.14 Creativity and Practicality
2.15 Endorsements

Now, we'll pick up where we left off. Without further ado, let's get started.

2.16 * TESTING

What makes for great advertising? It's simple—a compelling message that quickly motivates your prospects to become customers and your customers to make repeat and additional purchases and to refer their friends, family, and associates to your business. However, finding that message can take some testing.

Your Guerrilla Marketing is an investment that you want to be as profitable as possible. Your goal, of course, is to invest as little as possible to generate (or exceed) your profit goals.

There are many ways to test your advertising. For example, we addressed email in Volume 1, Section 4.35, "Email Split Testing." In this section, we'll focus on other advertising testing options, such as:

- Surveys
- Opinion Polls
- Focus Groups
- Split Testing

- Multivariate Testing

A significant difference between testing options is whether you're seeking quantitative results or qualitative results. Split testing, multivariate testing, and opinion polls provide quantitative results (i.e., the numbers). Focus groups, on the other hand, provide more qualitative results (i.e., behavior and observations). Surveys that allow for open comments can provide both quantitative and qualitative results. Let's consider two examples of surveys:

- Monadic design is focused on asking multiple questions about one advertising option/design
- Sequential monadic design is focused on asking multiple questions about two or more options/designs

According to SurveyMonkey, a monadic design is more likely to result in a short questionnaire, which can increase the completion rates. A sequential monadic design can limit the number of questions you can ask about each option/design with the intention of keeping the survey short and, thus, the completion rate high. Fortunately, SurveyMonkey offers ad testing templates to help you get started.

As we addressed in Volume 1, Section 2.8, "Advertising Keys to Success," it's important to know that nearly everyone fancies themselves as a marketing and advertising expert. As a Guerrilla marketer, you'll hear a lot of opinions about your advertising, but you know the opinions that matter the most are that of your customers who have purchased your product(s) or service(s) and your prospects who have not yet made a purchase.

When you're evaluating the results of your testing, it's critical to consider whose opinion you're listening to. Listening to the opinions of people (e.g., non-targeted focus groups, your employees, friends, family, etc.) who have not purchased or are unlikely to purchase your product(s) and/or service(s) can have valuable insights, but those opinions and insights should be kept separate.

It's the opinion of those that have purchased or are likely to purchase your product(s) and/or service(s) that provide the most valuable insight. Hearing directly from your customers and/or prospects helps to keep your ideas, creativity, marketing, and advertising focused on a profitable outcome.

Therefore, if you're testing outside of your customers, it's important to collect some basic data (i.e., age, income, gender, profession, etc.), along with the answers, to ensure that you're separating the responses. At the same time, you may find new prospect opportunities among those showing a strong likelihood (see Section 6.30, "Consumer Intention") to purchase your product(s) or service(s), who have a different set of characteristics than what you've been considering as your target audience/prospects.

What might you consider testing?
- Call to action effectiveness (i.e., Do they clearly understand the action you wanted them to take, and are they motivated to take that action?)
- Copy effectiveness (i.e., Do they find your copy compelling?)
- Image/video effectiveness (i.e., Could they relate to and were motivated by the images and video in your advertising?)
- Color effectiveness (i.e., Do they find one color more appealing?)
- Brand recognition (i.e., If they were already aware of your business/brand, do they immediately realize the advertising or marketing was your business/brand?)
- Brand awareness (i.e., Do your advertising/marketing make them notice and become aware of your business/brand?)
- Brand favorability and/or credibility (i.e., Have you piqued their interest; do they think your expertise is worth consideration, and is your business top-of-mind for new purchases and/or repeat or additional purchases?)
- Brand advantage (i.e., Do they know what is unique about your business/brand?)

Utilizing direct, clear, and concise questions with simple and minimal answer options (e.g., a strongly agree or disagree scale) will help your response rates, regardless of which testing option you're considering. The quicker it is to provide input, the more likely your prospects and customers will be to complete the survey. An open comment field can also help your business receive qualitative information and results.

When it comes to split testing, there are many tools available to help you test your advertising. It can begin as simple as A/B testing, which can be done on online platforms, such as:
- Facebook: allows for testing in Ads Manager regarding variables, such as images, videos, ad text, age and gender, saved audience, placement, customer variables (e.g., multiple variables), and more
- Google: allows for experiments with search and display network campaigns. Google also allows for ad variation testing with text and URLs
- LinkedIn: offers A/B testing in their campaign manager with sponsored content and direct sponsored content

Equally, there are simple split testing methods that work with most forms of advertising, such as:
- Unique phone numbers
- Unique URLs
- Unique QR codes
- Unique coupon codes
- Unique pricing or offers

For more advanced testing (e.g., multivariate testing of three or more elements), there are several services available. The following are a few services to get to know:
- Voxco: an online and offline ad testing tool that allows your business to test concepts, copy, messages, logo, and packaging. Their tools can, in part, help you understand the intent of your customers and their perception of your brand as you test video, print, and text advertisements
- Zappi: an advertising and innovation testing platform that helps your business test, with standard or custom audiences, your advertising, naming, products, packaging, etc. Their tools can help your business understand both the sales uplift and longer-term brand influence and give your business testing results to utilize and improve your advertising for the greatest effectiveness
- Qualtrics: offers tools to test audio, video, text, and image concepts with the right audience, from the concept of your advertising and marketing to its performance over time. Their machine learning tools help to discover the insights provided by your prospects and customers in open-text responses

Testing is an ongoing activity. From pre-testing your concepts (e.g., products, packaging, advertisements, etc.) to split testing your existing advertising, ongoing testing helps your business maximize your results over the long term.

2.17 * ATTRIBUTION

Marketing attribution is growing in importance, and although it was once focused mainly on large businesses with large budgets, it's more accessible for SMBs today. The goal of marketing attribution is to determine which of your marketing tactics are creating sales. It's expected that several of your tactics are working together to create sales, and marketing attribution can help identify how your marketing tactics are working together.

In Volume 1, we addressed marketing attribution, specific to marketing tactics, such as:

- Volume 1, Section 2.4, "Podcast Advertising"
- Volume 1, Section 2.5, "Television Advertising and Appearances"

In addition, we addressed attribution marketing more broadly in Volume 1, Section 2.8, "Advertising Keys to Success."

In this section, we'll expand and go deeper. After all, there are many layers of marketing attribution analysis. When you dive deeper into analysis, you can find golden information. For example, you can determine which of your marketing efforts are influencing your most ideal customers.

If you've not already done so, take the time to define your ideal customers. See Section 8.50, "Ideal Customers," for assistance.

Your marketing tactics that influence your ideal customers might be different than what you believe based on looking at your higher-level data. If, for example, only 20 percent of your customers (See Volume 1, Section 6.12, "The 80/20 Rule") are what you define as your ideal customers, what influences them can easily get lost in the data and percentages—unless you dive deeper into your results. You may find that a tactic at the bottom of your results (which are based on percentages) appears to be unimportant (i.e., not influencing sales). However, with a deeper dive, you may find that a very high percentage of your ideal customers (i.e., that 20 percent of your customers) are influenced by that tactic.

To provide another example: your marketing attribution and analysis may find that only 10 percent of your email marketing is creating sales. At first glance, you may decide that your email marketing is not working, and therefore, you need to make changes. That decision could be devastating for your business if you don't dive deeper to analyze that 10 percent to determine what percent of your ideal customers are in that group. Perhaps that 10 percent is generating 80 percent of your referrals.

An alternate example is on the other end of the percentage scale. What if you see that a particular social media platform is generating 40 percent of your sales. At first glance, you may decide to increase your marketing with that social media platform. If you make that decision without diving deeper into that 40 percent, you may not realize that they are your least ideal customers (e.g., one-time purchases, high return rates, high chargeback rates, low ratings, costly from a service perspective, etc.) and attracting more of them can be devastating for your profits and the longevity of your business.

Marketing attribution can certainly help your business determine how to keep refining your marketing to maximize your sales and profit results. However, marketing attribution requires careful analysis to make accurate determinations of which marketing tactics are working (i.e., driving profits) so you can do more of them. Careful analysis will also help you determine what's not working so you can improve or eliminate those marketing tactics.

Attribution marketing can take on many forms. At its simplest level, it's effective communication within your business, such as between customer service, sales, and marketing. According to Marketo, "Organizations with tightly aligned sales and marketing departments see 36% higher customer retention and 38% higher sales win rates."

When your business is ready to increase your marketing attribution, there are many resources available. In. Volume 2, Section 2.12, "Measurement and Analysis," we provided examples of tools that can help with measurement and attribution, and those are worth repeating and expanding:

- Nielsen Marketing Effectiveness Tools (multichannel along with non-marketing factors measurement and attribution)
- iSpot.tv (television measurement and attribution)
- TVEyes (television and radio measurement)
- Claritas (multichannel measurement and attribution)
- Cision (media monitoring and attribution)
- News Exposure (multichannel monitoring and data analysis)
- Marketo Engage (multichannel measurement, data analysis, and their Bizible product is designed for B2B)

To analyze the results of marketing attribution you need an accurate understanding of:

- Your ideal customers (see Section 8.50, "Ideal Customers")
- Customer lifetime value (see Section 8.44, "Customer Lifetime Value (CLV or LTV)")
- Your financials (see Section 1.14, "Business Foundation")
- Your referrals (see Volume 1, Section 8.25, "Referral Programs")
- Your robust CRM system (see Section 4.61 "Customer Relationship Management Platforms (CRMs)")

Similar to the adage "look before you leap," when it comes to making changes based on your marketing attribution and analysis, take a deep dive and analyze your results before you leap. That means, for example, choosing split testing to test your hypothesis instead of making dramatic changes right away. In addition to Section 2.16, "Testing," also refer to Volume 1, Section 2.8, "Advertising Keys to Success," and Section 4.35, "Email Split Testing," for more information.

The benefits of your attribution marketing are understanding how to:
- Increase your appeal to your ideal customers
- Identify which of your marketing tactics are most appealing to your ideal customers
- Identify the marketing messages that compel and motivate your ideal customers, which can reveal powerful information, such as words/terms/phrases, products, features, and services that are most appealing

There are numerous marketing attribution models. For example, Google Ads offers a variety of attribution models for search, YouTube, and display ads to help you determine the amount of credit to give each of your customers' multiple interactions with your advertising. They also offer a model comparison report.

To better describe attribution models, Marketo offers valuable marketing attribution model examples, including:
- First-touch: "It assigns complete credit for conversion to the marketing effort that first brings a customer in." An important consideration is ". . . it measures only top-of-funnel marketing efforts and provides no real visibility into important touchpoints that happen later in the sales funnel."
- Last-touch: ". . . inverts first-touch attribution by focusing on the final touchpoint that leads to a sale." An important consideration is ". . . it tracks only bottom-of-funnel marketing activity. It is not useful for measuring the channels that bring customers to your brand in the first place."
- Linear: ". . . a simple multi-source attribution model that aims to identify all key touchpoints that were relevant in driving a purchase. Once those touchpoints are identified, equal weight is assigned to each one." An important consideration is ". . . if some interactions were more important than others, this model won't reveal the most influential ones."

As you evolve into more advanced models (e.g., position-based, w-shaped, time decay, etc.), percentages (or weights) are assigned to various touchpoints to determine their impact and effectiveness.

Regardless of how simple or complex the marketing attribution model is that you choose, the value of the data is for the purpose of helping your business succeed now and for the long term.

It's important to remember the adage, "garbage in . . . garbage out" for the purpose of keeping your focus on obtaining and utilizing accurate and high-quality data. If your data is anything less (i.e., garbage in), the decisions you make and actions you take are compromised (i.e., garbage out). With accurate and high-quality data and effective analysis, you can make successful hypotheses and decisions that translate into actions that improve your sales and profits.

2.18 * OPTIMIZATION

Guerrilla Marketing thrives when you're continually optimizing your efforts. By tracking the effectiveness of your marketing tactics and following up, you'll be able to:
- Improve or remove what's not working
- Identify and do more of what is working
- Identify new tactics to add, based on what's working

After all, the more you do well, the harder life is for your competition. Therefore, your business needs to consider the components of optimization to ensure that you're combining the right data with the right tools, testing, and scaling.

Key Performance Indicators (KPIs)

Key performance indicators are the metrics that businesses use to measure and monitor their success. Once your business determines the results you want to achieve, you can determine and focus on the correct indicators to keep you on course. Examples are:
- CAC: Customer acquisition cost
- CPA: Cost-per-action
- CPC: Cost-per-click
- CPL: Cost-per-lead
- CPM: Cost-per-mille (thousand)
- CPV: Cost-per-view

- CR: Conversion rate or, alternately, customer retention
- CRO: Conversion rate optimization
- LTV/CLV: Lifetime value or customer lifetime value
- MQL: Marketing qualified leads
- NPS: Net promoter score
- Payroll percentage
- PPC: Pay-per-click
- Revenue
- ROAS: Return on ad spend
- ROI: Return on investment
- Social: Follower growth, likes, comments, clicks, shares, etc.
- SQL: Sales-qualified leads
- Website traffic: Total, organic, referral, etc.

Tools

Optimization relies, first and foremost, on reliable high-quality data. It then relies on the right tools to measure and monitor your performance and identify opportunities for improvement. Examples of those tools are:

- Marketing automation platform (see Volume 1, Section 4.34 "Email Autoresponder Platforms," and Section 4.61, "Customer Relationship Management Platforms (CRMs)")
- Attribution (see Section 2.17, "Attribution," and Section 4.62, "Digital Attribution")
- Analysis tools, such as:
  - Google Analytics
  - Kissmetrics
  - Segmetrics
- Dashboards, such as:
  - Tableau
  - Qlik
  - Microsoft Power BI Desktop
  - Domo
  - Klipfolio

Segmentation

While your prospects and customers have things in common, they also have significant differences. Those differences could be due to:
- Demographics
- Geography
- Psychographics
- Technographics and firmographics (see Volume 2, Section 4.50, "Digital Account-Based Marketing")
- Consumer behavior (see Volume 1, Section 6.9, "Consumer Behavior")
- Mindset (see Volume 2, Section 6.17, "Consumer Mindset")

The more you know about your customers, the greater the opportunity you have to increase your appeal by segmenting them into groups with similar characteristics and customizing your marketing and advertising (e.g., messages, media type, etc.) to have greater appeal.

For example, you may find that certain customers buy a particular category of products very quickly in response to your advertising on a particular social media platform. By segmenting those customers, you can customize your marketing to appeal to their desire for that product category, make it easy for them to act immediately, and perhaps utilize retargeting.

An important group to segment is your ideal customers (see Section 8.50, "Ideal Customers") to ensure your marketing efforts are focused on continually delighting them and motivating referrals.

Testing

See Section 2.16, "Testing," and Volume 1, Section 2.8, "Advertising Keys to Success."

Implementation and Scaling

The goal of your testing is to, of course, find statistically significant results. That means you're confident the results are not substantially influenced by underlying factors. Those other factors may consist of:
- Sampling errors, which can result from the:
  - Sample size: for example, what is statistically significant in a group of 500 people may not be significant when the group size is increased to 5000 people

- o Variations of the prospects and/or customers in the test group: for example, your test group could have something in common that is uncommon in your total database of prospects and/or customers
- Other errors can be a result of bias, timing, and intention vs. action. For example, if your testing method is a survey, people will respond with intention, which may or may not tightly correlate with their actions. Therefore, you may receive a favorable indication in the survey that your respondents would buy your new product, but do they take action once your new product is available?

By scaling your implementation, you'll gain confidence in the accuracy of your testing prior to your full implementation. When you scale your implementation, you'll, for example, increase the size of your audience from 500 to 1000 and re-measure your results. Assuming the results are the same, you'll continue to increase your audience size and continue to measure your results through full implementation.

Conclusion

Have you ever reviewed your data and realized what you should do but haven't taken the steps to do it? Concerns and fears regarding the unknown will often lead people to indecision. Limiting thoughts—such as "Why fix what isn't broken?"—are all too common.

When it comes to marketing decisions, there are rarely absolutes. However, one absolute is that not taking well-thought-out action is the same as standing still in a fast-changing world, which means you're falling behind.

2.19 * ALTERNATE OUT-OF-HOME (OOH AND DOOH) ADVERTISING

In Volume 1, Section 2.7, we addressed billboard advertising. In this section, we'll address alternate out-of-home (OOH) advertising opportunities to reach your prospects and customers who are on the go.

While traditional billboard advertising is an effective means for certain businesses to reach and motivate their prospects and customers, there are numerous additional opportunities. Alternative OOH options include digital opportunities (referred to as DOOH) that allow you to be dynamic with your creativity.

DOOH advertising opportunities allow your business to rotate different messages, utilize dynamic images and video, easily target geographies, and utilize shorter timeframes and programmatic buying. Your creativity can shine with a variety of options. According to Clear Channel Outdoor, some options are: "social media integration, countdowns, day/weekparting, live updates, conditional content (weather, temperature), Outdoor Connect/RSS WiFi/Touch-Screen, and more."

If DOOH advertising is well-suited for your business and your prospects, be sure that your retail outlets are aligned. For example, if you're using rich video creative in your DOOH, your prospects and customers will expect (consciously or subconsciously) continuity when they enter your physical business location or go to your website.

Therefore, your rich video advertising is ideal when it's met with consistent video headers on your website and throughout your content. Equally, your video advertising is ideal when it's met with consistent video displays at your physical retail location, such as in your window displays, on point-of-sale signage, on displays, etc. That consistency builds familiarity; familiarity builds trust, and trust creates sales, repeat purchases, and precious referrals, which is the fuel for your long-term success.

There are a variety of alternate OOH and DOOH options to consider as your business seeks to attract and motivate your prospects and customers to take action, such as:

- Airplane banners (pulled behind)
- Mapping kiosks and/or service centers at venues, retail centers, etc.
- Mobile digital or wrapped boards (e.g., trucks with mounted or pulled behind digital panels, box trucks and semi-trailers using wraps, etc.)
- Custom vehicles (e.g., Red Bull marketing vehicles, LandShark mobile hot tub, etc.)
- Sidewalk-mounted digital panels in cities, busy beach areas, venues, etc.
- Elevators (e.g., wraps, video panels, decals, etc.)
- Pop-up kiosks
- Decals (e.g., sidewalk, steps, escalators, doors, etc.)
- Robots
- Transit advertising

- o Busses and bus shelters
- o Airports
- o Rail and stations for commuter and long-haul
- o Automobile (e.g., taxi, rideshare, private service, etc.)
- o Gas (or charging) stations

There are several companies to be familiar with when you're considering alternate OOH and DOOH advertising, such as:

- Lime Media: which, according to the company, has the largest fleet in the US, with three-screen digital board box trucks. The screens can display static images or videos. With geo-targeting, your creativity can be featured on all three screens to promote your business and your compelling call to action. They also have options for mobile showrooms, pop-up shops, and sampling vehicles. Whether it's around your physical business locations, at events or tradeshows, or in heavy pedestrian traffic areas, these options can help your business shine—on a small scale or a large scale
- Clear Channel Outdoor: offers a wide range of OOH and DOOH options to help you target your prospects and customers in the US and in multiple markets around the globe. Their Radar system provides a suite of solutions and digital insights to help businesses target and measure their advertising. According to Clear Channel Outdoor, Radar "... leverages anonymous, aggregated mobile location data to help advertisers understand consumer mobility, behavior and true campaign impact."
- Rolling Adz: offers a large nationwide fleet of GPS-tracked mobile billboards that reach consumers seven days a week. Based on the size of your buy, you have the option of exclusivity in your market. According to Rolling Adz, "Our data partners along with our beacon application provide impression reports, user engagement, frequency, and enable you the ability to retarget consumers with online ads."

When you refer to Volume 1, Section 2.7, "Billboard Advertising," you'll find we detailed why it's important to make every inch of the creativity you use in your advertising work for your business. When you clearly communicate your compelling message, you'll motivate your prospects and customers to act.

Regardless of whether you use OOH or DOOH, your compelling message must be concise (eight or fewer words), clear, readable at all times (e.g., no matter the time of day, weather conditions, etc.) and free of distractions. To be free of distractions, any images and words you use are focused on delivering one easy and compelling message and call to action. Additionally, the use of a QR code and a dedicated landing page make it easy for your prospects and customers to respond to your compelling call to action.

You'll find a growing list of tools, resources, and examples at gMarketing.com/Club to give you a head start with OOH and DOOH advertising.

SECTION III

Guerrilla Minimedia Marketing

GUERRILLA MINIMEDIA MARKETING

Your Guerrilla Minimedia Marketing lets your talent, Guerrilla Creativity, and style shine. You can color outside of the lines and be extraordinarily unconventional with your Guerrilla Minimedia Marketing. However, to be effective, your efforts must be built on a strong foundation and be consistent with all of your marketing.

When you align your Guerrilla Minimedia Marketing with your Guerrilla Marketing plan, USP, Guerrilla Creative and Advertising strategy, Guerrilla ten words, and Guerrilla Company Attributes and Attitudes, you're engaging in intelligent and effective marketing.

As a Guerrilla marketer, you know that your marketing efforts work together—just like each instrument in a band that, when playing the same song in perfect harmony, creates extraordinary music. Your goal is simple: Clearly and consistently communicate your compelling marketing messages (e.g., your competitive advantages, USP, etc.) as you address your prospects' and customers' pain points to generate profits.

Resist the temptation to communicate many different and/or disconnected marketing messages. When you communicate too much, you're communicating nothing at all. Your prospects and customers have limited attention spans, which means you must make every word in your marketing message(s) compelling. Each marketing message should compel your prospects and customers to engage with your business and make a purchase or learn more.

Additionally, resist the temptation to communicate marketing messages that are interesting to you but irrelevant for your prospects or customers. Your goal is to be compelling, engaging, and motivating.

- 3.1   Interior Design and Signage
- 3.2   Exterior Signage
- 3.3   Vehicle Wraps
- 3.4   Business Cards
- 3.5   Digital Templates and Stationery
- 3.6   Personalization
- 3.7   Telephone Marketing
- 3.8   Easy Contact
- 3.9   A Vanity Phone Number
- 3.10 Directory Advertising

3.11   Postcards
3.12   Classified Advertising
3.13   Shared Advertising
3.14   Coupons and Coupon Sites
3.15   Cash Back/Point-Shopping Portal Sites
3.16   Community Advertising
3.17   Traveler Advertising
3.18   Niche Out-of-Home Advertising
3.19   Events, Conferences, and Trade Shows
3.20   Shopping Deals on TV
3.21   Canvassing and Street Teams

In Volume 2, we addressed:
3.22   Promotional Item Advertising
3.23   Promotional Item Marketing
3.24   Drone Marketing
3.25   Mapping
3.26   Receipt Marketing
3.27   Retail Location Selection
3.28   Product Labels
3.29   Shopping Bags

Now, we'll pick up where we left off. Without further ado, let's get started.

3.30 * SHOP THE BLOCK

Guerrilla marketers know that collaboration (see Volume 1, Section 7.6, "Fusion/Affiliate Marketing and Collaboration") and relationship building (see Section 9.29, "Relationship Builder") are great ways to make their business shine while putting their Guerrilla Creativity (see Volume 1, Section 1.2, "Guerrilla Creativity") to use.

Fortunately, online-only businesses have the same opportunity as those with physical business locations to collaborate for a cross-promotional shopping event. Therefore, whether your block is online or on the map, there are numerous opportunities to collaborate with other businesses to help each business succeed.

For example, there are national (US) programs that promote small business shopping (online and at physical business locations), such as:

- Small Business Saturday
- Shop Small with American Express

According to Salesforce, "Sixty-seven percent of SMB leaders say community support has been important to their company's survival." You have the opportunity to create successful shop-the-block events that appeal to consumers who want to support community businesses. Successful shop-the-block events are:

- Clearly defined among the participating businesses
- Easy to understand, compelling, and motivating for your prospects and customers
- Inclusive of like-minded businesses that share a passion for high-quality products, services, and customer service excellence and, therefore, will be of benefit to each other's prospects and customers
- Inclusive of like-minded businesses that value cross-promotional marketing (see Volume 2, Section 8.36, "Cross-Promotion) and its benefits for each business
- Inclusive of community-focused organizations (e.g., Chamber of Commerce, neighborhood groups, online social groups, etc.) along with your PR and media relationships
- Well-advertised and marketed with each participant's customers and prospects, such as:
  o Email marketing (begin with Volume 1, Section 4.31, "Email Marketing")
  o Social media
  o On-site marketing, such as physical business locations utilizing exterior signage to create shopping districts and promote special shopping events (see Volume 1, Section 3.2, "Exterior Signage")
- If possible, inclusive of supplemental paid advertising to well-targeted prospects (begin with Volume 1, Section 4.2, "Paid Digital Advertising")

Shop the Block Online

By gathering a group of like-minded and complementary businesses (e.g., products and/or services), a date can be determined for the businesses to come together online (e.g., Clubhouse, Zoom, webinar, etc.). Each business promotes the event to its database as a coming together of expertise to address the pain points or pleasure points of their prospects and customers. It's an opportunity for each business to build expertise and credibility (see Volume 1, Section 6.3, "Your Expertise and Credibility") and, therefore, must be carefully curated and executed.

The online event could be short, multi-hour, or even multi-day. A hosting structure would be set, which could be one person that acts as the curator and provides a continuity thread between each of the presentations. Each business receives a time slot to present compelling information and stories around their product(s) or service(s) along with special offers that are only available to people that attend the online event.

Online shop-the-block events work well for e-commerce businesses as well as for coaches, consultants, trainers, service providers, and other complementary businesses. The key is to work with businesses that share your standard of service and similar prospects and customers. The businesses benefit from the sales opportunity and by building relationships and awareness of the businesses to each database, along with offering each other implied or direct endorsements.

Shop-the-Block Physical Business Locations

By working together and with community organizations and leaders, along with your PR and media relationships, physical business locations can create events supporting their small businesses, such as:

- Entertainment events with local performers (e.g., music, theater, recreation activities, etc.)
- Taste of town events that encourage people to try local and participating restaurants that are offering special promotions (e.g., pre-fixed menus, cooking demonstrations, discounts, specialty offerings, etc.)
- Scavenger hunt, passport book, or coupon book promotions. Online or with a designated check-in area, shoppers are given a coupon book and/or passport book or scavenger hunt list to fulfill (by visiting each business) to win or earn a prize. There are several apps that can be customized for this, such as:
  o Scavify
  o Eventzee
  o Actionbound

- Target-specific events, which are, for example, exclusive to residents of a particular building (office or residential), neighborhood, or geographic area (see Volume 1, Section 4.26, "Geofencing," for relevant information)

To be successful, your events are designed to bring prospects and customers to the participating businesses, not to create an event that competes with the businesses, which is a common miscalculation. For example, a group of businesses would not want to put an event together that brings in food vendors that compete with the participating restaurants. Instead, the group of businesses would want to set up sampling options at booths and/or by using street teams (see Volume 1, Section 3.21, "Canvassing and Street Teams") to entice prospects to enjoy the participating restaurants.

Conclusion

Working with other like-minded businesses in the area (or online) is easier than one might think, and it's an effective way for a Guerrilla marketer to succeed by being unconventional and unleashing the power of collaboration. A Guerrilla marketer collaborates with other businesses and together, they drive and motivate their customers and targeted prospects to benefit from each of the businesses. Therefore, everyone involved in the collaboration is motivated to get creative and help each other succeed.

3.31 * POP-UP

Guerrilla marketers thrive by being unconventional, engaging, and unexpected. Pop-ups are a great way to accomplish those objectives. They are also a great way to meet your prospects and customers where they are. Consider that pop-ups are great opportunities with:
- Local events
- Venues (airports, plazas, malls, etc.)
- Collaborating with other businesses (see Volume 1, Section 7.8, "Fusion/Affiliate Marketing and Collaboration") to host reciprocal pop-ups at each other's businesses

- Collaborating with other businesses with win-win options that may not be reciprocal but delight your or their customers
- Retailers that sell your product(s) or service(s) and would benefit from showcasing your business at their location (i.e., online or physical location businesses)

Pop-ups are typically thought of as an option only for physical retail locations, but they are also an opportunity for online-only businesses. After all, online Fusion/Affiliate marketing is a form of a pop-up.

An example of an online pop-up is a social takeover. With a social takeover, a brand or influencer takes over another person's (or business's) social account for a short period of time. A social takeover captures the two sets of followers and can be a very powerful form of collaboration in an ephemeral style. An example of this in television is where a guest host takes over a show for an episode or multiple episodes. It helps draw new people to the show and to the guest host. This model can be used on social accounts, podcasts, and more.

Pop-ups not only give you the opportunity to generate sales, but they also give you news worth sharing. That sharable news is great content for your PR and media contacts (see Volume 1, Section 7.8, "Public Relations (PR)"). That sharable news is also news worth sharing with your prospects and customers.

Your business can utilize a pop-up to generate additional sales for your existing business (online and/or offline). For example, if you own a restaurant that is only open for dinner service, hosting pop-ups at neighboring office buildings to sell box lunches (or other menu options) is a great way to let your prospects experience your food and keep your business top-of-mind with your customers. If selling lunches is not an option, a mid-afternoon "snack-attack" or "energy booster" pop-up and give-away may be a welcome and compelling option.

Pop-ups are also a great way to test the market when you're considering a new retail location. Additionally, when you've selected a location, pop-ups are a great opportunity to begin promoting your business prior to opening the new retail location. With a pop-up in the new location or area of the new location, you can either begin selling your product(s) or service(s) or host samplings (see Volume 1, Section 7.10, "Giveaways and Sampling") and/or giveaways of your promotional items (see Volume 2, Section 3.22, "Promotional Item Advertising," and Section 3.23 "Promotional Item Marketing"), demonstrations, etc.

As we referenced in Section 2.19, "Alternate Out-of-Home (OOH and DOOH) Advertising." Lime Media is a resource to be aware of, with numerous options for mobile showrooms, pop-up shops, and sampling vehicles.

The key to making your pop-up effective is your consistent marketing. Everything your prospects and customers see and/or sense should clearly market your business (e.g., uniforms, signage, packaging, giveaways, etc.). As you're looking at pop-up options, think of your options with the end in mind. Make a list of what you want your prospects and customers to remember and the action you want them to take because of your pop-up. Then work backward to ensure your marketing is aligned to your goals. For example, depending on your goals, does your marketing:

- Clearly promote your uniqueness (see Volume 1, Section 1.3, "Unique Selling Proposition (USP)")
- Compel and motivate your prospects and customers
- Clearly identify your business when your prospects and customers share their experience with their friends, family, and associates
- Clearly tell your prospects and customers the action you want them to take
- Clearly tell your prospects and customers how to reach you (e.g., a QR code, the location of your physical business, your website, etc.)
- Deliver a memorable experience that will keep your business top-of-mind
- Deliver a five-star experience (see Volume 2, Section 6.18, "Five-Star") that motivates your customers to leave a glowing review of your product(s) and/or service(s)

Guerrilla marketers tend to the tiny, supercharged details that can generate big profits. By beginning with the end in mind, you'll find it easy to identify each of those supercharged details that will make your pop-up marketing efforts successful.

3.32 * EXPERIENTIAL MARKETING

Experiential marketing is an opportunity to engage your prospects and customers, often in unexpected ways. Creating meaningful and memorable experiential marketing is only limited by your creativity and your knowledge of your prospects and customers. You have limitless options for your Guerrilla Creativity (see Volume 1, Section 1.2, "Guerrilla Creativity") to shine, and the following are some examples:

Sampling

Sampling is a time-proven method of experiential marketing. After all, as a consumer, you walk up to the bakery case because you want to buy something, and then you begin to tell yourself why you shouldn't (e.g., I don't know if it tastes good; I need to lose weight; I should just make that at home, etc.). Along comes a friendly sales associate with an engaging free sample, and your roadblocks and excuses fly out of the door as you purchase a dozen of those baked goods.

Sampling is a great way to take something static (e.g., the bakery goods behind the glass) and turn it into an experience. There are many options for sampling when you're not face-to-face with your prospects and customers, such as package inserts, scratch-and-sniff stickers on packaging, or scent strips or samples used as inserts in print advertising. Many products can be sampled in advertising, such as perfume and beauty products (creams, make-up, etc.).

Augmented Reality (AR) and Virtual Reality (VR)

AR and VR are fantastic ways to engage your prospects and customers in an immersive experience that's memorable and compelling. That experience doesn't require them to come to you (i.e., face-to-face) because there are many ways for you to bring memorable and immersive experiences to them.

We have previously addressed several AR and VR examples and options that you want to be familiar with, such as:
- Direct mail (see Volume 1, Section 2.1, "Direct Mail")
- Magazine advertising (see Volume 1, Section 2.6, "Magazine Advertising")
- Physical business locations design and signage (see Volume 1, Section 3.1, "Interior Design and Signage," and Section 3.2, "Exterior Signage")
- Vehicles (see Volume 1, Section 3.3, "Vehicle Wraps")
- Business cards (see Volume 1, Section 3.4, "Business Cards")
- Events (see Volume 1, Section 3.19, "Events, Conferences, and Trade Shows")
- Catalogs (see Volume 1, Section 5.7, "Catalogs")

- Product labels (see Volume 2, Section 3.28, "Product Labels") that entertain and/or bring your product to life

There are several other options for your business to use AR and VR to make your marketing engaging and experiential for your prospects and customers, such as:

- Entertainment: Lego, for example, has an AR app that brings their specific product sets to life. After assembling an AR-specific product set, their customers use the app on their smart devices for a fully immersive experience that takes the product interaction and entertainment to a new level. They also offer other AR/VR options
- Gamification: Retailers are making shopping more fun by enticing their prospects and customers to collect tokens or points as they shop. Those points or tokens can be redeemed for discounts, goods, experiences, or services
- Product Experiences such as:
  - Virtual fitting rooms and try-ons for apparel, accessories, and cosmetics (both with a smartphone and/or in-store with specialized mirrors)
  - Virtual styling with everything from apparel to home interior goods and design goods that allow users to experience a product as a try-on or added in their space (e.g., placing a vase, wall color, piece of furniture, artwork, etc., in their home or business)
  - Customization and "designed by you" options

AR and VR can excite and motivate your prospects and customers. It can also close the gap between expectations and reality to improve customer experiences and satisfaction.

Events and Location

From a fashion show to a pop-up (see Section 3.31, "Pop-Up") to a demonstration (see Volume 1, Section 5.1, "Presentations, Speeches, Consultations, Demonstrations, and Seminars) you can bring your products to life for your prospects and customers.

You can also take your product(s) or service(s) to where your prospects and customers are (e.g., community events, trade shows, etc.). When you create an engaging experience, you invite them to interact with and experience your business as they never have before. From games to AR and/or VR experiences, relaxation, and creating something (e.g., an art wall, a building project, etc.), you can create an experience they will remember. See Volume 1, Section 3.19, "Events, Conferences, and Trade Shows," for ideas. Also see Section 2.19, "Alternate Out-of-Home (OOH and DOOH) Advertising," for ideas.

Collaboration

Guerrilla marketers think of where and when experiencing their products or service would be the most engaging, and they then find a partner to help bring their product or service to life at just the right time. For example:
- Tonal and Nordstrom
- Lululemon and The Mirror

Collaborations can be big or small and be equally experiential and impactful. Physical business locations can partner with their neighboring businesses to create experiential and motivating experiences. For example, the businesses collaborate with a combined street team approach to distribute samples from each business all at once or in a rotating fashion (see Volume 1, Section 3.21, "Canvassing and Street Teams"). For more ideas, see Volume 1, Section 7.6, "Fusion/Affiliate Marketing and Collaboration."

3.33 * PROOF

Trust is hard to earn, and it's just as hard to maintain. Therefore, Guerrilla marketers understand the importance of proving their trustworthiness, quality, exclusivity, and relevance to their prospects. They also understand the importance of continually demonstrating those qualities to their customers to maintain their trust.

When you're focused on maintaining their trust, you're increasing the likelihood they will not only make additional and repeat purchases, but will also refer their friends, family, and associates. Guerrilla marketers make no mistake about the value of their customers to fuel their long-term success. Therefore, Guerrilla marketers keep their toolbox filled with ways to prove their trustworthiness, quality, exclusivity, and relevance to their prospects and customers at every opportunity, such as:

- Ratings and reviews from your customers and from organizations, such as the Better Business Bureau (see Volume 1, Section 8.20, "Testimonials, Reviews, and Ratings," and Volume 2, Section 6.18, "Five-Star")
- Testimonials and stories (see Volume 1, Section 5.6, "White Papers, Testimonials, and Sharing")
- Quantities, such as your approximate number of customers, your social reach, etc.
- Memberships and organizations, such as trade and industry groups, community organizations, etc.
- Endorsements (see Volume 2, Section 2.15, "Endorsements")
- Causes and purpose (see Volume 2, Section 9.17, "Purpose-Minded")
- Competitions and awards, which prove your best qualities, whether they are skills-based or popularity-based
- Rankings that show your expertise
- Exclusivity created by price, patents, access, etc.
- "As seen on" in the case of your video or television appearances or "As heard on" in the case of podcasts or other audio presences (see Volume 1, Section 2.5, "Television Advertising and Appearances," and Volume 2, Section 5.13, "Reality TV")
- Free trials (see Volume 1, Section 7.11, "Free Trials and Consultations") and sampling (see Volume 1, Section 7.10, "Giveaways and Sampling")
- Warranties and guarantees (see Volume 1, Section 7.13, "Warranties, Guarantees, and Service Programs")
- Demonstrations (see Volume 1, Section 5.1, "Presentations, Speeches, Consultations, Demonstrations, and Seminars")

If your business is selling and marketing B2B, also refer to Section 4.63, "Online B2B Networking."

Guerrilla marketers seek to be extraordinary, unconventional, and innovative, and they aren't afraid to tell their stories in compelling ways. For example, when you find a great review online that shares a use for a product that is new to you or that you're not promoting, share it with your customers (e.g., email, social media, etc.). For example, share a review as, "We were blown away and impressed with Amy's creative use, and we think you might be too . . . Thanks, Amy—you made our day, and we salute you!"

Section IV

Guerrilla E-Media Marketing

GUERRILLA E-MEDIA MARKETING

Guerrilla E-Media Marketing encompasses many online Guerrilla Marketing tactics, tools, and tips, including those used in social media marketing, paid online advertising, your website, email marketing, creating revenue streams, SEO, viral marketing, data privacy, cybersecurity, and so much more.

Guerrillas view online marketing as an opportunity to not only generate sales but also build and nurture relationships. A Guerrilla marketer views a prospect or customer who walks into their retail store or physical location just as they view their online prospects and customers. Each prospect and customer is unique and desiring personalized service that inspires them to make new and repeat purchases and provide precious referrals.

With the right Guerrilla E-Media Marketing tactics, grounded in a strong foundation of Guerrilla Marketing (see Section I) and aligned with your Guerrilla Media (see Sections II, III, V, and VI) and Non-Media (see Section VII) efforts, Guerrilla Company Attitudes (see Section IX), and Guerrilla Company Attributes (see Section VIII), your business will be far ahead of the competition. That alignment builds valuable familiarity with your prospects and customers. And when you avoid inconsistencies, your business is sidestepping unnecessary and expensive disruptions and roadblocks in your marketing. In Volume 3, Section 4.57, "Marketing and Sales Funnels," we'll dive deeper into the best ways to see how your marketing compels your prospects and motivates them to become customers.

Your prospects and customers have expectations, and it's the job of your business to meet and exceed those expectations with every single interaction you have with those prospects and customers. Your Guerrilla E-Media Marketing efforts provide the opportunity to learn more about your prospects and customers and deliver personalized marketing that exceeds their expectations.

When it comes to Guerrilla Marketing, your goal isn't to do more things; your goal is to do more of the right things and do them very well. That means that when you find something that you think will be effective in reaching your prospects, you must evaluate your own skills to make sure that your marketing effort is done well. You may need to learn new skills, and you may need to reach out to find skilled and talented people to help you.

In Volume 1, we addressed:

4.1 Data Privacy and Cybersecurity

4.2	Paid Digital Advertising
4.3	Display, Search, and Native Advertising
4.4	Video Advertising
4.5	Retargeting (or Remarketing) Advertising
4.6	Influencer Marketing
4.7	Cost and Measurement of Digital Advertising
4.8	Your Website
4.9	Website Hosting Platforms
4.10	Contact Us and About Us Pages
4.11	Your E-Commerce Website
4.12	Conversion Rate Optimization (CRO)
4.13	Your Mobile App
4.14	Viral Marketing and Social Media
4.15	Sweepstakes, Giveaways, Challenges, and Competitions
4.16	Social Media
4.17	Online Groups, Chat Rooms, and Forums
4.18	Search Engine Optimization
4.19	On-Page SEO
4.20	Search Engine Keywords
4.21	Off-Page SEO
4.22	Google My Business
4.23	Directory and Search Engine Listings
4.24	Revenue Streams and Channels of Revenue
4.25	Webinars
4.26	Geofencing
4.27	Ebooks, Self-Publishing, and Electronic Brochures
4.28	Courses
4.29	Membership Programs
4.30	Your Podcast
4.31	Email Marketing
4.32	Email Address
4.33	Email Signatures
4.34	Email Autoresponder Platforms
4.35	Email Split Testing
4.36	Video and Audio Email
4.37	List Building

4.38   Abandoned Cart Emails
4.39   Cold Email Outreach
4.40   Personalized Email
4.41   Email Deliverability
4.42   Email Infrastructure
4.43   Email Content
4.44   Email List Management

In Volume 2 we addressed:
4.45   Voice Search
4.46   Enhanced Images and Descriptions
4.47   Message Bots
4.48   YouTube Connected TV
4.49   WhatsApp
4.50   Digital Account-Based Marketing
4.51   Text Message Marketing
4.52   Twitter
4.53   Push Notifications
4.54   Referral Sites
4.55   Social Media Monitoring
4.56   Discovery Ads

Now, we'll pick up where we left off. Without further ado, let's get started.

4.57 * MARKETING AND SALES FUNNELS

The concept of a marketing or sales funnel is used to describe and map your prospect's journey to becoming a customer. Whether your prospect is walking in the door of your physical retail location or landing on your website, they are on a sales and marketing journey. Your marketing and sales funnels will map the journey they are on, which consists of:

- Awareness (i.e., brand awareness) of your business

- Recognizing your business and the product(s) and/or service(s) associated with it (i.e., brand recognition)
- Compelling their interest in your product(s) and/or service(s)
- Motivating their consideration of your call to action
- Taking action

As your prospects flow through your sales funnel, your call to action is the important step that must motivate them to take a desired action (e.g., download an ebook, make a purchase, share with friends, etc.) and become your customer.

Marketing and sales funnels are used to describe and map many different journeys that your prospects and customers take with your business. For example, they are utilized to map the journey that your:

- Prospects go through on the way to providing their contact information and becoming a lead for your business
- Prospects go through on the way to becoming a customer of your business
- Customers go through on the way to purchasing an additional product from your business
- Customers go through on the way to upgrading their service plan or subscription plan (see Volume 1, Section 4.29, "Membership Programs," and Volume 2, Section 5.16, "Subscriptions") with your business
- Customers go through on the way from receiving service (e.g., customer service) to making an additional purchase
- Customers go through on the way to referring their friends, family, and associates to your business

Sales and marketing funnels have been around for many years. However, the importance of sales and marketing funnels became mainstream with the growth of online direct response marketing and the ability to:

- Automate many of the steps with sales and marketing automation software (see Volume 1, Section 4.34, "Email Autoresponder Platforms," and Section 4.61, "Customer Relationship Management Platforms (CRMs)")
- Track each step in the sales or marketing funnel
- Analyze the effectiveness of each step and split test options (see Volume 1, Section 2.8, "Advertising Keys to Success," and Section 4.35, "Email Split Testing") to improve your engagement, motivation, and results

At a minimum, the idea is to compel and motivate prospects through a sales funnel comprising of a lead magnet, sales landing page, and checkout page. From that point, a wide variety of more complex funnels can be developed and utilized to find the right solution for each of your prospects by offering upsells and down-sells to motivate them to become your customer.

Whether you're just getting started or you want to enhance your existing sales funnel, where do you begin? Guerrilla marketers use all of their research and customer knowledge (begin with Volume 1, Section 1.1, "Research and Knowing) to determine what combination of products, services, offers, and promotions will appeal to the needs and pain points of their prospects. With that determination, it's time to build a sales funnel that maps how to successfully deliver those offers to their prospects and motivate them to become customers.

As an example, a doctor is seeking to sell health supplements to address particular pain points shared by his/her prospects. Therefore, prior to becoming a customer, they include the following in their sales funnel to appeal to their prospects:

- A quiz/health assessment that their prospects opt in to receive the results
- An opportunity to book a telehealth (or in-person) consultation
- A free sample of the health supplement that becomes a monthly subscription program unless the prospect elects to cancel it

This sales funnel describes and maps the process by which leads are acquired and prospects progress through a series of online and potential one-on-one experiences on their journey to becoming a customer.

As another example, an expert in weight loss is seeking to sell supplements, training, and coaching that address the pain points of his prospects and results in the fitness and weight loss they desire. To explain the expert's methodology and build their credibility, they have written a book. To sell the book, supplements, training, and coaching to their prospects, their sales funnel may include:

- A quiz that assesses the prospects' pain points and needs, and then they opt in to receive the results
- Offering the book for free. The offer is a free+shipping offer, which means prospects are offered the book for free when they pay $6.95 for shipping costs. Any buyer of the book is a buyer and no longer a lead or prospect; they are now considered a customer
    o Upon purchase of the book, a series of complimentary products and services, such as supplements, training, and coaching are offered

- o Social and community opportunities are offered for the expert to build relationships (see Section 9.29, "Relationship Builder") with their customers and within the expert's community

Sales funnels serve to automate and replicate a perfect selling situation to address the needs of as many of your prospects as possible. They are a very powerful systemization tactic to ensure each of your leads get the same experience and the same opportunity to buy each time.

The key is to first decide if a funnel can work for your product(s) and/or service(s) and then decide which technology to use. The common types of sales funnels are:

- Book funnels
- Free plus shipping
- Quiz funnels
- Assessment funnels
- Book an appointment funnels
- E-commerce funnels

Funnels are not for every situation; however, they apply to many more use cases than people initially realize. Consider how a properly conceived and designed sales funnel could help your business. There are a dizzying array of funnel tools out there that either stand beside or operate within your website.

If you have a hosted WordPress website, there are numerous plugin options for building your sales funnels. If you have a non-WordPress site or are looking for more options, there are many standalone marketing automation options. See Volume 1, Section 4.34 "Email Autoresponder Platforms," and Section 4.61, "Customer Relationship Management Platforms (CRMs)," for more information.

Regardless of what technology you choose, a sales funnel can seek to effectively replace a person-to-person sales process, or it can lead to a person-to-person opportunity as a step within the funnel. With a sophisticated sales and marketing automation platform, you can incorporate numerous one-on-one activities, such as:

- Social selling (see Section 4.59, "Social Selling")
- Appointment setting
- Demonstrations
- Proposals
- Negotiation steps
- Follow-up

The more expensive it is for your business to attract leads and prospects, the more important your sales funnel is to maximize your profits. Therefore, a robust sales and marketing automation platform will help you actively track and analyze every step in the process to maximize your results.

Creating successful sales and marketing funnels brings together:
- What you would like your prospects and customers to do
- What your prospects and customers are likely to do
- Analyzing what they did

If you only consider what you would like your prospects and customers to do, you'll miss many opportunities. Your knowledge of your prospects and customers can help you identify where they are (see Volume 2, Section 6.16, "Meet Prospects and Customers Where They Are") so you can meet them there. Additionally, careful tracking and analysis of your sales funnel will help you identify the holes in your funnel—where you're not compelling, motivating, or meeting your customers' desires.

Very small tweaks to a funnel can yield significant changes in profitability. It could be as simple as timing or follow-up, or it could be more challenging, such as changing trends and/or finding the right message at the right time, Therefore, it's essential to continually analyze and test improvements and solutions (e.g., split testing) to drive maximum return on investment from the lead-generating efforts.

4.58 * OPT-IN FORMS

Guerrilla marketers tend to the tiny, supercharged details that can generate big profits. Your online opt-in forms are one of those supercharged details. Your opt-in forms feed into your autoresponder and CRM (see Volume 1, Section 4.34, "Email Autoresponder Platforms") to turn interactions into connections and relationships with your prospects and customers.

Opt-in forms are placed conspicuously on your website and on special squeeze pages (i.e., a form of a landing page that is dedicated to driving email opt-ins), and opt-in forms should be placed on a variety of pages and portions of the website, such as:
- Landing pages

- Your homepage
- Blog posts
- Pop-ups
- Exit-pops

Utilizing well-placed opt-in forms is a must to turn your prospects who visit your pages into customers. When your prospects choose to opt in, you have a golden opportunity because they have opened the door and are giving your business the chance to motivate them to make purchases.

There are several choices to consider when creating your compelling opt-in forms.

Timing

We've all landed on a webpage and are immediately interrupted with an opt-in form. When you've compelled your prospects to visit your site (e.g., in response to an online ad, article, press release, etc.) the immediate appearance of your opt-in form can be a distraction and result in them quickly leaving your website. Most opt-in forms will allow you to choose when the form appears (e.g., immediately, after a specified amount of scrolling, after a set period of time, at the anticipated exit, etc.). A Guerrilla marketer is keenly aware that their compelling content, product(s), or service(s) are what must first interest your prospect before they are motivated to opt in.

Location

Your opt-in form can be a pop-up, pop-over, sidebar, widget, and/or menu option. You can choose multiple locations to make it as easy and convenient as possible for your prospects to opt in whenever they are motivated to do so.

Ease of use

Your opt-in forms should be clear, simple, and free of distractions. The form has one purpose, which is to encourage your customers and prospects to join your email list. It's also a great practice to make it easy to close or dismiss the opt-in form if your prospects choose to do so. When you choose to have your opt-in form in more than one location (e.g., sidebar and an easy menu option), you'll make it easy for those prospects to opt in when they feel motivated to do so. It's also important to ensure that your opt-in forms are mobile-friendly in all aspects. You may consider requiring only email addresses or first names and email addresses. If you choose to add more fields, be aware that the more fields you require, the more information you can gather; however, it adds more friction, which often lowers the opt-in percentage.

Single Opt-In or Double Opt-In and reCAPTCHA

reCAPTCHA is a service offered by Google that helps to reduce spam with your opt-ins, and it can be used with single opt-in forms or double opt-in forms. While single opt-in forms are the easiest for your prospects, double opt-in forms (i.e., the prospect enters their email address, receives an email, and has to click a link to confirm their opt-in) are the most ideal for ensuring correct email addresses, a clean email list, reduced spam complaints, etc. See Volume 1, Sections 4.37, "List Building," and 4.44, "Email List Management."

Conclusion

While there are several considerations when it comes to creating high-performing opt-in forms, decisions can be confidently made with split testing. Split testing will help you determine the most appealing options for your prospects and customers. You can easily set up split tests with your opt-in forms to find the most appealing options for your prospects and customers and the most effective placement, timing, and required fields. See Volume 1, Sections 4.12, "Conversion Rate Optimization (CRO)," and 4.35, "Email Split Testing," for more information.

4.59 * SOCIAL SELLING

Social selling is the online version of offline networking and cold calling. Social selling focuses on driving awareness of your business (i.e., brand awareness) and sales by building rapport and relationships that are person to person (or peer to peer).

Social platforms (e.g., Facebook, LinkedIn, Pinterest, Instagram, TikTok, Twitter, etc.) make it easy for your business to see and be seen by your ideal prospects and customers. Social selling utilizes those platforms and a Guerrilla marketer's successful relationship-building skills (see Section 9.29, "Relationship Builder") to help them stand out.

A quality social-selling initiative is filled with value, interaction, an interest in people (see Volume 1, Section 9.6, "Honest Interest in People"), rapport-building, and soft selling. Guerrilla marketers don't make the mistakes that other businesses do. Everything goes wrong for businesses that use a social platform as a pitch-zone and for hard selling. That means the business doesn't have a relationship with their prospects (hence the business is a stranger to the prospects), and the business is constantly promoting its product(s) or service(s) and adding little to no value to the social dialogue.

People often use social platforms primarily for entertainment. Therefore, to break through and compel them, you can present your marketing in an entertainment-focused manner and one that is focused on a specific action that you want them to take. Consequently, you can let your Guerrilla Creativity (see Volume 1, Section 1.2, "Guerrilla Creativity) shine and measure your results by the actions they take.

Your prospects and customers use social platforms for different reasons and hard selling is not the way to attract them, especially those who are casual users. Instead, social selling is the time for your consistent and appealing Guerrilla Company Attitudes (see Section IX) to shine. Consider sharing information, statistics, memes, jokes, polls, and other engaging and inspiring content (see Section 5.19, "Creating Sharable Content," for more ideas) to build consistent awareness of your business and its personality and uniqueness. The term edu-tainment was coined to help describe this blend of information with entertainment.

Organic content is engaging for your prospects, and it can move them from awareness of your business (i.e., brand awareness) to helping them recognize (and helping your customers recall) your business and the product(s) and/or service(s) associated with it (i.e., brand recognition). Once your prospects are familiar with your business and your customers recall your business, they are more likely to make purchases.

Both online and offline, building rapport is the key to selling and creating relationships. It may be easiest to think about it from an offline perspective. For example, if you're a sales agent and you attend a birthday party, you'll likely view it as being filled with potential clients. However, they are at the party to celebrate a birthday, not to purchase what you're selling. Therefore, going from saying hello, straight to a hard sell sales pitch is not a good idea. Word spreads quickly at the party, and everyone knows to avoid you and your sales pitch.

Instead, organic conversations—including asking people how they know the person celebrating their birthday (i.e., finding people in common who might be your customers), asking what they do for a living, and asking about their interests (i.e., finding common experiences and pursuits)—allows you to build rapport and get to know each other before they are receptive to your selling.

There is time to soft sell once a positive rapport is established. That time may not be at that birthday party, but your rapport has opened the door for a later opportunity. That opportunity is greatly enhanced when you refer to your friends in common (who are your customers) and how your product(s) or service(s) relate to their job and/or interests that you learned about at the birthday party. Telling stories instead of selling (see Volume 1, Section 6.5, "Stories Sell") sets your business apart.

All the same elements of that offline birthday party experience apply to your online social-selling opportunity. Therefore, you're wise to, first, build rapport and a relationship with all new contacts. Your rapport and relationships lead to soft selling (e.g., your USP, problem-solving, providing solutions, etc.) opportunities.

There are platforms and tools that can help you manage social selling that you'll want to become familiar with, such as:

- LinkedIn: offers a Social Selling Index dashboard (in Sales Navigator) to assess your performance and find ways to improve over time. According to LinkedIn, social-selling leaders yield multiple benefits, such as:
  - "Social selling leaders create 45% more opportunities than peers with lower SSI
  - Social selling leaders are 51% more likely to reach quota.
  - 78% of social sellers outsell peers who don't use social media."
- Hootsuite Inbox: allows your business to organize private and public messages across multiple social platforms in one inbox. They also offer collaboration tools to ensure that messages are being directed to the best-qualified person. With filters and saved responses, you can work and respond efficiently

When looking at tools for social selling, they are often blurred together with social commerce (see Section 4.60, "Social Commerce"). To be effective with your social selling, it's important to maintain a distinction between the interactive dialogue and relationship-building of social selling and the promotional approach of social commerce.

4.60 * SOCIAL COMMERCE

The number of social commerce buyers is steadily increasing in the US, according to eMarketer. The dramatic increase in 2020 is expected to normalize with growth continuing. They project US social commerce buyers to be 96.1 million in 2022 and 101.1 million in 2023. Although those numbers are a small percentage of the overall ecommerce figures, social commerce is a growing trend and a worthwhile opportunity for many Guerrilla businesses.

According to the research from eMarketer, "Apparel/accessories remains the largest category for social commerce, but consumer electronics, cosmetics, home decor, and consumer goods are also key players. Brands featuring new and differentiated products and/or aspirational imagery are best suited for the social commerce environment."

Social commerce allows your prospects and customers to buy your product(s) or service(s) within the social media platforms. In Volume 2, Section 7.23, "Expanded Distribution," we addressed social media selling platforms as an option to increase your sales. Additionally, in Volume 2, Section 4.49, "WhatsApp" and Section 4.48, "YouTube Connected TV," we addressed how these platforms are enabling numerous opportunities, including social selling, for your business.

Additional examples of social commerce options are:
- Facebook and Instagram shops, which are easily set up in your Facebook business profile and from your Ecwid dashboard and can be configured to sync with your ecommerce store. With Shoppable tags on your Instagram page, you'll connect to your Facebook store
- Pinterest has a partnership with Shopify, which allows Shopify merchants to upload catalogs and turn products into shoppable pins
- TikTok Shopping has also partnered with Shopify to add a shopping tab to their TikTok profile (with a TikTok for business account). Shopify

merchants can sync their product catalogs to create a mini-storefront that connects with their online store checkout

Social commerce allows for interaction along the sales and marketing funnel journey (see Section 4.57 "Marketing and Sales Funnels"). Social commerce can also remove the barriers and roadblocks between social discovery of a product and purchasing the product.

On social platforms, your prospects and customers are often looking for product(s) and service(s) used by and recommended by people they know, like, and trust. That discovery may happen organically (e.g., user-generated content) or by paid advertising efforts. Either way, social commerce can reduce the number of steps required to make a product purchase.

For example, social media influencers, from micro-influencers to mega-influencers (see Volume 1, Section 4.6, "Influencer Marketing"), have loyal followers that will consider buying the latest skincare, clothing, or other products or services that they recommend. With the use of social commerce, the barriers are removed, and by doing so, it helps increase the number of purchases.

If your product(s) or service(s) is an appealing category for social commerce, your business has an easy opportunity to increase its profits.

4.61 * Customer Relationship Management Platforms (CRMs)

Customer Relationship Management Platforms (CRMs) are a must for most businesses. Your ability to seamlessly manage your marketing and customers in one system will set your business apart.

In Volume 1, Section 8.31, "Systems and Automation," we addressed the different levels of marketing automation to put to work for your business. In summary:

- Light versions of marketing automation are auto-responders (e.g., Get Response, Constant Contact, MailChimp, and AWeber), and we addressed the pros and cons that you'll want to be familiar with. Also see Volume 1, Section 4.34, "Email Autoresponder Platforms"

- More robust versions of marketing automation are Customer Relationship Management (CRM) systems. CRM systems will help you manage your marketing, customers, and transactions in one system. Examples of CRM systems are:
    - Sales Force
    - Infusionsoft/Keap
    - Marketo
    - Zoho CRM
- As your business grows, an Enterprise Resource Planning (ERP) service offers CRM services plus automation for the entire business, including financials, inventory management, re-stocking, etc. Companies, like Sales Force, offer these services, or there are industry-specific ERPs that can be cost-effective because they narrow their focus specifically to the needs of the businesses in your industry

It's important to find a system that matches your capabilities and is easy for your business to fully utilize and grow with. Your business only benefits from the capabilities of a CRM system, when you're able to use those capabilities. A system that overreaches the technical know-how and/or interest of your business can result in under-utilization of the available functions and lost time spent learning, resolving challenges, and correcting mistakes.

Just as with the three bears, you don't want to choose a bed (i.e., a CRM system) that's too hard, as we just outlined. You also don't want to choose a bed (i.e., a CRM system) that's too soft. A CRM system that's too soft might be fast and simple, but it can leave your business behind when it comes to the capabilities of your competition. Finding the bed (i.e., a CRM system) that's just right for your business means factoring in numerous important considerations, such as:

- Ease of use
- Integrations with your existing systems
- Growth capabilities
- Storage and user limits and related costs
- Automation
- Personalization capabilities
- Journey capabilities for your sales and marketing funnel (e.g., action-based stops, path changes, etc.)
- AI
- Learning resources and support for set-up and operation of the system

- Cross-device (e.g., mobile or desktop) and platform (e.g., different browsers, email, etc.) recognition for singular prospect and customer identification

Choosing a CRM system that matches your capabilities and is easy for your business to fully utilize and grow with will help your business seamlessly, delighting your prospects and customers today and long into the future.

4.62 * DIGITAL ATTRIBUTION

It's becoming increasingly difficult to attribute sales or leads to a particular Guerrilla E-Media Marketing tactic, especially as you utilize more and more tactics. The cause of this is due, in part, to growing privacy concerns, the changes in privacy laws/policies, and an aggressive desire for data.

Guerrilla marketers are keenly aware of the need to understand what is working with their marketing and advertising efforts. In Section 2.17, "Attribution," we addressed the importance of attribution regarding your Guerrilla Maximedia Marketing efforts. When your business is deploying multiple marketing tactics, including Guerrilla Maximedia Marketing, you're encouraged to carefully review that section.

However, many businesses focus their marketing efforts on Guerrilla E-Media Marketing tactics only, and therefore, their concern is digital attribution modeling. Simply put, if you don't know what's working, you can't do more of it and continually refine it to keep improving your results. Equally, if you don't know what's not working, you can't improve it or know to stop doing it. Both scenarios make for expensive marketing investments and digital attribution can help.

Because you want to know what's working and what's not with your marketing and advertising efforts, you'll want to attribute your sales, opt-ins, and other important actions to their specific cause (i.e., marketing and advertising tactics). An important consideration is the timing of your marketing tactic, to attribute it as:

- The first touch or the first advertisement that your prospect or customer interacted with before making a purchase

- The last touch or the last advertisement that your prospect or customer interacted with before making a purchase
- Linear, or attributing each advertising tactic along the path equally

The timing of the advertising is important, and that data should be viewed independently. For example, if your prospect sees two advertisements—one last week and one today immediately before their purchase—which advertisement gets the credit or attribution? If you chose to attribute the sale to the last advertisement, you may be missing the value of the first advertisement, the impact of their creative differences, or the power of repetition (see Volume 2, Section 1.10, "Guerrilla Marketing Repetition").

Therefore, the best digital attribution assigns a weighted ratio to the touches or successful advertising tactic. For example, there are two models that Google uses:

- Time decay gives more weight to the more recent clicks (i.e., those closest to the purchase, lead generation, etc.) and declining (over time) credit to prior clicks
- Position-based attribution gives equal credit to the first touch and last touch and distributes credit for each of the clicks in between

Additional digital attribution models are:

- View through attribution (VTA) or impression tracking. This attribution model accounts for advertisements that your prospects and customers viewed but did not click
- Click-through attribution (CTA), which accounts for advertising that your prospects and customers clicked

Attribution also helps your business be more accurate with your key performance indicators (KPIs), such as return on ad spend (ROAS). It's important to know how much you spent to turn a prospect into a customer. The better you can attribute your advertising to leads and sales, the better you can manage your marketing investments.

The most common method for accumulating data for digital attribution has been the cookie-based method. With cookie-based attribution, a person sees an advertisement and clicks on it. As a result, a cookie is dropped on their browser. When they make a purchase, at that time or later, the cookie helps to close the loop for the advertiser. Therefore, the advertising is credited with having stimulated the sale. However, cookie-based attribution is rarely that simple.

The challenge is your prospects and customers are surfing, browsing, and shopping across multiple devices. Your prospects and customers are also using privacy-centric browsers, such as Brave and Firefox. They are also using devices such as Apple, whose Safari browser makes tracking difficult.

Multiplying those issues is the growing complexity of privacy rules, regulations, and laws. See Volume 1, Section 4.1, "Data Privacy and Cybersecurity," for more information. With all issues considered, Guerrilla marketers have a true challenge when it comes to digital attribution.

You'll find that most digital advertising platforms have digital attribution capabilities. When it comes to using that information to determine your ROAS, you want to understand the calculation methodology (i.e., first touch, last touch, VTA, CTR, etc.) to determine the certainty of the data for your business.

As your digital advertising and marketing efforts increase, you'll want to look at tracking platforms to help you consistently track your performance across each advertising network. See Section 2.17, "Attribution," for examples.

4.63 * Online B2B Networking

Guerrilla marketers know putting their social-selling skills (see Section 4.59, "Social Selling") to work will boost their B2B networking and sales results. Social selling gives you and your business the opportunity to be engaged early in the buying cycle of your prospects.

Hosting and attending targeted Meetups is a great way to combine your online and one-on-one marketing talents. See Volume 1, Section 7.1, "Organizing and Hosting Meetups," for ideas to bring like-minded people together for meaningful networking.

Your business has numerous tactics available to you such as geofencing, IP-based targeting, retargeting, etc. Be sure to see Volume 2, Section 4.50, "Digital Account-Based Marketing," for valuable tactics and the tools you need to help your business get noticed at the right time.

We'll focus on LinkedIn for the remainder of this section because according to LinkedIn, they are the top platform for lead generation with four out of five of their members driving business decisions and over 750 million professionals that are users. That is an audience and an opportunity that you want to compel and motivate to engage with you and your business.

The challenge is making your business stand out and be noticed by your prospects. Fortunately, Guerrilla marketers understand how to make LinkedIn work for them.

Profile

When it comes to your profile, there are best practices for helping you and your business stand out. For example:
- Utilize a background photo (currently LinkedIn recommends a background photo size of 1584 x 396 pixels)
- Set a custom URL (in the View Profile setting, go to Edit Public Profile and URL)
- Add links to external content such as websites, social media, etc.
- Focus on SEO by optimizing the words you use to help your profile be found in searches (see Volume 1, Section 4.19, "On-Page SEO")
- Leverage endorsements

Connecting

As we addressed in Volume 2, Section 5.15, "Connections," there are several LinkedIn tactics that will help you and your business establish and/or grow your valuable connections:
- Build a network that is focused on your goals (e.g., industry experts, peers, colleagues, prospects, customers, etc.)
- Ask a connection of yours to introduce you to a particular connection of theirs, with whom there is mutual interest and value. It's far more valuable to receive the benefit of an endorsement or implied endorsement that the introduction will provide
- When you're sending an invitation to connect, take the time to use the "personalize invite" tool. This is your time to mention where you may have met or to let them know that you appreciate the information they shared, and you would like to know more

Content and Sharing

You are your content in the eyes of your prospects and customers, and Guerrilla marketers never lose focus on that powerful reality. You build influence and relationships with your sharing, listening, engagement, and appreciation. This is your opportunity to be intentional and utilize your focus to make your content and marketing shine. To do so, you'll want to:

- Create value by understanding and focusing on the needs (i.e., pain points), desires (i.e., pleasure points), and interests of your prospects and customers
- Clearly communicate your uniqueness (see Volume 1, Section 1.3, "Unique Selling Proposition (USP)") and your "why"
- Create and share valuable information on a daily basis (even multiple times per day). That valuable information could be a customer experience, a tip, a tactic, or a particular tool that is valuable to you and that you believe will also be valuable for your audience. Valuable content is focused on them (i.e., your audience/prospects) so strive for a mix of company and non-company compelling content. For more ideas see Section 5.19, "Creating Shareable Content"
- Comment, like, and share other people's posts. Be sure that the post is aligned with your Guerrilla Company Attributes (see Section VIII) and Guerrilla Company Attitudes (see Section IX) so that it's building your valuable credibility

Promote

LinkedIn has a suite of advertising opportunities available to help your business be noticed. For example:

- Sponsored content, which are native ads
- Sponsored messaging
- Text ads, which are PPC or CPM
- Dynamic ads that are personalized automatically

You can measure and improve your performance with LinkedIn's campaign manager tool that puts everything you need in one platform. Refer to Volume 1, Section 4.3, "Display, Search, and Native Advertising," for additional information regarding digital advertising types and options.

Performance

To continually improve your online B2B networking you want to monitor, measure, and redirect. By doing so, you'll continually be doing more of what works and improving or removing what isn't working.

You don't have to go it alone. LinkedIn offers a Social Selling Index dashboard (in Sales Navigator) to assess your performance and find ways to improve over time. According to LinkedIn, social-selling leaders yield multiple benefits, such as:
- "Social selling leaders create 45% more opportunities than peers with lower SSI.
- Social selling leaders are 51% more likely to reach quota.
- 78% of social sellers outsell peers who don't use social media."

You can also utilize sharing tools (See Volume 2, Section 5.18, "Sharing Tools") to easily share across multiple platforms. When you're sharing valuable video and audio content, see Volume 2, Section 5.17, "Video and Audio Broadcasting," to reach the largest audiences.

If you or your business are not currently utilizing LinkedIn for your online B2B networking, now is the time to jump in and put these tactics to work for your business.

4.64 * SOCIAL LINKING

Many social platforms allow you to provide a useful link for your audience to connect with your valuable content. Commonly, the link is in your bio or on a story and/or post.

The social platforms typically limit their users to one link to avoid clutter and spam. The challenge, is how do you utilize one link to direct your unique audiences with content that is created to be appealing to them?

Equally, how can you utilize one link to multiple offers, opt-ins, resources, business entities, and more? Fortunately, Guerrilla marketers know the answer is to use a landing page with multiple links.

You can build a dedicated page on your business website to hold this "directory" of links. By doing so, you can make it easy for a person to go from your social profile to one of many of your engagement options. To be effective, this page will be carefully curated.

After all, your audience that is linking from a social media platform already knows, likes, and/or trusts you. Therefore, you don't want to treat them like a stranger, as many businesses and people do when they simply link to their home page.

This page is your opportunity to build your relationship and, therefore, for you to put your authentic and engaging business personality forward. The page should be quick and easy for your audience to engage further with your brand.

Consider including on your link page opt-in options, contact options (e.g., a meeting scheduler), products, offers, links to your other social profiles, etc. Think of this link page as an extension of the social profile that the link is posted to. It's your opportunity to extend the conversation and build the relationship (see Section 9.29, "Relationship Builder"). Think of it as your opportunity to open your audience to the rest of your online footprint. It is the gateway to more engagement with you.

An alternative to building your own dedicated page is to use a service that provides robust and easy options to dazzle your audience. There are free and paid services, and a few examples are:

- Linktree
- Leadpages
- InfluencerSoft

These services can turn your link page into a launchpad with ease. Beyond links, many of them offer services, such as customization, collecting payments (e.g., tips, donations, etc.), integrations, analytics, and insights.

Social linking is a tiny, supercharged detail. Guerrilla marketers tend to the tiny, supercharged details that can generate big profits.

4.65 * ARTIFICIAL INTELLIGENCE (AI) OVERVIEW

Artificial intelligence (AI) is having a sweeping impact on marketing in many areas, from automated/algorithmic advertising management to creating marketing and advertising copy and content. AI is not simply about efficiency; it's also about seeing and thinking differently and, thereby, creating new ideas.

AI is rapidly growing, and it's important to be aware of how it can help your business succeed. Accenture offers an explanation: "Artificial intelligence is a constellation of many different technologies working together to enable machines to sense, comprehend, act, and learn with human-like levels of intelligence. Maybe that's why it seems as though everyone's definition of artificial intelligence is different: AI isn't just one thing."

The MIT Sloan School of Management further explains, "When companies today deploy artificial intelligence programs, they are most likely using machine learning—so much so that the terms are often used interchangeably, and sometimes ambiguously. Machine learning is a subfield of artificial intelligence that gives computers the ability to learn without explicitly being programmed."

Decades ago, it was unthinkable that programmed robots would disrupt industries by performing many of the tasks involved in manufacturing. For example, in the production of automobiles, where robots have the ability to accurately and efficiently perform repeat tasks, there's been a disruption in the manufacturing process. Today AI is disrupting the marketing world.

Just as with any new technology, there is hype and misrepresentation regarding the uses of AI. However, Guerrilla marketers use knowledge to help them sort through the options that exist for AI to help market and advertise more profitably.

There are many platforms that promote their use of AI as their USP. However, their use of AI may not be unique and may not be necessary because:
- Not all claims of AI usage or application is AI; many times it may simply be an algorithmic (i.e., formula-based) software
- Not all AI methods are better than non-AI options

After all, just because you can automate and replicate a process, it does not mean it is the best process. Therefore, it's important to realize that AI does not guarantee the best results. For example, AI in software is built with the inherent biases and assumptions of the creators, and those assumptions may be good or they may not. You may find that it works as intended, or it may have significant issues and blind spots.

Often a company will tout AI as a feature and list the associated benefits of it for their customers. When you look deeper, you may realize they are simply talking about algorithms that are being represented as AI. Those algorithms are just formulas that manage "if this happens, then do that" scenarios. They are using simple formulas, not different technologies working together to enable machines to function at human-like levels.

It's rather confusing, but Guerrilla marketers are armed with knowledge to help them wade through the hype and loose interpretations of AI to find real solutions that use AI for clear benefits.

One of the easiest ways to distinguish AI is the application of machine learning. With machine learning, AI "learns" with human-like capabilities by different technologies working together and with new input and data. A feedback loop is meant to provide a path for the AI to "learn" and, consequently, become better.

In the marketing context, the ideal solutions would have a machine learning feedback loop to improve the performance of the decision-making over time. This is similar to how a human learns and grows their capabilities by trial and error and feedback.

The growth of AI in marketing is creating advancements in, for example, message bots (see Volume 2, Section 4.47, "Message Bots"). According to Hubspot, in 2021, 47 percent of responding marketers are using bots for marketing efforts.

Additional examples include creating powerful marketing copy for websites, advertisements, and more by using natural language processing. According to the MIT Sloan School of Management, "Natural language processing is a field of machine learning in which machines learn to understand natural language as spoken and written by humans, instead of the data and numbers normally used to program computers. This allows machines to recognize language, understand it, and respond to it, as well as create new text and translate between languages."

AI, in other areas, has become able, for example, to create entire transcripts in your voice and likeness and, alternately, to create unique art. Perhaps, the most compelling application of AI and machine learning today is in the management of digital ad campaigns (see Section 4.68, "AI and Marketing Performance").

A Guerrilla marketer knows that it's important to continually grow their knowledge of AI and its capabilities. Being aware of how AI can help make marketing easier and more profitable can make your business more successful. In the following sections, we'll share many of the growing capabilities of AI.

4.66 * AI MARKETING COPY AND CONTENT

Guerrilla marketers know they need an endless supply of powerful copy for their advertising and marketing content efforts. After all, when you think about your sales funnel (see Section 4.57, "Marketing and Sales Funnels"), the flow of copy from advertisements to landing pages, sales pages, emails, social posts, etc., you quickly realize the massive amount of copy it takes for a prospect to become a customer and for your customers to make additional and repeat purchases and make precious referrals of their friends, family, and associates.

The challenge for marketers is not only the amount of powerful copy they need for their marketing and marketing content efforts presently; it's also the need for continual testing to improve their results, which requires a steady flow of new copy. The constant need for fresh copy can be a significant investment. At present, talented copywriters are employed to create powerful copy by bringing together many important components, such as:

- The needs and pain points of your prospects and customers
- The USP and benefits of your business
- Consumer mindset knowledge (see Volume 2, Section 6.17, "Consumer Mindset")
- Consumer behavior knowledge (see Volume 1, Section 6.9, "Consumer Behavior")
- Competitive knowledge (See Volume 1, Section 7.2, "Benefits and Competitive Advantages")
- Your call to action

With that input, copywriters work their magic to create copy that compels and motivates your prospects to become your customers and your customers to make repeat purchases. However, there are many human issues that affect the process, such as turnaround time, engagement level, availability, price, etc.

Alternately, many SMBs cannot employ a full-time copywriter, are not aware of or comfortable with outsourcing options, or simply choose to write their own copy instead of using a professional copywriter.

Is AI a possible solution for the endless supply of powerful copy needed for their advertising and content marketing efforts that Guerrilla marketers need? Fortunately, the capabilities of AI and machine learning are perfectly suited.

Dozens of platforms have launched to leverage some of the great advances in AI in recent years. OpenAI, is on a mission to ". . . ensure that artificial general intelligence (AGI)—by which we mean highly autonomous systems that outperform humans at most economically valuable work—benefits all of humanity." In doing so, they have made significant progress in the ability of AI to both interpret and generate text.

Through various generations and improvements, the models have become better and better each time, while incorporating billions of data points. The companies that have begun leveraging this capability are able to provide online tools to create advertising copy and marketing content for emails, blog posts, and more.

One of the first software-driven, copy-generating platforms was created by one of the top direct response copywriters, Jon Benson. The system he created was able to use proven persuasive copy frameworks and rewrite them for specific products, services, or offers. Over time, the formulaic approach was enhanced by the use of true AI, using AI data models and machine learning. The platform is called CopyPro.

CopyPro differs from other notable platforms because it starts with proven direct response copy that is supplied by talented copywriters and regenerates it for the user's specific offer. It keeps the proven and effective persuasion language patterns and flow of the copy intact, which is an important advantage. Additionally, CopyPro has integrations with several marketing automation platforms, which provides the needed feedback loop for AI and machine learning. With the feedback from the marketing automation platforms, the software knows how the copy performs in the real world, and it uses that information to continually become better.

Join us at gMarekting.com/Club for additional tools and services to consider. For example, ConversionAI and Jarvis and other tools can be used for creating short ads for Facebook or long-form content for blog posts.

As with any copy-generating service, it's important to be aware these tools work best when you know how to elicit the desired output. Your business can use these services to create effective copy faster. However, effective copy, in part, requires the important components listed earlier in this section (e.g., your USP, the pain points of your prospects and customers, etc.); therefore, you may find that you want to tweak the generated copy to make it better suited for your business to shine. However, to clarify, tweaking does not mean second-guessing the copy (as unnecessary changes could weaken its effectiveness); it simply means ensuring accuracy.

The capabilities of AI and machine learning are perfectly suited for generating effective advertising and marketing copy, which is an advantage that Guerrilla marketers are wise to explore and utilize. As more data is consumed by the learning models, the copy gets better and better. In Volume 4, Section 4.74, "AI Selling," we'll dive deeper into the developing options to improve your sales and profits.

4.67 * AI AUDIO AND VIDEO

Can you believe everything you hear? AI is currently transforming what you hear. Utilizing AI and machine learning, machines can learn from and be trained by your voice.

By simply reading a passage from a book, AI can be put to work. The result is the creation of entirely new audio content in your voice. While that sounds interesting, it can be hard to imagine the benefit for a Guerrilla marketer. But imagine the possibilities of using this AI and machine learning application for voice generation to create radio ads, telephone greetings, on-hold messaging, personalized messages to prospects and customers, and so much more.

AI is also gathering momentum in the production side of audio. According to Pro Sound News, "When it comes to audio workflows, there are three main areas where AI is starting to have an impact: assisted mastering, assisted mixing and assisted composition." Also, they point out the ability for AI, post-production, to reduce the speed to market: "Sound engineers can use AI to speed up and simplify baseline tasks, enabling them to focus on the high-value aspects that require more creativity."

Can you believe everything you see? Companies have also emerged to create AI-generated video content. According to CNBC, an AI TV anchor in China was launched in 2018, and ". . . the new anchor learns from live videos and is able to work 24 hours a day, reporting via social media and on the Xinhua website."

AI-generated video is being developed for marketing purposes as well. An example company is Tavus. With the ability to connect to your marketing automation platform (see Volume 1, Section 8.31, "Systems and Automation") or CRM platform (see Section 4.61, "Customer Relationship Management Platforms (CRMs)"), Tavus can generate personalized videos. Those videos use your image and voice and can be used for personalized (see Volume 1, Section 3.6, "Personalization") marketing efforts with your prospects and customers.

This is just the beginning. Today, it requires you to record a video, record a training script with a special microphone, and other nuances. They then create a template that the AI fills in with AI-generated personalized words and even alter the video to approximate the mouth movements of those word variations.

To answer the question, "Can you believe everything you hear and see?" AI is making it more difficult than ever before to know what's real. On the downside, there are numerous demonstrations of the audio and video capabilities of AI to create deep fake videos. Though the videos appear very real, they are not.

For more tools and resources, see Section 4.69, "AI Creativity."

4.68 * AI AND MARKETING PERFORMANCE

The analytical power of AI and machine learning has had the largest impact on managing advertising campaigns and marketing performance. AI is utilized for machine adjustments to budgets, testing creative, and optimizing combinations (e.g., creative, copy, targeting, etc.). With the utilization of AI, the results can provide greater abilities than humans. Additionally, the system can run 24/7 and adapt quickly to changes in the market.

Many advertising platforms offer some form of advertising testing and optimization to better the advertising performance on the platform. AI is also utilized for programmatic buying. Programmatic digital advertising buying, as defined by Strategus, "is the process of purchasing online advertising impressions through automated platforms, allowing advertisers to aggregate, book, flight, analyze, and optimize the ad campaign." The process is less time-consuming and more capable of reaching the right prospects and optimizing performance.

Examples from prior sections include:
- Responsive search ads that use the power of machine learning (an application of AI) to deliver ads that are customized for what your prospects are searching for (see Section 4.73, "Responsive Search Ads")

- DOOH advertising opportunities allow your business to rotate different messages, utilize dynamic images and video, easily target geographies, and utilize shorter timeframes and programmatic buying (see Section 2.19, "Alternate Out-of-Home (OOH and DOOH) Advertising")
- LinkedIn Dynamic Ads are automatically personalized to engage your prospects (see Section 4.63, "Online B2B Networking")

Chatbots and message bots are also increasing marketing performance. As we addressed in Volume 2, Section 4.47, "Message Bots," some message bots are utilizing AI and others are not. The non-AI message bots are script-based. They simply use programmatic questions and responses (i.e., scripts). Therefore, the responses from your prospects and customers will result in the same scripted responses from the bot.

AI-powered chatbots can handle high volumes and can engage in small talk while they track orders, provide product details, and answer common questions. There are several AI-powered chatbot providers to be familiar with, such as:

- Vee24: offers basic chatbot capabilities along with several advanced options, such as the ability to upsell and co-browse to guide your prospects and customers to relevant web pages. They can also provide proactive nudges to engage your prospects and customers and route to live agents upon request. They utilize machine learning to enable the chatbots to get smarter over time, utilizing a variety of data sources
- IBM Watson Assistant: with deep learning, machine learning, and natural language processing capabilities they offer basic chatbot capabilities and several advanced options, such as providing relevant selections to your prospects and customers. They can also ask prospects and customers for clarifying context. With the ability to interact on any channel (e.g., phone, SMS, web, or any messaging platform), you can meet your customers however they want to communicate

The analytical power of AI and machine learning has had a large impact on managing advertising campaigns and marketing performance, and advancements are ongoing. In Volume 4, Section 4.74, "AI Selling," we'll dive deeper into the developing options to improve your sales and profits.

4.69 * AI CREATIVITY

From music to art, AI is changing the world of creativity. Those changes are empowering Guerrilla marketers to promote their uniqueness in new ways. Whether creativity is your business (e.g., art, music, content, etc.) and/or your business can benefit from greater creativity in your marketing, AI can deliver new creativity for your business.

As AI is creating new possibilities for your creativity, there are several examples to be aware of, such as:

- Deep Dream Generator: allows you to take different images that become combined to create unique and "dream-like" new images
- Fotor: offers GoArt – AI Photo Effects, which turns your photos into a variety of different classical painting styles to transform your photos into artwork
- Runway: allows you to reimagine your video content and marketing. Their Sequel product offers video editing powered by machine learning, and their ML Lab product offers a catalog of machine learning models
- Magenta: combines music, art, and machine learning. For example, their Magenta Studio offers tools for "cutting-edge machine learning techniques for music generation." Alternately, their Quick, Draw! dataset provides millions of open-source drawings and doodles that were contributed by people playing with their game
- DearDiary: allows you to type anything (e.g., feelings, thoughts, goals, stories, etc.) and transform it into music as you type. The music that you've created can then be shared with a link
- Zendo: allows you to upload images and teach it to identify and locate objects in the image, which can transform your approach to visual tasks
- Play: utilizes AI for voice generation from text. From podcasts to voiceovers, there are numerous applications to enhance your creative marketing efforts and increase your accessibility and engagement

Every day, with the power of AI, new options are being developed to make creativity easier and more accessible. Guerrilla marketers are wise to pay attention to creative advancements utilizing AI.

4.70 * NIMBLE

A Guerrilla marketer knows the key to long-term success is to be both agile (see Volume 2, Section 9.13, "Guerrilla Agile Mind") and nimble. The question is, why is the need for being nimble paramount for the long-term success of your business?

More often than not, there are issues in your business that throw you curveballs, and you and your business need to be able to pivot. As an example, consider for a moment the various platforms and technologies that you rely on in your marketing and advertising efforts. Consider both the free (e.g., Facebook. TikTok, Google, etc.) and paid platforms and technologies you use in conjunction with your organic or paid advertising and marketing.

Each of those platforms and technologies has its own terms of service. What would happen if you found yourself in a situation (regardless of whether the issue is or isn't valid) where your account is suspended or shut down?

The possible reasons for the suspension vary widely. Perhaps it was a user complaint or the result of an automatic algorithmic-based decision that is intended to combat fake news, propaganda, and harmful and/or unwanted content. Even when you understand the terms of service of a platform and are in compliance, you could, for example, find yourself in a situation where a problem with your paid advertising account leads to your entire business or personal account being suspended. Any of these reasons pose a degree of uncertainty for any business.

It's often very difficult and time-consuming—sometimes even impossible—for an account to be reinstated. Many of the platforms can "sniff out" a new account, and if they determine you're setting up a replacement account, they can elect to lock you out forever.

If your business relies on your free organic posts and your account is shut down, your entire sales funnel (see Section 4.57, "Marketing and Sales Funnels") and ability to acquire customers may consequently be shut down. Imagine having your business appear to disappear after building an audience. For these reasons, it's advisable to limit or refrain from posting content that is likely to be problematic. As a businessperson, it's time to decide to stay above a certain level and maintain professionalism. You may even want to have multiple social accounts "owned" by different people as a form of redundancy. However, do not try to create fake user accounts, as those can land you in trouble.

A nimble Guerrilla marketer expects the best. However, they don't ignore the importance of being prepared for unexpected curveballs. Therefore, Guerrilla marketers know it's a best practice for their business to never have all their eggs in one basket.

When you and your business are nimble, you're diversifying the sources and platforms that you utilize for reaching and interacting with your prospects and customers. You're also nimble as you, for example, realize a platform that works for you now may indeed no longer be useable in the future, so you're regularly experimenting and testing new options.

For more information, also see Volume 2, Section 8.40, "Profit Out of Lemons."

4.71 * TIMING

Guerrilla marketers think of marketing as pieces to a puzzle. Each piece is a complete and compelling message. However, the more pieces your prospects and customers recall (i.e., they have consciously and subconsciously collected them), the more they are putting the pieces together, which is creating a bigger picture that motivates them.

At this point, they want to see your entire picture (i.e., the completed puzzle), and they visit your website, ask friends, and/or visit your physical business location. As they accumulate and put more of the pieces together, your consistency is showing them that the pieces fit together in a compelling entire picture that they can't resist.

Think about businesses that you know, like, and trust. You know numerous facts and pieces of information about them. However, it's unlikely that you learned all of that at one time. It's far more likely that you learned that information while collecting one or more puzzle pieces at a time, and you put those pieces together, consciously and subconsciously.

Think about an image of the sun rising over a desolate beach. Now picture that image as a puzzle. There are numerous pieces that would look alike—the pieces that make up the sand, sky, ocean, or sun, having the same colors as those that fit next to them. For example, there may be ten puzzle pieces of the sand.

You don't have to place them in sequential order, but you have to realize their consistent attributes that provide the clues they are pieces of the sand. This is similar to how consistency and repetition are required for your prospects to put the puzzle pieces together and notice your business. As the pieces reveal a desirable image, your business becomes appealing to consumer behavior (see Volume 1, Section 6.9, "Consumer Behavior") and:

- Speaks their buying language
- Addresses their pain points and pleasure points

Then, your prospects become compelled and motivated to put more of the pieces together and become your delighted customer.

If your business is marketing a bunch of disconnected pieces and nothing fits together for your prospects, your business isn't creating a compelling or memorable picture. Your disconnected puzzle pieces are afloat in the sea of marketing that your prospects and customers are exposed to every day.

Guerrilla marketers know that timing is everything when it comes to your prospects and customers putting your compelling puzzle together. Therefore, to reach, compel, and motivate your prospects and customers, your business wants to be where they are at just the right time.

When it comes to online marketing, your business has five key opportunities to reach them and compel them to notice your business and motivate them to take the action you desire: Those five key online moments are while they're:

1. Scrolling and reading
2. Sharing
3. Browsing
4. Researching
5. Ready to buy

When your business consistently and repeatedly appears in front of your prospects at those key moments, opportunity is knocking and the pieces to the puzzle are coming together. Now is the time for all your Guerrilla Marketing tactics to work together. Therefore, let's look at each opportunity, and how your puzzle pieces are coming together, to be more powerful than any one puzzle piece is on its own.

While They're Scrolling and Reading

This is the perfect opportunity for your Guerrilla Marketing to shine with your engaging content and discovery ads. With Discovery ads, a single Google ad campaign allows your business to reach your prospects as they interact across the different Google platforms. For more information, see Volume 2, Section 4.56, "Discovery Ads."

At the same time, your native advertising (see Volume 1, Section 4.3, "Display, Search, and Native Advertising") is leveraging the power of Guerrilla Marketing consistency and repetition and is working to supercharge your marketing.

Sharing

Your Guerrilla Marketing is paying dividends when your customers and prospects are sharing what makes your business unique and compelling. Their testimonials are, typically, the most powerful marketing tactic your business has and the best sign that your Guerrilla Marketing is consistent and sets your business apart from the competition. That sharing can have many motivations, such as those that we have addressed:

- Volume 1, Section 5.6, "White Papers, Testimonials, and Sharing"
- Volume 2, Section 5.18, "Sharing Tools"
- Section 5.19, "Creating Sharable Content"
- Volume 2, Section 7.18, "Customer Loyalty"
- Volume 1, Section 8.25, "Referral Programs"

While They're Browsing, Researching, and Ready to Buy

When your prospects and customers are in these stages—browsing, researching, or ready to buy—Guerrilla marketers are ready too. During the time they are browsing and researching, your prospects and customers are open to new information. This is a great time for your USP to shine and compel your prospects to notice your business and your customers to recall your business by setting your business apart with what makes it unique. At the same time, your ratings and reviews will become a key source of information that influences your prospects and your customers (see Volume 1, Section 8.20, "Testimonials, Reviews, and Ratings").

As your prospects and customers are browsing, researching, and ready to buy, all of your online marketing puzzle pieces are working to your benefit. Some of the key pieces are:

- Paid ads and retargeting ads, including:
    o Volume 1, Section 4.2, "Paid Digital Advertising"
    o Volume 1, Section 4.3, "Display, Search, and Native Advertising"

- Volume 1, Section 4.4, "Video Advertising"
  - Volume 1, Section 4.5, "Retargeting (or Remarketing) Advertising"
  - Volume 2, Section 4.56, "Discovery Ads"
- Email marketing, beginning with Volume 1, Section 4.31, "Email Marketing," and the subsequent sections
- Influencer and social media marketing, including:
  - Volume 1, Section 4.6, "Influencer Marketing"
  - Volume 1, Section 4.14, "Viral Marketing and Social Media"
  - Volume 1, Section 7.3, "Buzz and Shares"
  - Volume 2, Section 4.55, "Social Media Monitoring"
- Your website, app, and mapping, including:
  - Volume 1, Section 4.8, "Your Website"
  - Volume 1, Section 4.11, "Your E-Commerce Website"
  - Volume 1, Section 4.13, "Your Mobile App"
  - Volume 1, Section 4.22, "Google My Business"
  - Volume 1, Section 4.26, "Geofencing"
  - Volume 2, Section 3.25, "Mapping"
- Your SEO and CRO
  - Volume 1, Section 4.12, "Conversion Rate Optimization (CRO)"
  - Volume 1, Section 4.18, "Search Engine Optimization," and the subsequent sections

Without going further, you have an idea of all the puzzle pieces that you want your prospects and customers to be exposed to as they're browsing, researching, and ready to buy the product(s) and service(s) that your business sells.

Conclusion

While timing unquestionably matters, so does the power of consistency and repetition, both of which are a "super-power" for your timing. When your prospects are exposed to compelling, consistent, and repeated marketing and advertising at the right time (e.g., during those five key online moments), they put the pieces of the puzzle together and become familiar with your business.

You are either top-of-mind, bottom of mind, or out of mind (i.e., not in mind). The goal is to be top-of-mind when the buying decision is going to be made. To be top-of-mind, consistency, timing, and repetition matter.

Your customers don't need to become familiar with your business, but they benefit because you're helping them recall your business and keep it top-of-mind,

By doing so, your business can not only motivate additional and repeat purchases, it can also encourage them to share and/or provide precious referrals of their friends, family, and associates.

4.72 * UNSUBSCRIBE

When you hold your prospects' and customers' data, you must let them opt out and/or unsubscribe. With the needs of your prospects and customers in mind and the knowledge that privacy concerns and government privacy laws are getting stricter, a Guerrilla marketer seeks an easy process.

With your email list, text message marketing, and push notifications, a prospect or customer who has opted in to receive your messages may, at some point, decide they want to reduce the frequency of messages, or they are seeking more relevant emails based on their needs and desires. Many businesses don't want to or choose not to offer their prospects and customers the ability to easily manage their preferences, which leaves them no choice but to unsubscribe.

Guerrilla marketers appreciate and facilitate their prospects' and customers' ability to easily manage their preferences. By doing so, your prospects and customers are telling your business how to personalize your communications with them, which is a tremendous advantage and opportunity for your business.

Guerrilla marketers understand the importance of meeting their prospects and customers where they are (see Volume 2, Section 6.16, "Meet Prospects and Customers Where They Are"), and by making it easy for them to manage their preferences, they are telling you, as a Guerrilla marketer, where they are and how your business can be more appealing to them. They may, for example, only want to receive emails and notifications for:
- Sales and promotions
- New products and/or services
- Specific product and/or service categories

For those prospects and customers that still choose to opt out, it's a good practice to ask them to share the reason why as an optional (not required) multiple choice and/or open type box.

Your email marketing system will usually force the inclusion of an unsubscribe link in your email messages. The more advanced options of reducing frequency and managing preferences are typically in the platform's help documentation and may require some special setup within the system.

It's a good idea to familiarize yourself with the capabilities and decide which you want to implement to give your prospects and customers the best possible options that are also easy to use.

A typical email footer will include the sender's name, email address, and physical address—plus an unsubscribe link that is necessary to be compliant with CAN-SPAM and similar laws, which are subject to change at any time. With the addition of a "manage my email preferences" link, you're immediately letting your prospects and customers know that you value and respect them and their desires. The simple option of being able to manage their preferences increases their desire to stay engaged with your business instead of opting out entirely.

People might desire to have all of their data deleted from your business, and that poses an even larger challenge for small businesses to comply with GDPR, CCPA, and others. If you market or sell to areas covered by special privacy laws (e.g., The European Union), you need to create a process for complete removal of personal data and a response to that request as well as designating a privacy contact in your business. These data laws carry steep penalties, and you want to establish and maintain compliance.

4.73 * RESPONSIVE SEARCH ADS

If your prospects and customers frequently find your business in their search results, Guerrilla marketers are wise to be familiar with responsive search ads. When your prospects and customers are researching, they have a high level of interest and buying intent, and you want your business to be the answer they are looking for (even if they don't know it).

Google offers responsive search ads, which allow you to create dynamic and adaptable ads. By being adaptable, your business can be the answer as your prospects search. For example, when your prospects and customers search by category for your product(s) or service(s), such as "best affordable . . .," it's a perfect time for your business to be found in the answers (e.g., search results).

According to Google, your business will "Enter multiple headlines and descriptions when creating a responsive search ad, and over time, Google Ads will automatically test different combinations and learn which combinations perform best. By adapting your ad's content to more closely match potential customers' search terms, responsive search ads may improve your campaign's performance."

Responsive search ads use the power of machine learning (an application of AI) to deliver ads that are customized for what your prospects are searching for. Your multiple headlines and descriptions will be used to generate those ads. With the tools and tracking that are offered, you'll receive valuable input regarding your selections and tracking for your results. Additionally, these flexible ads are adaptable to the device of the user.

To be effective, the headlines and descriptions must work well together to capture your prospects' and customers' attention and interest. When your prospects and customers click your ad, it's time for your consistency to shine. For example, when your existing customers click your ad and find their way to your website, your consistent marketing will help them instantly recognize and trust your business, based on their prior interactions and purchases. That recognition and trust significantly increase the chances for additional sales and repeat purchases.

When your business has the opportunity to say the right thing at the right time, you're supercharging your marketing. Guerrilla marketers utilize opportunities to be more effective with less effort.

SECTION V
Guerrilla Info-Media Marketing

GUERRILLA INFO-MEDIA MARKETING

Guerrilla Info-Media Marketing encourages businesses to leverage the appeal of valuable information in their marketing. Whether it's the information you currently possess or the information that you learn along the way, information is a powerful marketing opportunity for any business.

People seek information every day, and the more interesting, appealing, fascinating, entertaining, and relevant information a business provides, the more fulfilling it is for the people seeking that information. From the news to social media, blogs, podcasts, and videos, the right information in the right place gives a business the opportunity to deliver the story of their business, expertise, USP, and the benefits of their product(s) and/or service(s). Many businesses are discovered, not based on their latest promotion, but instead based on the information they provide.

Utilizing Guerrilla Info-Media Marketing tactics improves both offline and online marketing efforts. Online, a website that is packed with useful information is attractive and engaging to prospects and customers, and it's advantageous for SEO. Offline, information-filled catalogs, consultations, and demonstrations are also engaging to prospects and customers.

When utilized in combination, the tactics of Guerrilla Info-Media Marketing work together to create authenticity, fascination, consistency, and trust. Those are the cornerstones of a successful and thriving business. Guerrilla marketers know that consistency builds familiarity; familiarity builds trust, and trust creates sales, repeat purchases, and precious referrals, which is the fuel for long-term success.

Guerrilla Info-Media Marketing is your opportunity to build important connections and relationships with your prospects, customers, vendors, suppliers, employees, community members, and media contacts—and attract Fusion/Affiliate marketing partners (refer to Volume 1, Section 7.6, "Fusion/Affiliate Marketing and Collaboration"). All those connections and relationships fuel the growth of your business over the long term.

In Volume 1, we addressed:

5.1   Presentations, Speeches, Consultations, Demonstrations, and Seminars
5.2   Customer Data and Studies
5.3   By-Product
5.4   Blog and Newsletter Copy
5.5   Know-How

5.6   White Papers, Testimonials, and Sharing
5.7   Catalogs
5.8   Brochures
5.9   Books, Ebooks, and Downloads
5.10 Certifications, Surveys, and Quizzes
5.11 Infomercials

In Volume 2, we addressed:
5.12 Menus and Options
5.13 Reality TV
5.14 Variety and Modality
5.15 Connections
5.16 Subscriptions
5.17 Video and Audio Broadcasting
5.18 Sharing Tools

Now, we'll pick up where we left off. Without further ado, let's get started.

5.19 * CREATING SHARABLE CONTENT

To understand how to create powerful online content that people want to share, Guerrilla marketers first seek to understand how to compel them. When you understand how to appeal to the needs of your prospects and customers (see Section 6.25, "Appealing to Needs") and their emotions (see Section 6.23, "Appealing to Emotions"), you can develop and deliver powerful content.

Guerrilla marketers view sharing as a dialogue with their prospects and customers. Your content is your opportunity to talk "with" people not "to" people or "at" people. Your goal is to build relationships (see Section 9.29, "Relationship Builder") and in the process, learn more about your customers and prospects.

With the goals in mind of creating powerful and sharable content and building relationships, Guerrilla marketers seek to understand why people share content. To understand the sharing mindset, we'll explore two perspectives that provide valuable insight. With that valuable insight, you can examine or re-examine your content and content-sharing efforts to see what modifications you can make to increase sharing and build valuable relationships.

First, Shutterstock has identified five main explanations regarding why people share on social media.

"To Convey Our Identity"

People have a desire to share as a means of conveying both their real identity and the identity that they want people to see. The reward or gratification is the likes and follows.

"To Nurture Relationships"

People enjoy sharing information or ideas that they think is of mutual interest and/or will benefit others while building and strengthening relationships.

"For an Incentive"

Ethical bribes (see Volume 2, Section 7.22, "Incentivize," for more information) motivate likes and sharing in exchange for a discount of other promotional offers or benefits.

"To Feel a Sense of Belonging"

"In effect, engaging in an online community and receiving feedback for our actions can provide us with social validation and a greater sense of connection."

"To Advocate Great Content"

People enjoy sharing information that evokes emotion (laughter, beauty, inspiration, etc.) and helps them meet new people and stay connected.

To expand the understanding of why people share on social media, let's look into a *New York Times* study that further evaluates the psychology of online sharing. The *New York Times* research found six sharing personality types.

"Altruists"

Altruists share content to let others know they are thoughtful and that they care about others.

"Careerists"

Sharing content to create conversation, debate, and provoke useful recommendations defines a Careerist. At the same time, Careerists seek credit for their sharing, and they like to share information from others as they network (professionally and personally) to create contacts and relationships.

"Hipsters"

Seeking to be the first to share content and wanting to start a conversation, debate, or controversy motivates Hipsters. They view themselves as having an online identity and want to stay connected to the world and like-minded people.

"Boomerangs"

Boomerangs seek to be the first to share content, and they desire validation and a reaction (e.g., comments that are negative or likes).

"Connectors"

As the name implies, Connectors seek connections with their sharing. They often share entertaining content and other content (e.g., coupons, restaurants, etc.) that will bring them together in person with like-minded people.

"Selectives"

When sharing information of value with a particular person, a Selective seeks a response and appreciation for the sharing of information, which they believe the recipient would not have found on their own.

As you compare these six sharing personality types with what you know about your customers and prospects, their motivations tell you how you can create powerful content that grows and improves your relationship.

For example, is your business taking the time to respond to and/or share what your customers are posting? If your customers and prospects have "Careerist," "Hipster," and "Boomerang" personality types, you're building relationships when you provide them with the validation and connection they seek. Equally, with your comments and responses, their networks (which are likely similar to your prospects and customers) are getting to know your brand/business on a more engaging level.

This is the time for your consistent Guerrilla Marketing and repetition to shine. See the following sections for more information:
- Volume 2, Section 1.9, "Guerrilla Marketing Consistency"
- Volume 2, Section 1.10, "Guerrilla Marketing Repetition"
- Volume 1, Section 9.11, "Consistency"

A traditional marketer doesn't see the opportunity and power of creating a dialogue and building relationships through sharing, consistency, and repetition. Fortunately, a Guerrilla marketer does see that value. Therefore, you seek to motivate your prospects and customers to share your powerful content. To better understand the sharing mindset, the *New York Times* research also identified the top motivations for sharing content online.

- The *New York Times* found the primary motivation is to share "valuable, enlightening and entertaining content" to those they care about and to improve those lives. Also:
    - "94% consider the value and utility" of the information they will share
    - "90% share to help someone have a positive experience (or avoid a negative one)"
    - "89% share to help others save money"
    - "50% share to inform others about products they know the recipient to be interested in and possibly change their opinion or motivate them to act"
- They found that people are seeking to define themselves and receive validation. To that point, "68% share to define themselves both to others and themselves"
- "To grow and nourish their relationships" and, therefore, "73% share content online to help them connect with others with the same interests"
- Self-fulfillment, which means 69 percent find that "sharing information makes them feel more involved in the world"
- To support a cause or brand they believe in and, therefore, 84 percent seek to "support causes or brands they care about"

Keeping this research in mind will help you share relevant and valuable information and content with your customers and prospects, and they will want to share it with their friends, family, and associates.

Now that you know what motivates people to share, let's look at a few ideas to further increase your opportunity for sharing to make your marketing work harder for your business.

Fortunately, the *New York Times* research provided some valuable recommendations to marketers, and those recommendations, in part, are:

- Make your content appeal to what motivates consumers to share information with others
- Consumers seek to trust the source, accuracy, and motivation behind the content they share
- Simplicity matters. Clear and straightforward content is more likely to be appealing and successfully shared
- Consumers with a sense of humor enjoy sharing it. Consumers have a vested interest in the reaction and responses to the humor they share in order to find enjoyment
- Embrace a sense of urgency. If your content will be shared, it must be shared quickly
- Consumers like to share their comments to your business and the response (or lack thereof) from your business (i.e., brand). Therefore, be prepared for your responses (from your business) to be shared

Now that you have insight into the sharing mindset of your prospects and customers, you can create powerful and relevant content that they are eager to share. With your powerful and sharable content, you'll want to combine it with the right tools. In Volume 2, Section 5.18, "Sharing Tools," we provided valuable ways to make online sharing easy. Those tools will help you turn your valuable content into connections with your customers and prospects. Reference Volume 1, Section 5.6, "White Papers, Testimonials, and Sharing," and Section 7.3, "Buzz and Shares," for more sharing information. Also, reference Volume 1, Section 4.43, "Email Content," and the two sections that follow (Section 5.20, "Creating Personalized Content," and Section 5.21, "Creating Sellable Content") for more content creation information.

5.20 * CREATING PERSONALIZED CONTENT

Guerrilla marketers know personalization is a key to selling content. They also know long gone are the days when personalization simply meant using the names of your prospects. Your prospects and customers are looking for your business to focus on their needs so they can achieve the opinion that "this business understands me and what I'm looking for."

How does a Guerrilla marketer gather the information they can utilize for personalization? Simply put, your every interaction is an opportunity to gather the needs, desires, and preferences of your prospects and customers to compel and motive them. Consider what you learn from their:

- Buying behavior
- Advertising responses (e.g., the creative they responded to and the resulting actions taken)
- Opt-in forms
- Quizzes or assessments that, based on their responses, lead to a customized and personalized download to specifically address their concerns
- Buying behavior related to collaboration efforts (see Volume 1, Section 7.6, "Fusion/Affiliate Marketing and Collaboration")
- Browsing behavior
- Survey responses
- Likes and shares
- Social platform preferences
- Bot interactions
- Loyalty and reward program activities
- Referral program activity
- One-on-one conversations
- Split testing preferences
- Gift purchases, which allow you to send annual reminders and suggestions when you offer valuable options to personalize the gift (e.g., occasion, recipient name, etc.)

Your business can enhance that information with data appending services that help you learn more about your prospects and customers. As we referenced in Section 8.54, "Customer Segmentation," the data may include everything from attribute information to online and offline behavior.

It's imperative that you only work with highly credible data appending services because the success or failure of your business relies on it. The security of the information you provide and the quality of the information you receive are critical for your success.

With your information in hand, how do you make effective use of it? Guerrilla marketers know there are some keys to success.

One Silo

The more systems you have in your business, the greater your need is for seamless integration. Most businesses have significant amounts of data to use for personalization, but they're in different systems that aren't integrated with or don't interact with (i.e., different silos) their marketing system (e.g., CRM platforms, ERP platforms, marketing automation platforms, etc.). As you grow your data, consider using a data lake (aggregation pool) or another container to hold the information so that it can easily feed into your marketing engine.

Don't Assume; Ask

"Are you interested in . . .?" is a powerful question to ask your prospects and customers, especially with online marketing. Have you ever accidentally clicked on a link or a product on a website and it set off a barrage of re-targeting and follow-up emails? While those marketing tactics are effective, they can be more effective when you ask a question instead of making assumptions.

When you make an assumption and turn it into a statement (e.g., "Here is the . . . you want"), you can repel instead of attract your prospects and customers. Alternately, consider asking an engaging question. Think of this as magnetizing your message instead of pushing your agenda. By doing so, you're inviting a dialog that helps you learn more and deliver greater personalization that attracts your prospect and customers. For example:

- Would you like to see similar products?
- Would you like to see additional colors?
- We noticed your interest in . . . and we'd love to know what you think of . . .

Additionally, Guerrilla marketers consider more robust measures are possible. For example, ask your customers if they would like to create a profile so you can cater to their needs and desires. According to research by Accenture, "83% of consumers are willing to share their data to enable a personalized experience as long as businesses are transparent about how they are going to use it and that customers have control over it." Of course, when capturing that information, data security is paramount (see Volume 1, Section 4.1, "Data Privacy and Cybersecurity").

Delivering Personalization

Once you've gathered information to utilize for personalization, it's time to deliver compelling and motivating personalized marketing.

- PURLs: these are personalized URLs and can be very effective at drawing interest by using the person's name, such as firstname-lastname.website.com (e.g., Bob-Smith.[insert domain name].com), which would point to a personalized landing page using the person's name and other attributes to "speak" to them
- Dynamic fields: by passing identifiers in dynamic ads or emails, you can personalize the webpages they see when they click where the dynamic fields show recent products searched for, salutation, and even targeting offers based on birthdays or other attributes.
- Mail merge/data merge: merging data from your database into the marketing pieces (direct mail, email, digital ads, ringless voicemail, etc.) can turn a boring "one-size-fits-all" message into a "this message is specific for me"
- Video: you can create custom, personalized videos based on user input or data. This can be done with multiple videos in a series that plays or is skipped, based on user input.
- AT&T provides a good example: they use a dynamic presentation to explain your bill and it is complete with real data from your actual bill. This creates an immersive, powerful education tool to reduce customer service burden and increase satisfaction. New customers are often confused with bills, and this technology strives to reduce the frustration
- Browsing intent and cart abandonment emails that ask questions instead of making assumptions
- Retargeting advertising: see Volume 1, Section 4.5, "Retargeting (or Remarketing) Advertising"
- Omnichannel: consistent promotion in email, social platform advertising, etc.

Additionally, choose-your-own-adventure tools, such as LeadsHook, allow you to custom-tailor the user experience based on actions/inputs. For example, with a weight-loss offer, you might gather information that informs you the user identifies as male, mid-fifties, moderately obese, and a busy professional. With this information, the tool can change the colors on the website and change the marketing copy to "speak" to a busy professional who is in their mid-fifties, complete with pop-culture references and more.

Conclusion

All of the knowledge you gather for the purpose of personalization should be used with caution to avoid being invasive (e.g., utilizing personal information that the prospect or customer knows they did not provide to your business). Your goal is to create interactions with your prospects and customers that are delightful and build relationships.

5.21 * CREATING SELLABLE CONTENT

Creating sellable content is an opportunity for Guerrilla marketers to shine with their expertise (see Volume 1, Section 6.3, "Your Expertise and Credibility") and creativity. Your goal is to convince them of your expertise, show them how to make their lives better, and motivate them to buy in and take action.

How do you make your content as compelling and motivating as possible? Guerrilla marketers keep their prospects and customers in focus as they create their content; therefore, they:

- Offer modality (see Volume 2, Section 5.14, "Variety and Modality")
- Appeal to each learning style (see Section 9.28, "Skilled Thinking")
- Develop relatable content, which means understanding consumer mindsets (see Volume 2, Section 6.17, "Consumer Mindset") and where their prospects and customers are (see Volume 2, Section 6.16, "Meet Prospects and Customers Where They Are")
- Understand and connect with their prospects' and customers' pain points and show them how they can relieve those pain points with their expertise (see Volume 1, Section 6.4, "Bet the Solution")

- Promote their USP (see Volume 1, Section 1.3, "Unique Selling Proposition (USP)") and other uniqueness (see Volume 2, Section 8.39, "Uniqueness")
- Appeal to their prospects' and customers' senses (see Section 8.45, "The Power of Color," Section 8.46, "Appeal to the Senses," and Volume 2, Section 4.46, "Enhanced Images and Descriptions")
- Utilize the power of AI (see Section 4.66, "AI Marketing Copy and Content," and Section 4.67, "AI Audio and Video")
- Appeal to their needs (see Section 6.25, "Appealing to Needs") and emotions (see Section 6.23, "Appealing to Emotions")

As you think about creating sellable content, it's important to know the types of high-quality content that are appealing. For example, consider creating content that delivers:

- Expertise and skills (e.g., recipes, fitness, sewing, magic, coaching, etc.)
- Education (e.g., languages, certification courses, etc.)
- Analysis
- Research and survey data
- Creativity and artistry (e.g., music, photography, artwork, greeting cards, apps, etc.)
- Customized and personalized information, product(s), or service(s) based on your prospects' and customers' specific needs and desires (see Section 5.20, "Creating Personalized Content")
- Digital services (e.g., software, copywriting, graphic design, etc.)

When you've developed your unique, creative, and compelling content, it's time to turn your attention to the ways to deliver your sellable content. Fortunately for Guerrilla marketers, it has never been easier to deliver content, and you have many options, such as:

- Memberships (see Volume 1, Section 4.29, "Membership Programs," and Volume 2, Section 5.16, "Subscriptions")
- Masterminds
- Webinars (see Volume 1, Section 4.25, "Webinars")
- White labeling and licensing (see Volume 2, Section 7.23, "Expanded Distribution")
- Courses (see Volume 1, Section 4.28, "Courses")
- Books, which are published or self-published (for a direct relationship with your customers) and sold as, for example, "free plus shipping" for

physical book copies and/or downloadable ebooks (see Volume 1, Section 4.27, "Ebooks, Self-Publishing, and Electronic Brochures")
- Free content that is advertising-supported (television programs, radio programs, websites, blogs, podcasts, etc.)
- An app (see Volume 1, Section 4.13, "Your Mobile App")
- Third-party selling platforms, such as Amazon, Shopify, Etsy, Udemy, Skillshare, Thinkific, etc.)
- Social commerce (see Section 4.60, "Social Commerce")
- Broadcasting free video and audio to compel and motivate prospects and customers to want more (see Volume 2, Section 5.17, "Video and Audio Broadcasting," and Section 8.42, "Leveraging Social Live Broadcasting")
- Utilizing collaboration (see Volume 1, Section 4.6, "Influencer Marketing," Section 7.6, "Fusion/Affiliate Marketing and Collaboration," and Section 7.8, "Public Relations (PR)")

Sellable content can have many advantages, such as low cost of creation, low overhead cost, flexibility, adaptability, and high profit margins. Creating sellable content is also an opportunity to think about leveraging your by-product (see Volume 1, Section 5.3, "By-Product) to diversify yourself and your business or businesses.

5.22 * ADVERTORIALS AND MAGALOGS

Guerrilla marketers know a key to selling their content is the way in which they present their content. Advertorials and magalogs bring together the power of print marketing and your content.

If you don't utilize print advertising in your selection of marketing tactics, you may not be aware of the power of print advertising. In a 2021 study by Insider Intelligence and eMarketer, nearly half of the US adult respondents find print, TV, and radio advertising trustworthy over online advertising. That compares to 19 percent that find social media advertising trustworthy, 30 percent that find websites trustworthy, and 38 percent that find search engines trustworthy.

Advertorials, in print, are akin to native advertising online. Similarly, advertorials follow the look and feel of the content in the publication in which they appear, but they do disclose that they are an advertisement. When well crafted, your content in the advertorial will be directly related to and compatible with the content of the publication. The goal of an advertorial or magalog is for your business to provide compelling content and garner an implied endorsement (see Volume 2, Section 2.15, "Endorsements") from the publication in which they appear.

A magalog is a short-format combination of a catalog and a magazine. Its goal is to sell products through an attention-getting cover (designed like a magazine with a main image and story teasing copy), engaging stories, and high-quality images.

The goal of an advertorial or magalog is to increase your credibility (see Volume 1, Section 8.14, "Credibility") and build trust with your prospects and customers. After all, trust creates sales, repeat purchases, and precious referrals.

Advertorials and magalogs are the time for your expertise to shine (see Volume 1, Section 6.3, "Your Expertise and Credibility," and Section 8.18, "Subject Matter Expert (SME)"). This is the time for soft selling and:

- Sharing your USP (see Volume 1, Section 1.3, "Unique Selling Proposition (USP)")
- Telling your story (see Volume 1, Section 6.5, "Stories Sell")
- Telling compelling stories, such as those of your customers (who want to participate) and examples of your service(s) or product(s) effectiveness
- Case studies and testimonials (see Volume 1, Section 5.6, "White Papers, Testimonials, and Sharing")
- Conveying and connecting with prospects' and customers' pain points
- Being the solution (see Volume 1, Section 6.4, "Be the Solution")
- Sharing your credibility (e.g., ratings, reviews, "as seen on . . .," etc.)
- Utilizing an assumptive close (e.g., "I know you'll want to . . . and here is how") and telling the reader exactly what action you want them to take

Magalogs are a powerful marketing tactic used, for example, by a financial investment business to promote investment opportunities by sharing macro trend stories and other compelling content. Other effective uses can be in healthcare (e.g., cosmetic, pain treatments, etc.) and by content marketers (e.g., books, courses, etc.).

In addition to appearing in print publications (newspapers, magazines, etc.), as an inline advertisement or insert, magalogs and reprints of advertorials can be used in direct sales, tradeshows, conferences, and direct mail to compel and motivate your prospects and customers.

5.23 * CREATING SOCIAL DESIRE

Guerrilla marketers know the value of stoking social desire, instead of just garnering social attention. When you're creating social desire, you're motivating your prospects to make a purchase and become your customers.

For example, a pizza shop sells and promotes a two-foot slice of pizza. Their customers love to purchase the giant slice of pizza and share their photos online with their followers and those of the pizza shop. The pizza shop receives a lot of social attention that is tied to people making a purchase. That is stoking social desire that makes the cash register ring.

It's easy to get caught up in the battle of garnering attention online and lose sight of the goal, which is to garner attention that stokes a desire for your prospects to purchase your product(s) and/or service(s) and share that purchase with their followers and your followers. How can your business create social desire? Here are some ideas to get your Guerrilla Creativity (see Volume 1, Section 1.2, "Guerrilla Creativity") flowing:

- Crowdsourcing photos in your online reviews (see Volume 2, Section 4.46, "Enhanced Images and Descriptions")
- Challenges (see Volume 1, Section 4.15, "Sweepstakes, Giveaways, Challenges, and Competitions")
- Offering "outrageous" products or services that your prospects want to purchase and share
- Creative packaging that promotes easy sharing as your customers are opening your product
- Offering social badges that your customers are eager to share, such as a social badge for successfully completing an online course (see Volume 1, Section 5.10, "Certifications, Surveys, and Quizzes")
- Selling your products on social platforms (see Section 4.59, "Social Selling," and Section, 4.60, "Social Commerce")

As you're coming up with creative ideas, remember to stay focused on ideas that result in purchases of your product(s) and/or service(s). It's easy to come up with an idea for an outrageous product or service that garners social attention.

For example, a retailer can create a very expensive product that is aligned with and draws attention to their consistent Guerrilla Company Attributes (see Section VIII) and Guerrilla Company Attitudes (see Section IX). That very expensive product creates a desire for their prospects to share the story and/or visit their store to see and take a photo of/or with the product. While that attention does have value, attention alone is not the goal. A Guerrilla marketer keeps their focus on winning ideas that result in a desire to purchase your product(s) and/or service(s), one that turns into sales and profits.

Your customers and prospects can give you ideas when you take the time to evaluate the other purchases they share. You'll not only want to look at what the products are, but you'll also want to look at what those businesses are doing to promote sharing of their products.

SECTION VI

Guerrilla Human-Media Marketing

GUERRILLA HUMAN-MEDIA MARKETING

Guerrilla Marketing embraces the realism that you're marketing with every bit of contact your business has with people (internally and externally). Therefore, you utilize your marketing knowledge and insight, and in doing so, you're being intentional with your marketing.

Guerrilla Human-Media Marketing harnesses the power of marketing know-how, consumer and customer behavior, and the role that you and your employees play in your marketing. Marketing is a series of moving parts. When they work together, they move your business forward. When they don't work together, your business is stalled.

The moving parts of your marketing are not just your social posts, blog, website, advertisements, product(s), and/or service(s). The moving parts are also the human components, which are optimal when they're a consistent element of your marketing.

The ability to present yourself well, be engaging and appealing, and delight your prospects and customers—while remaining consistent with every other aspect of your marketing—are the goals of a Guerrilla marketer. If that task sounds daunting, remember that it's far better to do a few things very well than to do many things poorly, and a successful Guerrilla marketer tells instead of sells.

Therefore, it's wise to ensure that the moving parts of your Guerrilla Human-Media Marketing are working in beautiful harmony to maximize the results of all of your marketing efforts. After all, the best advertisement can rarely overcome an interaction with a business that has employees with poor relationship and selling skills. Also, if you're marketing a story or solution that your prospects don't relate to, the register is not ringing.

Guerrilla marketers take the time and put energy and creativity into mastering the tactics of Guerrilla Human-Media Marketing. Getting all of the moving parts of your marketing working together is a simple and powerful tactic. It's just as easy for people to do marketing well as it is for them to do it poorly. Guerrilla marketers intentionally choose the tactics that work, and they execute them well to move their business forward and create profits.

In Volume 1, we addressed:

6.1   Your Employees and Representatives
6.2   Business Attire and Uniforms
6.3   Your Expertise and Credibility

6.4	Be the Solution
6.5	Stories Sell
6.6	Appealing to Opinions
6.7	Designate and Delegate
6.8	Guerrilla Marketing Insight
6.9	Consumer Behavior
6.10	Sales Training
6.11	Satisfied and Delighted Customers
6.12	The 80/20 Rule
6.13	Your Guerrilla Self
6.14	Evolution
6.15	Connection and Interaction

In Volume 2, we addressed:

6.16	Meet Prospects and Customers Where They Are
6.17	Consumer Mindset
6.18	Five-Star
6.19	Touch Points
6.20	Influence
6.21	Human Billboards and Directionals
6.22	Be Stickie and Compelling

Now, we'll pick up where we left off. Without further ado, let's get started.

6.23 * APPEALING TO EMOTIONS

Guerrilla marketers appreciate the art and science of marketing and remain lifelong students of the changing process. Appealing to emotions is a significant factor that explains why marketing and advertising works. Appealing to emotions allows your business to go beyond customer satisfaction and achieve long-lasting customer connections.

According to *Psychology Today*, "A brand is nothing more than a mental representation of a product in the consumer's mind. If the representation consists only of the product's attributes, features, and other information, there are no emotional links to influence consumer preference and action. The richer the emotional content of a brand's mental representation, the more likely the consumer will be a loyal user."

It's important to remember that while appealing to emotions is a great way to attract your prospects' and customers' attention, you still must motivate them to act. First, your prospects become aware of your business (i.e., brand awareness), and second, they recognize your business and the product(s) and/or service(s) associated with it (i.e., brand recognition). Once they do, your call to action must then motivate them to take a desired action (e.g., download an ebook, make a purchase, refer a friend, etc.). Your marketing efforts are ideal when they appeal to each aspect (brand awareness, brand recognition, and action) at the same time.

Appealing to your prospects' and customers' emotions is an important way to create that brand awareness, brand recognition, sales, customer loyalty, and profits. We've addressed many of the ways to appeal to the emotions of your prospects and customers, such as:

- Meeting them where they are (see Volume 2, Section 6.16, "Meet Prospects and Customers Where They Are")
- Appealing to their senses (see Section 8.46, "Appeal to the Senses")
- The power of color (see Section 8.45, "The Power of Color")
- Telling stories (see Volume 1, Section 6.5, "Stories Sell")
- Your enthusiasm (see Volume 1, Section 9.1, "Passion and Enthusiasm," and Section 8.16, "Amazement")
- Your position in your customers' minds (see Volume 1, Section 8.8, "Intelligent Positioning")
- Relationships (see Section 9.29, "Relationship Builder")
- Exclusive experiences (see Section 7.24, "Exclusive Experiences")

Your business appeals to your prospects' and customers' emotions with their senses (sight, touch, smell, taste, and hearing) and by tapping into the basic human emotions, which are identified by Frontiers: "There are four kinds of basic emotions: happiness, sadness, fear, and anger, which are differentially associated with three core affects: reward (happiness), punishment (sadness), and stress (fear and anger)."

Your marketing may need to help shift your prospects' and customers' emotions. For example, your marketing can appeal to your prospects' and customers' emotions by first appealing to and connecting with them and the emotions they are currently feeling (e.g., sadness or anger, which are also described as their pain points). With that connection, your marketing can then show them how your high-quality product(s) and/or service(s) can take them to the emotional states they desire (e.g., happiness). Examples of possible marketing messages are:

- "I've been exactly where you are, and I know how defeated I felt; that's why I created . . ."
- "Are you frustrated with . . .? Now you can . . ."

Keep in mind that when your marketing needs to help shift your prospects' and customers' emotions, your marketing must stay on the emotional journey with them to establish a long-lasting relationship. Once your customers have achieved a happy outcome, your marketing needs to be connecting with their happy emotions. If your marketing is only speaking to where they were (e.g., sad, angry, etc.), you're no longer appealing to their emotions based on where they are now.

Alternatively, your marketing may just need to move them within the range of a particular emotion. For example, if your prospects' and customers' emotions are happy, your marketing should meet them where they are (i.e., happy) and show them how your high-quality product(s) and/or service(s) can make them even happier. Examples of possible marketing messages are:

- "Celebrate your success by . . ."
- "You deserve a . . ."

It's important to be aware that emotions run on a low-to-high scale, and if your marketing is at the wrong end of the scale, you can miss connecting with your prospects and customers. For example, if your ideal prospects and customers are somewhat unhappy about a problem that your business solves and your marketing is speaking solely from a high level of unhappiness, they can easily dismiss or disregard your marketing efforts as being too extreme.

Your customers that make a rich emotional connection with your business are more likely to be loyal to your business and make repeat and additional purchases and refer their friends, family, and associates, both of which pave the path for the long-term success of your business.

Understanding what appeals to your prospects and customers can begin by simply examining what they share online and your knowledge and observations from your interactions with them. It can also result from advertising responses, surveys, opinion polls, the content they share and like, etc. With your robust

CRM system, you can begin tagging and segmenting your customers, which we'll address further in Section 8.54, "Customer Segmentation."

When your marketing appeals to your prospects' and customers' emotions, that rich connection makes them interested in knowing more about the personality of your business. In 6.24, "Business Personality," we'll dive deeper into how your marketing works.

6.24 * BUSINESS PERSONALITY

Guerrilla marketers are intentional about their marketing, and therefore, they consciously create the personalities of their businesses. They do so through their marketing efforts and their consistent Guerrilla Company Attributes (see Section VIII) and Guerrilla Company Attitudes (see Section IX).

As a Guerrilla marketer, you focus your efforts on understanding your prospects and customers from the perspective of:
- Demographics
- Psychographics
- Consumer mindset (see Volume 2, Section 6.17, "Consumer Mindset")
- Consumer behavior (see Volume 1, Section 6.9, "Consumer Behavior")
- Pain points and pleasure points
- Personality

At the same time, your prospects and customers are evaluating and seeking to understand the personality of your business as they become aware of your business (i.e., brand awareness), recognize your business and the product(s) and/or service(s) associated with it (i.e., brand recognition), and contemplate the action you want them to take.

According to *Psychology Today*, "Research reveals that consumers perceive the same type of personality characteristics in brands as they do in other people. And just as with people, they are attracted more to some personality types than others—attractions which are emotion-based, not rational."

In Volume 1, Section 8.1, "Brand," we explained that your brand is generally recognizable by your visual and graphic representation (e.g., your logo, tagline, jingle, etc.). The personality of your business comes from multiple fac-

tors. As we addressed earlier, those factors include your Guerrilla Company Attributes (see Section VIII) and Guerrilla Company Attitudes (see Section IX). They also include:
- The words in your marketing
- The personalities of the people featured in your marketing
- The personalities of the people in your business (e.g., sales, customer services, etc.)
- What your prospects and customers sense (see, touch, smell, taste, and hear) when they interact with your business (see Section 8.46, "Appeal to the Senses")
- The emotions your prospects and customers experience (see Section 6.23, "Appealing to Emotions") as a result of your marketing and their interactions with your business
- Your USP (see Volume 1, Section 1.3, "Unique Selling Proposition (USP)")
- Reviews of your business and, therefore, the opinions of others because consumers often trust strangers more than they trust a business (see Volume 1, Section 8.20, "Testimonials, Reviews, and Ratings," and Volume 2, Section 6.18, "Five-Star")
- Referrals from their friends, family, and associates (see Volume 1, Section 8.25, "Referral Programs")

In simple terms, you can think of your brand as the image your prospects and customers see when they encounter your employee(s) in their uniform. What your prospects and customers feel is related to the personality of your business, which is created by the marketing and advertising that your prospects and customers have experienced and everything that happens once that same employee (in their uniform) begins speaking.

Guerrilla Marketing is a 360-degree consistent methodology that weaves through every aspect of your business for the purpose of, in part, helping you identify and present a consistent, authentic, engaging, and appealing business personality. Just as people are generally not attracted to other people who have inconsistent and unengaging personalities, they are not attracted to businesses that have inconsistent and unengaging business personalities.

6.25 * APPEALING TO NEEDS

When interacting with and marketing to your prospects and customers, it's important to understand their needs. That understanding begins with understanding basic human needs.

To understand human needs, people often turn to Maslow's hierarchy of needs, which is explained by SimplyPsychology as, ". . . a motivational theory in psychology comprising a five-tier model of human needs, often depicted as hierarchical levels within a pyramid. From the bottom of the hierarchy upwards, the needs are: physiological (food and clothing), safety (job security), love and belonging needs (friendship), esteem, and self-actualization. Needs lower down in the hierarchy must be satisfied before individuals can attend to needs higher up."

While most of the levels are self-explanatory, it's worth pointing out that self-actualization is akin to the process of reaching your full potential. Therefore, for the purpose of effective marketing, it's important to understand the needs of your prospects and customers. It's also valuable to point out that their needs change over time, and their lower needs may only be partially fulfilled when they are tending to higher needs.

When you consider your customers' needs now and combine that with the knowledge that they are reaching for their full potential, you can frame your marketing message to first meet them where they are (see Volume 2, Section 6.16, "Meet Prospects and Customers Where They Are"). Once you've done so, you can help them see and feel where they can be with your product(s) and/or service(s) by the stories your business tells (see Volume 1, Section 6.5, "Stories Sell").

If your business is marketing products and/or services that appeal to multiple hierarchical levels, you can quickly see that vastly different messages may be appealing. For example, if you're marketing clothing, you may easily require three different brands to appeal to prospects and customers focused on their needs for "safety," "belonging," or "esteem." Why? Because what appeals to each of them is vastly different. Your prospect focused on "safety" is looking for low-cost, durability, and value. On the other hand, your prospect who is focused on "esteem" is looking for luxury and prestige that might make them feel successful, which is then reinforced as they impress others.

When you understand the needs of your prospects and customers, your business will create and/or deliver appealing products and services with features that motivate them to make ongoing purchases, share their delight, and refer their friends, family, and associates.

6.26 * CONVERSATION STARTERS

Guerrilla marketers know that how conversations start with prospects and customers has a lot to do with determining if their prospects will become their customers and if their customers will make additional and repeat purchases.

It's easy for your attention to turn to just one conversation, but there are many conversations to consider. Think about each way the conversation gets started in your business. For example:

- Through your email marketing
- As they enter your physical retail location
- With pop-ups on your website
- During live chats
- Through message bots (see Volume 2, Section 4.47, "Message Bots")
- Face-to-face with a trade-show team, sales representative, customer service representative, etc.
- On the phone
- Through social media

If you're not already aware, there is no single correct way to get the conversation started. Your customers are not clones. They each have their own paths to meeting and engaging with your business, and they bring their own needs, mindset (see Volume 2, Section 6.17, "Consumer Mindset"), behaviors (see Volume 1, Section 6.9, "Consumer Behavior"), and an assortment of other things on their minds that likely have nothing to do with your business. Equally, some have eighty things to do on any given day, and some have nothing to do other than interact with your business. With that in mind, where do you begin?

First, break out of traditional, expected patterns but don't make your prospect or customer uncomfortable. It's important to remember that the conversation is about your prospect or customer, and your focus should be on them. Therefore, avoid any unnecessary multi-tasking that unintentionally makes you appear uninterested in them and their needs.

When it comes to sales opportunities, your prospects and customers are seeking to satisfy their own needs (i.e., pain points or pleasure points), which are their primary concerns. Once your business has shown them how you can meet their needs, they're looking for reasons to believe they should make a purchase, and they want to feel smart for having done so. A Guerrilla business strives to make each customer feel smart for having chosen them. Therefore, your business can break out of traditional patterns to get the conversation started.

Traditional Business	Guerrilla Business
"Hi," "Hello," etc.	"It's great to see you, [adding their name, if you know it, is ideal]."
"How can I help you?" "What brings you in today?"	*If they don't know you:* "My name is Penelope, and I'm delighted to help you with anything you need. You picked a special day to stop by." *If they do know you:* "You always have great timing, and you picked a special day to stop by."

A simple, non-invasive, unexpected, and genuine compliment can be a great way to break out of the traditional conversation patterns that attempt to make prospects immediately start answering questions, which can be a repellent. Instead, recognizing them with a non-invasive and unexpected compliment can put your prospects and customers at ease. When that compliment is connected with a quick, open-ended, intrigue-oriented statement (e.g., "You picked a special day to stop by."), you can become magnetic and motivate them to want to engage in conversation. However, it's your prospect's or customer's response, or non-response, that will give you the indication as to how to proceed with a productive conversation.

Here are examples of how some businesses utilize effective conversation starters:

- Luxury hotels rely on their valets to capture their customers' names, which they relay to the desk to allow for personalized service. When the customer arrives at the desk, the conversation starts with the customer's name and knowledge of their reservation, and that's a great conversation starter. How do the best ones do this? They read the last name from the

luggage tags and radio to the front desk. It's smooth and effective at delivering that five-star feeling
- Personalized emails get the conversation started. In your email marketing, according to Campaign Monitor, "Readers are 26% more likely to open emails with personalized subject lines."
- When it comes to service conversations, your customers are looking for quick and accurate information and validation that they were smart to make a purchase with your business. The more personalized the experience (e.g., thanking them for being a customer for ten years), the more engaging and validating it is

Guerrilla marketers don't just think in terms of how their business gets the conversation started with their prospects and customers externally, they also focus on how conversation starters happen inside their business. How do you get the conversation started with your employees? Those conversation starters set the tone for the conversations they have with each other and the conversations they have with your prospects and customers. Therefore, Guerrilla marketers intentionally model the conversation starters they want their employees to have with their customers and prospects.

Some well-regarded hotels and resorts require a request to be responded to with some version of "my pleasure." They know this makes the requestor feel respected and that their request is not a problem. In fact, one response to eradicate from your business is "not a problem." Though it's commonly used, the issue with this phrase (and similar phrases) is how the subconscious mind works.

As we addressed in Section 1.13, "Consumer Decision-Making," carefully choose your words because when you tell your prospects and customers not to do something (e.g., don't think about a pink elephant), their subconscious mind will conjure up that image (i.e., a pink elephant). Negative commands are not processed by the subconscious mind.

Listen for this the next time you are out to eat and ask the server for something. Very often, when you thank them, the response is "not a problem." It's best to choose your words carefully and, therefore, not introduce the word "problem" in this way.

Once you have the conversation started, what comes next makes all the difference when it comes to turning a prospect into a customer and motivating a customer to make an additional purchase and provide precious referrals of their friends, family, and associates. We'll address what comes next in the conversation in Section 6.27, "Calibration."

6.27 * CALIBRATION

In Section 6.26, "Conversation Starters," we addressed numerous options to help your business open the door to a conversation with your prospects and customers. Now that the door is open, it takes just as many skills for the conversation to turn your prospects into customers and motivate a customer to make an additional purchase and provide precious referrals of their friends, family, and associates.

There are numerous conversation preferences that your prospects and customers have, which include:

- Open conversations: many prospects and customers want to have an open-ended conversation before "getting down to business." For those prospects and customers, that's an important component to building a relationship. It's ideal to quickly set the pace if a long conversation is not possible, and you want them to feel noticed and special instead of rushed. For example, "What a busy day we're having. I want to quickly help you so you don't have to wait."
- Direct conversations: many prospects and customers value efficiency, and it's a better relationship-builder than open conversations. These prospects and customers want to immediately "get down to business," and they may be open to a short conversation after completing "their business"

Regardless of the conversation style, it's important to remember that effective conversations rely on your ability to learn about and empathize with their unique pain points and share how your product(s) or solution(s) will address their pain.

In-Person Conversation Tools

In-person conversations offer the advantage of body language, which is a powerful tool when it comes to having productive conversations. There are several signs to guide you, providing cues regarding how the conversation is going:

- Engagement: the person is making direct eye contact, leaning in, smiling, breathing normally, etc.
- Losing engagement: the person is fidgeting, leaning out, not making direct eye contact, not smiling, sighing, and/or seeking other options to occupy their attention (e.g., reaching for their phone, looking at your products, etc.)

Those body language patterns provide valuable information to understand how to calibrate the conversation to keep it going well. For example, when you see signs that your prospect or customer is losing engagement, it's time to quickly turn the attention back to their needs. You never want to lose your focus on hearing and addressing their specific pain points.

At the same time, by subtly mirroring the body language of your prospects and customers, you can create a valuable connection as you seek to build a long-lasting relationship. From eye contact to body language, sound level, hand usage, and posture, you can subtly create a connection.

Online Conversation Tools

While online conversations lack the insight that body language provides, there are many other advantages you can utilize. The option for live chat is a great way to quickly answer questions, but for many of your prospects and customers, they associate that option with long waits. To overcome that concern, it's ideal to ask some questions before connecting. Your business can ask those questions through a sales page. For example:

- Do you want help with sizing?
- Are you looking for something special?
- Do you want help finding a gift?

A quality chatbot (see Volume 2, Section 4.47, "Message Bots") can be used to begin the conversation and then offer a live chat option. The advantage, for your business and your prospects and customers, is you'll utilize that quality chatbot and know where they left off with the chatbot. With that knowledge, you can pick up from that point, which feels personalized and is efficient and respectful of your prospects' and customers' time. Therefore, you'll begin the conversation with bridging statements, such as: "It's nice to talk to you, [insert name]. My name is [insert name], and I see you're looking at the [insert specific product name] and you have additional questions about finding the right size. This has a great fit; let's find the right size for you . . ."

If you're looking for additional chat platform ideas (beyond those in Volume 2, Section 4.47, "Message Bots"), become familiar with these options:

- GoSquared: offers a platform that allows you to see the pages your prospects and customers have viewed and for how long, which allows for a personalized response. They also provide tracking tools that allow your team to share comments and notes regarding prior interactions and provide an opportunity for highly personalized and relevant conversations. There are also options to include social media profiles and company information, which can be quite advantageous, especially for B2B selling and service
- Qualified: is purpose-built for Salesforce. If your business is B2B, this platform can provide rich information to help you have meaningful conversations with your prospects and customers. They offer the ability to monitor your website traffic and focus on visitors with specific criteria, identifying them as ideal potential customers (see Section 8.50, "Ideal Customers") and even routing that information to the correct sales representative

Conclusion

Internal success sharing is a must. With connected/sharing tools and platforms and in weekly (or at any interval you prefer) meetings, each employee shares successful conversations. By utilizing a structured format (e.g., what was the customer's pain point, and how did you address it?), you'll maximize the learning for everyone and maintain focus on conveying the most important aspects of what your employees learned.

Including some unsuccessful interactions can also be useful. With the use of role-playing, you can provide additional tools to help your sales and service professionals increase their conversation skills and delight your prospects and customers in the process.

Refer to Volume 1, Section 6.9, "Consumer Behavior," and Volume 2, Section 6.17, "Consumer Mindset," for additional helpful insight.

6.28 * INSIDE OUT

Guerrilla marketers are intentional with their marketing. Realize that you're marketing with every interaction you and everyone in your business have, inside and outside of your business. Therefore, by being intentional about it, you can reap the rewards.

Businesses are far more transparent than many realize. Your prospects and customers are consciously and subconsciously evaluating your business based on interactions. They notice how you and your employees interact, which means they notice:

- An enthusiastic business where everyone interacts with energy and excitement, and they notice a business that doesn't
- An encouraging business where everyone works together and shares resources and knowledge, and they notice a business that doesn't
- A complimentary business where praise is freely flowing from peer to peer, top to bottom, and bottom to top, and they notice a business where it isn't

Your prospects and customers notice if your business is not living up to their standards, and it will consciously and subconsciously create or alter their opinions of your business. When it's subconscious, they speak of your business with phrases, such as, "I don't know what it is about that place; it just doesn't . . ." That's a self-created roadblock that holds a business back.

It's all too common to encounter a two-faced business. Those businesses believe they can keep things behind closed doors. That means the business interacts internally differently from how they are expected to interact with prospects and customers. For example, many businesses believe, or act as if they believe, it's okay to have openly rude, abrupt, or otherwise disrespectful interactions with their employees (peer to peer, top to bottom, and bottom to top) and then turn to a prospect or customer with a pasted-on smile and say, "How can I help you?"

The reality is that your prospects and customers notice, are influenced by, and share their opinions about the inner workings of your business. When your business is different on the inside from what you want it to be on the outside, it impacts your prospects and customers, and they don't want to have a relationship with your business.

For example, if an employee is treated with a lower standard of conduct behind closed doors, they bring the impact of that different behavior with them as they interact with your prospects and customers. It's in their tone of voice, body language, and energy level.

Guerrilla marketers avoid creating roadblocks that hinder their success. By simply creating and maintaining a standard and an environment where everyone in the business treats each other as you want them to treat your customers, you're setting the tone for success from the inside out. In business, the adage "treat others as you wish to be treated" is better stated as "treat others as you wish for your prospects and customers to be treated."

After all, a business that has highly-satisfied customers, has highly-satisfied employees. Highly-satisfied customers make additional and repeat purchases, and they provide precious referrals of their friends, family, and associates throughout their long relationship with your business. At the same time, highly-satisfied employees want to remain with your business, and they promote your business everywhere they go and refer high-quality potential employees. That is a formula for the long-term success of your business.

Refer to Volume 2, Section 9.14, "Inspire," along with the other tactics in Section IX, "Guerrilla Company Attitudes," for more information about helping your business shine from the inside out.

6.29 * MOTIVATE

Your prospects are initially indifferent to your business, product(s), or service(s). As we addressed in Volume 1, Section 6.9, "Consumer Behavior," an important benefit of Guerrilla Marketing is to help you move your prospects from indifference or apathy to making a purchase. You can do everything right with your marketing and position your business with alignment to how consumers behave and still have prospects that like your business but don't become customers. Those prospects think favorably about your business and may certainly consider making a purchase at some point.

You've done your job; you've compelled these prospects to notice your business. They are aware of your business (i.e., brand awareness), and they recognize your business and the product(s) and/or service(s) associated with it (i.e., brand recognition). After all, they:

- Open your emails
- Visit your website
- Come to your physical business location
- Are engaged with your social media

But they are still a prospect and not a customer because you haven't been able to motivate them to make the transition. They haven't moved past indifference or apathy to make a purchase.

How do you motivate them to respond to your call to action? There are several options, such as:

- Prove yourself (see Section 3.33, "Proof")
- Use popularity (e.g., we are the number one . . ., our number one selling . . ., back by popular demand, etc.)
- Offer limited-time deals
- Promote limited quantity
- Market exclusivity
- Use newness or innovation
- Highlight creative partnerships
- Use testing

When you segment those long-time prospects, you can put your testing skills (see Section 2.16, "Testing," and Volume 1, Section 4.35, "Email Split Testing") to great use. Surveys are also a great option to help you learn more about your prospects' pain points, preferences, and desires to see personalized marketing efforts (see Volume 1, Section 2.8, "Advertising Keys to Success," Section 3.6, "Personalization," and Section 5.10, "Certifications, Surveys, and Quizzes").

You can also appeal to additional elements of consumer behavior and add conveniences, such as:

Reciprocity

When it comes to marketing, reciprocity "simply means that if a person does something for you, it's natural to want to return the favor in some way," according to Patchmatics. Therefore, free trials (see Volume 1, Section 7.11, "Free Trials and Consultations"), sampling, gifts (see Volume 1, Section 7.10, "Giveaways and Sampling"), personalization (see Volume 1, Section 3.6, "Personalization"), and handwritten thank-yous motivate your prospects to respond and feel the need to reciprocate.

Payment and Pricing Options

By simply adding or promoting your payment options (see Volume 1, Section 8.30, "Payment Methods"), you may be able to motivate your prospects. Easy and creative payment plans can make all the difference. Additionally, testing pricing options and offering upgrade opportunities (see Volume 1, Section 8.24, "Price and Upgrade Opportunities") can motivate your prospects.

Cross-Selling

When you have your prospects' attention, make the most of the opportunity by cross-selling. When you promote (online or in-person) other carefully selected options, you have the opportunity to broaden your appeal and motivate them to make a purchase. It can be as simple as making color options easily accessible to offering compatible products and/or best-selling options.

Conclusion

Your engaged prospects have the greatest likelihood to become your customers, and some additional and personalized attention may just provide the necessary motivation. Though you may not be able to motivate every prospect to become a customer, the tactics of Guerrilla Marketing will help find numerous options and opportunities to do so. In Section 6.30, "Customer Intentions," we'll address more ways and useful tools to help you motivate your prospects and customers.

6.30 * CONSUMER INTENTIONS

You may not know everything about your prospects and customers, and that's perfectly fine. When you can see the intentions of your prospects and customers, your business can increase its appeal.

Fortunately for Guerrilla marketers, there are many other businesses that know about consumer intentions. They are happy to share their expertise and collaborate with your business, to help you better market your business and increase sales and/or profits. Two examples of businesses to be familiar with are:

- Namogoo: helps your business appeal to your prospects and customers by delivering the most appealing custom promotions, removing distractions (including competing offers), increasing your personalization, and more. They combine their knowledge and data with your website (with integrations with many ecommerce platforms) and goals
- BrandLock: utilizes machine-learning-based solutions to help your business identify price-sensitive shoppers on your site so you can promote appealing offers, coupons, and options. They also help remove distractions (e.g., consumer browser-based extensions, malware, and adtech) to keep your prospects and customers engaged in your content and offers
- Konnecto: gives your business deep insight into the needs and digital behavior of your prospects and customers to identify all stages of their journey and find new opportunities to appeal to them. Their Go-To-Market Intelligence platform also gives insight into your competitors to understand those journeys

The more you understand the intentions of your prospects and customers, the more you can motivate them through every interaction with your business. When you're motivating your prospects and customers in a personalized way, you're well on your way to creating long-lasting relationships. According to Epsilon research, "80% of consumers are more likely to make a purchase when brands offer personalized experiences."

Section VII

Guerrilla Non-Media Marketing

GUERRILLA NON-MEDIA MARKETING

Low-cost opportunities abound with Guerrilla Non-Media Marketing tactics. These low-cost Guerrilla Marketing tactics take your knowledge, time, energy, and creativity and turn them into profits.

When implemented correctly, Guerrilla Non-Media Marketing tactics will generate long-lasting opportunities to tell the story of your business, share your USP, and give your prospects compelling reasons to become your customers. Equally, they give your customers a compelling reason to make repeat and additional purchases and refer their friends, family, and co-workers to your business.

Guerrilla Non-Media Marketing tactics are often far more memorable than other Guerrilla Media tactics. They provide your business with the opportunity to interact and connect with your prospects and customers. With that interaction, you have the ability to build long-lasting relationships with your customers that investments in paid advertising may not achieve.

When you engage in Guerrilla Non-Media Marketing tactics, you'll showcase the expertise of yourself or your business while sharing the benefits and advantages of your product(s) or service(s). These tactics utilize your relationship-building skills to forge productive arrangements with employees, customers, complementary businesses, industry contacts, media contributors, and community members. These relationship-building skills may be utilized online or in-person or a combination of the two.

Many businesses never take the time to engage in these non-media tactics, and that's great news for Guerrilla marketers. Once you realize the kind of success and profits you can generate from these Guerrilla Non-Media Marketing tactics, you'll want to include more of them in your Guerrilla Marketing plan.

Invest a bit of your knowledge, time, energy, and creativity in these Guerrilla Non-Media Marketing tactics and see how you can turn them into satisfying and profitable relationships for your business.

In Volume 1, we addressed:

7.1	Organizing and Hosting Meetups
7.2	Benefits and Competitive Advantages
7.3	Buzz and Shares
7.4	Gift Cards
7.5	Memberships
7.6	Fusion/Affiliate Marketing and Collaboration

7.7   Research
7.8   Public Relations (PR)
7.9   Offers and Promotions
7.10 Giveaways and Sampling
7.11 Free Trials and Consultations
7.12 Negotiations
7.13 Warranties, Guarantees, and Service Programs
7.14 Crowdfunding

In Volume 2, we addressed:
7.15 Know Your Surroundings
7.16 Leave Behinds
7.17 Returns and Exchanges
7.18 Customer Loyalty
7.19 Talk of the Town
7.20 Boxing
7.21 Customer Entertainment
7.22 Incentivize
7.23 Expanded Distribution
7.15 Know Your Surroundings

Now, we'll pick up where we left off. Without further ado, let's get started.

7.24 * EXCLUSIVE EXPERIENCES

Guerrilla marketers appeal to their prospects and customers with exclusive experiences that are unique, shareable, and memorable while making them feel noticed, recognized, special, and valued.

After all, to stand apart, be memorable (see Section 8.43, "Being Memorable"), and make rich connections (see Section 6.23, "Appealing to Emotions") with your prospects and customers, you must do things differently than a traditional business. A good place to begin is promoting your uniqueness with your

USP (see Volume 1, Section 1.3, "Unique Selling Proposition (USP)"). When you add exclusive experiences, you further set your business apart.

Exclusive experiences don't have to be complicated. Several ongoing exclusive experiences are your opportunities to make continual long-lasting impressions and rich connections that help to keep your business top-of-mind. The opportunities to market exclusive experiences are wide open—such as, exclusive:

- Sneak-peaks or behind-the-scene access that is only for your customers
- Additional access (e.g., reserved parking, private access, masterminds, high-end groups, coaching, mentoring, a customer lounge, etc.)
- Customer entertainment (see Volume 2, Section 7.21, "Customer Entertainment," for ideas regarding the many opportunities you have to entertain your customers)
- Skills classes (e.g., cooking classes, insider tips for using your product or service, etc.)
- Demonstrations (see Volume 1, Section 5.1, "Presentations, Speeches, Consultations, Demonstrations, and Seminars" for ideas)
- Tastings
- Discounts and sales
- Referral programs (see Volume 1, Section 8.25, "Referral Programs," for ideas and resources)
- Customer loyalty programs (see Volume 2, Section 7.18, "Customer Loyalty," for ideas and resources)
- Networking and sharing referrals among your customers, especially if your business is B2B (see Volume 1, Section 7.1, "Organizing and Hosting Meetups," and Section 4.63, "Online B2B Networking," for ideas)
- Patents, which means your product(s) or service(s), or an aspect of them, is exclusive to your business
- Customer entertainment (see Volume 2, Section 7.21, "Customer Entertainment," for ideas and resources)

Appealing exclusive experiences are everything that make your customers feel special and rewarded. By appealing to their emotions (see Section 6.23, "Appealing to Emotions"), it helps them remember your business and motivates them to make repeat and additional purchases and provide precious referrals of their friends, family, and associates. Something as simple as validating parking for your customers can make a positive impression that people remember and want to share.

Finding the right exclusive experiences requires matching your customer knowledge with your consistent Guerrilla Marketing Attributes (see Section VIII) and Guerrilla Marketing Attitudes (see Section IX). Often, the five or six smaller, ongoing things you do can make a greater impression than the one larger thing you do. Consider that according to Salesforce, "91% of those polled say they're more likely to make a repeat purchase after a positive experience, and 71% say they've made a purchase decision based on experience quality." Additionally, ". . . research found that 80% of customers now consider the experience a company provides to be as important as its products and services."

What is your business doing right now that is available only to your customers? Take the time to make a list. Now, take the time to consider how you're marketing the exclusive experiences you already offer your customers.

Are your customers aware of and participating in your exclusive experiences? Are you making your prospects aware of the exclusive experiences you offer your customers? What exclusive experiences can you add?

Guerrilla marketers seek rich connections with their prospects and customers. Never forget that a rich connection helps your customers remember your business and motivates them to make repeat and additional purchases and provide precious referrals of their friends, family, and associates.

In Volume 4, Section 9.36, "Enhanced Customer Service," we'll address opportunities to take your relationship with your customers to the next level.

7.25 * UNLIMITED

Unlimited programs and plans can have unlimited appeal for your prospects and customers. Unlimited programs and plans are considered hassle-free, and that perception removes roadblocks for your prospects. At the same time, it encourages customer loyalty. In the minds of your customers, they don't want to go through the perceived hassle of moving away from your unlimited program or plan.

Become familiar with these unlimited programs and plans and their details and restrictions:

- MyPanera+ Coffee subscription offers unlimited beverages

- Verizon, AT&T, and T-Mobile (along with other wireless service providers) offer unlimited data (and more) plans
- The Lauren Look, which is a wardrobe rental subscription offered by Ralph Lauren, offers unlimited monthly box exchanges

Car wash businesses often utilize unlimited car wash subscriptions to appeal to their prospects and customers. Fitness studios and gyms also utilize unlimited visits to increase the appeal of their memberships.

You may not have to create something new. You may already be offering something that is unlimited, but you're not promoting it as a valuable feature. For example, your warranty or service program (see Volume 1, Section 7.13, "Warranties, Guarantees, and Service Programs") may already include an unlimited element (e.g., "lifetime"), or it can be tweaked to include an unlimited element.

Unlimited programs and plans can be a great way to make your business easy to do business with (see Volume 1, Section 9.2, "Easy to Do Business With"). However, it's important to be aware that your customers and prospects value your unlimited program and/or plan in accordance with their consumption of it. For your prospects, they value your unlimited programs and/or plan based on their *perceived* consumption of it. At the same time, your customers value your unlimited program and/or plan based on their *real* consumption of them.

Therefore, encouraging the use and value of your unlimited program and/or plan is important to motivating your customers to remain loyal to your business. Equally, promoting the use of your unlimited program and/or plan by your customers (e.g., "over 10,000 cups of coffee poured so far, and we love to keep pouring") increases the perceived value of your prospects.

Be familiar with laws and regulations, especially regarding any restrictions you place in your unlimited programs and/or plans. Also be sure to polish your cross-selling skills (see Volume 1, Section 8.23, "Selection and Cross-Selling") to encourage your customers with unlimited plans to make additional desirable purchases. You also have a great opportunity, with an unlimited plan and/or program, to upsell your customers (not on an unlimited plan) to a more expensive subscription plan (see Volume 2, Section 5.16, "Subscriptions") that is unlimited.

Guerrilla marketers appreciate marketing opportunities with unlimited appeal for their prospects to become customers. When the same marketing opportunities also motivate their customers to make repeat and additional purchases and provide precious referrals of their friends, family, and associates, they are opportunities worth considering.

7.26 * UNEXPECTED

Guerrilla marketers know opportunity shines brightly when delivering something unexpected that delights their prospects and customers. Unexpected convenience and value motivate your prospects to become your customers. The unexpected also motivates your customers to make repeat and additional purchases and make precious referrals of their friends, family, and associates to your business.

What unexpected goods, options, services, and conveniences can your business deliver? Let's get your Guerrilla Creativity (see Volume 1, Section 1.2, "Guerrilla Creativity) stirring.

Valuable Service and/or Convenience

How delightful is it when you pull up to the valet and discover they offer full-service car washing (that you can purchase)? With no extra effort on your part, you can get more done that day. That's a service and convenience that you will share, talk about, and remember.

How unexpected is it when you bicycle to a community event and discover they have a bicycle valet service? That's a wonderful convenience and peace of mind. It's even more delightful when you discover they offer a bicycle tune-up service (completed while you're enjoying the community event) that you can purchase. Your day just got better, and you can't wait to tell your friends and family about the service and convenience.

Giveaways and Sampling

It's always interesting to receive a giveaway or sample. Guerrilla marketers know that making that giveaway or sample compelling motivates their prospects and customers to take action. See Volume 1, Section 7.11, "Free Trials and Consultations," for ideas and help to get the right giveaways and samples into the hands of your target prospects and customers.

Also see Volume 2, Section 7.16, "Leave Behinds," for ideas and examples of unexpected tactics to delight your prospects and customers.

Free Trials

Guerrilla marketers know free trials are often an unexpected way to lessen the resistance by removing roadblocks in the sales process and encouraging prospects to try your product(s) and/or service(s). During the free trial, your business builds the necessary trust with your prospect by delivering a quality product or service. Trust creates sales, repeat purchases, and precious referrals from your customers.

Opportunities

From hosting Meetups (See Volume 1, Section 7.1, "Organizing and Hosting Meetups") to exclusive experiences (see Section 7.24, "Exclusive Experiences"), there are numerous ways to offer unexpected opportunities for your prospects and customers. From networking to entertainment (see Volume 2, Section 7.21, "Customer Entertainment"), delivering valuable opportunities is a great way to delight your prospects and customers and make your business shareable, memorable, and worth recommending. After all, customers remember when (and with whom) they learned about or were connected with another person, business, or service that is valuable to them.

Conclusion

Guerrilla marketers know the unexpected is a way to break through the crowd of businesses vying for your prospects' and customers' attention. Your extra effort makes your prospects and customers feel noticed and special, and that means they want to share their experiences. They also remember your business and are motivated to recommend it to their friends, family, and associates.

Consider that there are numerous businesses that make the unexpected their business model. For example, several subscription-based businesses have attracted customers to whom they deliver boxes of unexpected items at regular intervals (e.g., Birchbox, BarkBox, Winc, etc.). Their customers are delighted to open their boxes and discover all of the unexpected items inside. What unexpected value or convenience can your business deliver to your prospects and customers?

7.27 * CUSTOMER SPOTLIGHT

Guerrilla marketers take every opportunity to place the spotlight on their customers. Your success is built on your customers, and at the same time, your success depends on their success.

Given that Guerrilla marketers value collaboration (see Volume 1, Section 7.6, "Fusion/Affiliate Marketing and Collaboration"), spotlighting their customers is a perfect win-win opportunity. In the spotlight, your customers receive praise, recognition, and validation of their choices to be your customers. Further, in the case of a business, they receive valuable marketing exposure.

Of course, your business will secure the express permission of your customers, as needed, to be featured to ensure a win-win opportunity and build a long-lasting relationship. Once you've done so, your business can spotlight their stories and their successes in your marketing efforts, such as:

- PR (see Volume 1, Section 7.8, "Public Relations (PR)")
- Blogs and newsletters (see Volume 1, Section 5.4, "Blog and Newsletter Copy")
- Infomercials (see Volume 1, Section 5.11, "Infomercials")
- Social media (refer to Section IV, "Guerrilla E-Media Marketing" and Section V, "Guerrilla Info-Media Marketing"
- Presentations (see Volume 1, Section 5.1, "Presentations, Speeches, Consultations, Demonstrations, and Seminars")
- Promotional materials (see Volume 1, Section 5.6, "White Papers, Testimonials, and Sharing," Section 5.7, "Catalogs," and Section 5.8, "Brochures")
- Advertising (e.g., online, television, radio, print, etc.)

When it comes to your advertising, your customers' testimonials and reviews are powerful influencers for your prospects. According to Semrush, "90% of people are much more likely to trust a recommended brand (even from strangers)."

The win-win opportunity that spotlighting your customers presents has added benefits for your business. For example, when your customers are placed in the spotlight, they will eagerly share their time in the spotlight with their friends, family, and associates—along with their valuable implied or direct endorsement of your business.

Additionally, your communication with your customers, as you're seeking their approval and creating win-win opportunities, provides a valuable chance to learn priceless additional information. You can learn more about your customers and their opinions regarding the positive and negative aspects of your product(s), service(s), and business.

Therefore, be sure to focus your attention on your ideal customers (see Section 8.50, "Ideal Customers"). The benefits of building a long-lasting relationship while receiving additional information, endorsements, and referrals from your ideal customers are truly priceless. In Volume 4, Section 9.36, "Enhanced Customer Service," we'll address opportunities to take your relationship with your customers to the next level.

7.28 * CYCLING

Guerrilla marketers know that any opportunity to expand their business, by participating in the product cycling process, is worth exploring. The product cycling process is a valuable by-product (see Volume 1, Section 5.3, "By-Product") opportunity for many businesses.

For numerous reasons, consumers are engaging in the cycling of products. There are several cycling options, such as:
- Upcycling: taking a product and altering it to find a different function or a more appealing appearance
- Recycling: keeping products out of landfills and reducing waste by converting products into new materials and products
- Reuse: selling gently used products to be used by another

If your business is selling products, participating in the cycling process gives your business the opportunity to positively interact with your customers and expand your appeal to new prospects or existing prospects that you may have considered a lower priority in your customer segmentation (see Section. 8.54, "Customer Segmentation," and 8.55, "Lead Scoring").

There are some great examples and ideas from businesses that are effectively participating in the cycling of products. For example:
- Best Buy: offers an ever-expanding recycling program that currently includes everything from appliances to computers, TVs, cell phones, and so much more. For many of the devices, they motivate new purchases by offering coupons for your in-store recycle items and the purchase of a new and similar device. Best Buy reports they have collected over two billion pounds of items to recycle.
- IKEA: is piloting a "Buy Back & Resell" service. According to IKEA they, "will give IKEA Family members the opportunity to sell back their

gently used IKEA furniture in exchange for IKEA store credit." By offering store credit and limiting participation to IKEA Family members (i.e., a free membership program that provides discounts, perks, and more), they are recognizing, rewarding, and engaging their customers
- URBN Brands: is participating in multiple re-use opportunities. URBN has a brand called Nuuly, which is "A lifestyle retailer dedicated to inspiring customers through a unique combination of product, creativity and cultural understanding." They have two programs:
    o Nuuly Rent is a subscription clothing rental program that includes clothing from URBN brands (e.g., Anthropologie, Free People, Urban Outfitters, etc.)
    o Nuuly Thrift is a resale platform that enables consumers to buy and sell clothing and accessories
    o The URBN brands, such as Anthropologie, then resell gently used items in conjunction with Nuuly

Guerrilla marketers take every opportunity to meet their prospects and customers where they are (see Volume 2, Section 6.16, "Meet Prospects and Customers Where They Are"), and the product cycling process is a great opportunity to do so.

7.29 * BLOCKCHAIN SOLUTIONS

Blockchain technology is often thought of solely with cryptocurrency. Fortunately, Guerrilla marketers know that it goes way beyond cryptocurrency and offers numerous advantages for their business.

IBM defines blockchain as ". . . a shared, immutable ledger that facilitates the process of recording transactions and tracking assets in a business network. An asset can be tangible (a house, car, cash, land) or intangible (intellectual property, patents, copyrights, branding). Virtually anything of value can be tracked and traded on a blockchain network, reducing risk and cutting costs for all involved."

As Guerrilla marketers prefer, getting to the "why" (see Volume 2, Section 8.37, "Inspect What You Expect") is what makes blockchain technology important. Blockchain technology provides transparency that is not easily accessible today. The easiest example of an industry that is dramatically improved with the transparency that blockchain provides is the food industry, specifically the food supply chain.

If you're a business that brings food to customers (e.g., a grocery store, restaurant, etc.), you want to know everything about the food that you're putting on a plate or putting in your customers' shopping bags. If your customer has an issue, such as a foodborne illness, blockchain technology can help your business be more capable of immediately identifying the source and quickly helping, if needed, to remove it from the supply chain.

There are many industries in which irrefutable transparency is of enormous value to improving quality. Beyond the food supply chain, a few other examples are the airline industry, the healthcare industry, and the automotive industry—along with other industries in which the integrity of the product it critical. As consumers are looking for more transparency, blockchain is becoming more valuable.

As an SMB, blockchain technology may be required for your product to make it to the consumer, as in the food supply chain example. Alternately, there are many other uses. Legalzoom offers many examples, such as:

- Authentication of products for businesses that rely on serial numbers and want to ensure that their products are not being counterfeited. Therefore, blockchain technology can provide authentication of your products, allowing your customers to know they are not being subjected to counterfeit products
- Digital identities on the blockchain help ensure that products are tied to their rightful owners
- Blockchain technology is the underpinning of cryptocurrency, which allows for currency to more easily work around the globe
- In Volume 1, Section 7.14, "Crowdfunding," we addressed the many options that are available to help your business grow. Blockchain technology, of course, powers cryptocurrency, which is an opportunity to raise funds both through acceptance of cryptocurrency and through the creation of your own cryptocurrency. Securing specialized cryptocurrency legal expertise is required
- If your business relies on records, such as the medical, automotive, or other supply chain businesses, blockchain technology makes that information secure, transparent, and accessible

- When hiring employees, blockchain technology can accelerate and simplify the exhausting and resource-intensive work of candidate verification. Instead of relying on subjective information (i.e., references) and self-reported credentials, you can rely on transparent information that verifies the quality of your candidates

A primary benefit of blockchain technology is smart contracts. IBM explains, "Smart contracts are simply programs stored on a blockchain that run when predetermined conditions are met. They typically are used to automate the execution of an agreement so that all participants can be immediately certain of the outcome, without any intermediary's involvement or time loss. They can also automate a workflow, triggering the next action when conditions are met." Examples of smart contracts are tokens, coins, and non-fungible tokens (NFTs).

There are numerous uses for NFTs in business. NFTs are explained by Inc. as: ". . . a digital asset that represents an array of virtual and physical things, which cannot be substituted or switched with a fake since they are created on a blockchain that can always be traced back to the original owner or creator. NFTs can be works of art, photos, music, videos, collectibles, memorabilia, contracts, coupons, certificates of authenticity, ID files, health records, and more."

An example of an NFT use is with items intended as single-use, such as coupons or tickets, which can be issued without the ability to be duplicated or tampered with by the recipient. Other examples are when raising capital and with fundraising (see Volume 1, Section 7.14, "Crowdfunding," and Volume 2, Section, 8.38, "Capital and Fundraising for Your Business/Idea"), which can be done with a smart contract and predetermined milestones. By doing so, your investor can track the funds they are investing in and which are only issued as those predetermined milestones are reached.

As an SMB, it's important to be aware that blockchain technology is early in its development, and there are many blockchain solutions being developed. Many of the solutions provide substantial advancements. However, as with any new technology, there are numerous uses being offered that don't necessarily offer benefits or improvements that outweigh the complexity and/or costs of applying blockchain technology. Therefore, it's important to evaluate any blockchain solution to determine its benefits and value for your business as compared to other solutions that could be faster, more efficient, and less costly.

7.30 * IRRESISTIBLE

Guerrilla marketers know making their business irresistible keeps them top-of-mind with their prospects and customers. Irresistible offers are very powerful and have been called "mafia" offers, as in, offers you can't refuse. An irresistible business achieves many other advantages, too, such as great ratings and reviews (see Volume 1, Section, 8.20, "Testimonials, Reviews, and Ratings"), being shareable online (see Volume 1, Section 7.3, "Buzz and Shares"), and referrals (see Volume 1, Section 8.25, "Referral Programs") of customers' friends, family, and associates to the business. Those advantages dramatically reduce your marketing investment.

There are many other options for making your business irresistible, such as:
- Promoting your uniqueness (see Volume 1, Section 1.3, "Unique Selling Proposition (USP)")
- Giveaways (see Volume 1, "Giveaways and Sampling," Volume 2, Section 3.22, "Promotional Item Advertising," and Section 3.23, "Promotional Item Marketing")
- Competitions (see Volume 1, Section 4.27, "Sweepstakes, Giveaways, Challenges, and Competitions")
- Noble causes (see Volume 1, Section 9.12, "Generosity," and Volume 2, Section 9.17, "Purpose Minded")
- A contagious passion (see Volume 1, Section 9.1, "Passion and Enthusiasm")
- Being easy and convenient (see Volume 1, Section 8.21, "Convenience," and Section 9.2, "Easy to Do Business With")
- Experiences (see Section 3.32, "Experiential Marketing," and Section 7.24, "Exclusive Experiences")
- Promotions

Promotions are a long-time-used and proven method for increasing sales with your customers and attracting prospects with irresistible offers. The formula for promotions that boosts your sales is simple: make the right people aware of your irresistible offers. Sounds simple—and it can be—but more often than not, it's a challenge.

Any great offer must connect with the pain points (i.e., needs) and pleasure points (i.e., wants) of your prospects and customers. Once it does, your call to action helps motivate them to take action right then. Most businesses think in

terms of discounts only, but there are other considerations to make your promotions irresistible, such as:
- Limited time
- Limited quantity
- Exclusivity
- Newness or innovation
- Creative partnerships

Any irresistible promotion is reliant upon the placement of your advertising and marketing to reach your prospects and customers at just the right time. When it comes to timing, there are a number of factors to consider, such as pay cycles (e.g., many people are paid at the beginning and middle of the month), holidays (i.e., those that are popular for shopping), and the time of day for your advertising. For example, if your prospects and customers work, consider what time of day you advertise or market to them. After all, the right advertisement with the right promotion falls flat when your prospects and customers never hear or see it due to the time of day you're advertising. See Volume 1, Section 7.9, "Offers and Promotions," for many more ideas to make your offers and your business irresistible to your prospects and customers.

The tactics of Guerrilla Marketing are designed to make your business irresistible. As you become familiar with the tactics in each volume, you'll easily be able to identify which ones will make your business irresistible to your prospects and customers.

SECTION VIII

Guerrilla Company Attributes

GUERRILLA COMPANY ATTRIBUTES

Your company attributes are the characteristics and qualities that your business displays to your prospects and customers, whether you realize it or not. By defining, embracing, and being intentional about your company attributes, you have a broad array of Guerrilla Marketing tactics at the ready. Those tactics work together to create compelling and robust marketing for your business that appeals to your prospects and customers and delivers to their expectations.

Taking intentional ownership and taking the time to define and outline your Guerrilla Company Attributes puts your energy and Guerrilla Creativity to great use. Without awareness and ownership of the power of your company attributes, you're not engaging in intentional and intelligent marketing.

You're marketing with every bit of contact and interaction you have inside your company and that your business has with the outside world. When you're intentional with your marketing, you're the conductor of a world-class orchestra, with every instrument in perfect harmony and creating beautiful music together with audiences that are eager to hear more.

Guerrilla marketers know that being intentional means they're engaged in intelligent marketing. Therefore, you're focusing on the powerful details that most businesses are completely unaware of or choose to ignore. Fortunately, your Guerrilla Company Attributes are not difficult to define or create and market.

When your company attributes are defined, you benefit from your awareness, and you choose to harness the power of consistency. Consistency throughout each of your Guerrilla Company Attributes is a no-cost way to gain a competitive advantage that makes your prospects take notice.

That advantage is available to new and existing businesses. If you're starting a new business, you have the advantage of defining and creating your attributes with intention and consistency from the ground up. If you already have a business, you can review your Guerrilla Company Attributes to find the tactics you're currently missing. When you find inconsistencies, fix them and reap the rewards.

The simple acts of consistently and repeatedly leveraging your Guerrilla Company Attributes, such as your logo, tagline, meme, jingle, color palette, typeface, and fonts create and compel your prospects to notice your business, and it creates familiarity. Pair that with consistently marketing what makes your business unique (i.e., your USP), what it stands for, your stellar ratings and reviews, and your innovation and quality, and your business is creating greater familiarity. As that familiarity turns into trust and is paired with your motivating call to action, it creates sales, repeat purchases, and precious referrals, which fuels the long-term success of your business.

In Volume 1, we addressed many of the important components of your Guerrilla Company Attributes, such as:

8.1	Brand
8.2	Name
8.3	Identity
8.4	Logo
8.5	Memes and Jingles
8.6	Tagline
8.7	Color Palette, Typeface, and Fonts
8.8	Intelligent Positioning
8.9	What Your Business Stands For
8.10	How Your Business Delivers
8.11	Innovation
8.12	Quality
8.13	Efficiency
8.14	Credibility
8.15	Special Orders
8.16	Amazement
8.17	Writing, Copy, and Headlines
8.18	Subject Matter Expert (SME)
8.19	Product Placement
8.20	Testimonials, Reviews, and Ratings
8.21	Convenience
8.22	Service
8.23	Selection and Cross-Selling
8.24	Price and Upgrade Opportunities
8.25	Referral Programs
8.26	Awareness
8.27	Winning
8.28	Connecting and Interacting
8.29	Follow-Up
8.30	Payment Methods
8.31	Systems and Automation

8.32   Subliminal Marketing
8.33   Lead Buying

In Volume 2, we addressed:
8.34   Conflict Resolution
8.35   Compensation
8.36   Cross-Promotion
8.37   Inspect What You Expect
8.38   Capital and Fundraising for Your Business/Idea
8.39   Uniqueness
8.40   Profit Out of Lemons
8.41   Spin-Off
8.42   Leveraging Social Live Broadcasting

Now, we'll pick up where we left off. Without further ado, let's get started.

8.43 * Being Memorable

What makes a business memorable? Being memorable begins with being recognized. First, your prospects become aware of your business (i.e., brand awareness), and second, they recognize your business and the product(s) and/or service(s) associated with it (i.e., brand recognition). Once they do, your call to action must then motivate them to take a desired action (e.g., download an ebook, make a purchase, etc.). Your marketing efforts are ideal when they appeal to each aspect (brand awareness, brand recognition, and action) at the same time.

Once your prospects have taken action to become your customers, what are the factors that make your business memorable and top-of-mind? Guerrilla marketers know the tactics of Guerrilla Marketing makes their business memorable. There are many Guerrilla Marketing tactics to consider. Here are just a few:

Uniqueness

What makes your business unique, makes it stand out and memorable. However, your business will stand out and be memorable only if you are communicating in a clear, compelling, and motivating way (see Volume 1, Section 1.3, "Unique Selling Proposition (USP)," and Volume 2, Section 8.39, "Uniqueness").

Consistency

Your business only gets a fraction of time to make an impression with your prospects and customers. When your marketing efforts are consistent, you turn scattered fractions of time into a memorable experience (see Volume 2, Section 1.9, "Guerrilla Marketing Consistency").

Repetition

Repetition and consistency work hand-in-hand. When you're repeating consistent marketing efforts, you make it far easier for your prospects and customers to recognize and then remember your business (see Volume 2, Section 1.10, "Guerrilla Marketing Repetition").

Solutions

Your prospects and customers are looking for solutions to their problems and pain points. When you deliver those solutions, they feel good about themselves and about your business (see Volume 1, Section 6.4, "Be the Solution").

Experiences

Experiential marketing is an opportunity to engage your prospects and customers, often in unexpected ways. Creating meaningful and memorable experiential marketing is only limited by your creativity and your knowledge of your prospects and customers (see Section 3.32, "Experiential Marketing").

At the same time, Guerrilla marketers appeal to their prospects and customers with exclusive experiences that are unique, shareable, and memorable while making them feel noticed, recognized, special, and valued (see Section 7.24, "Exclusive Experiences").

Images and Appealing to the Senses

In Section 1.13, "Consumer Decision-Making," we addressed the idea that the consumer mind relies on and trusts images. Additionally, in Section 8.46, we'll address "Appeal to the Senses" and in Section 8.45, "The Power of Color."

Authenticity

Guerrilla businesses think of authenticity as "walking the talk" in all aspects of their business. Consumers build trust with authentic businesses, and that trust keeps the business top-of-mind (see Volume 2, Section 9.16, "Authenticity").

Connecting and Interacting

Consumers remember businesses they have positive connections and interactions with, and they love to share those experiences by giving ratings and reviews (see Volume 1, Section 8.20, "Testimonials, Reviews, and Ratings") and referring their friends, family, and associates (see Volume 1, Section 8.25, "Referral Programs"). As they do so, they are building valuable relationships. In Section 9.29, "Relationship Builder," we'll address the importance of building long-lasting relationships. Also refer to Volume 1, Section 8.28, "Connecting and Interacting," Section 8.29, "Follow-Up," Section 9.5, "Responsive and Attentive," and Volume 2, Section 8.34, "Conflict Resolution," for examples and more information.

What You Stand For

First and foremost, customers remember businesses that stand for quality (see Volume 1, Section 8.12, "Quality"). In addition, many customers are also looking for a business that's contributing to the betterment of society and the environment. In Volume 1, Section 9.12, "Generosity," Volume 2, Sections 9.17, "Purpose-Minded," and 9.18, "Community Minded," you'll find ideas to help your Guerrilla Company Attitudes be memorable for your customers.

Conclusion

What makes your business memorable is all the consistent Guerrilla Marketing tactics that you utilize to delight your customers and compel them to share and talk about their experiences with your business. Guerrilla Marketing isn't a tactic, it's a 360-degree, consistent methodology that weaves through every aspect of your business. By being intentional and consistent, you're creating a business with longevity, and we salute your success.

8.44 * CUSTOMER LIFETIME VALUE (CLV OR LTV)

Guerrilla marketers care about their customers and are delighted at every opportunity to build relationships. They also know a profitable secret, which is that at least half of their marketing investment (time and money) should be focused on existing customers.

Why would you invest that much in your existing customers? Because you not only have an absolute appreciation for your customers, you also have a full understanding of the lifetime value of a customer.

The lifetime value (LTV) of a customer can also be referred to as *customer lifetime value* (CLV). Both terms refer to the financial calculation of a customer and the profit they represent for your business over time. Guerrilla marketers understand the power of measuring and tracking a customer's lifetime value as a KPI (key performance indicator). Looking at a customer's lifetime value goes beyond their initial purchase.

Many companies, large and small, see a customer as a one-time transaction. Therefore, they invest their marketing budget to constantly acquire new customers instead of nurturing and retaining their current customers. Guerrilla businesses build relationships with their customers, which results in future purchases and valuable customer referrals. The lifetime value of a customer calculation quickly demonstrates the higher cost of being transaction-focused vs. operating your business with a long-term relationship focus.

LTV or CLV accounts for what you deem to be important to the long-term success of your business, such as shares, likes, purchases, repeat and additional purchases, referrals, etc. Measuring the value of your customers over their "lifetime" with your business, by accounting for the revenue they generate and the associated costs, gives you two valuable pieces to your success puzzle. One, which customers should be handled with the greatest care and, two, which customers you want to "clone" (e.g., demographics, psychographics, etc.) and attract more of as they are your ideal customers (see Section 8.50, "Ideal Customers"). Alternately, it will help you see which customers you don't want to clone.

Guerrilla marketers know most customers are lost due to apathy, which is often the result of the customer being ignored after the sale. Therefore, by engaging in fervent follow-up after the sale, your business is building relationships and retaining customers for the long term.

Guerrillas utilize their marketing as an opportunity. It's an opportunity to help your prospects and customers see how they can succeed at attaining their goals and solving their problems (see Volume 1, Section 6.4, "Be the Solution"). That opportunity is top-of-mind when you're looking at what you can give to your customers (and prospects) to build valuable long-lasting relationships.

Here are some ideas:

- Webinars (see Volume 1, Section 4.25, "Webinars")
- Ebooks (see Volume 1, Section 4.27, "Ebooks, Self-Publishing, and Electronic Brochures")
- Blog and newsletters (see Volume 1, Section 5.4, "Blog and Newsletter Copy")
- Networking opportunities, such as in-person gatherings with Meetups (see Volume 1, Section 7.1, "Organizing and Hosting Meetups") or online with a private Facebook group for your customers and B2B networking partners (see Section 4.63, "Online B2B Networking")
- Demonstrations (e.g., Home Depot holds "How-to Clinics," and Williams Sonoma holds cooking/tasting demonstrations). See Volume 1, Section 5.1, "Presentations, Speeches, Consultations, Demonstrations, and Seminars" for more information
- Interviews/Guest Speakers/Lectures (see Volume 1, Section 6.3, "Your Expertise and Credibility")
- Free offerings from your carefully selected Affiliate or Fusion partners. Remember, you're building a relationship with your customer by giving much more than by selling. See Volume 1, Section 7.6, "Fusion/Affiliate Marketing and Collaboration," for more information
- Podcasts (see Volume 1, Section 4.30, "Your Podcast," for more information)
- Charitable efforts (see Volume 2, Section 9.18, "Community-Minded")
- Loyalty programs. A loyalty or rewards program is a great opportunity to build relationships with your customers, but they are typically focused on customer spending and/or membership fees, which are not necessarily seen as "giving" by your customers. However, these programs do have value and to be successful, they need to be seamless, frictionless, and fully integrated into the purchasing experience. For example, Amazon Prime is tied to your login, making the process simple for the customer

(e.g., no codes, expiration, points, etc.). See Volume 2, Section 7.18, "Customer Loyalty," for more information

If your product(s) or service(s) are often gifted by your customers, you have valuable customers and a great opportunity to build long-lasting relationships. Therefore, think about how to make it easier and more compelling for your customers to give a gift from your business by offering:

- Free gift wrapping
- Gift-ready packaging
- Gift-ready and re-usable shopping bags that make it fun, elegant, and/or easy for your customer to gift your product(s), and it's an added benefit for the recipient who enjoys re-using the bag, one with your well-placed advertising (see Volume 2, Section 3.29, "Shopping Bags," for more information)

If you're selling B2B, you build long-term relationships as you're talking to your customers about anything you can do to help their businesses, such as:

- Hold demonstrations (e.g., "Lunch and Learns" where you conduct your demonstrations while providing lunch for the participants) for their customers and/or employees. See Volume 1, Section 5.1, "Presentations, Speeches, Consultations, Demonstrations, and Seminars," for more information)
- Participate in their charitable causes/events (see Volume 2, Section 9.18, "Community-Minded")
- Put them in the spotlight (see Section 7.27, "Customer Spotlight") in your blog, newsletter, podcast, advertising, PR, etc.
- Provide valuable content (see Volume 1, Section 5.6, "White Papers, Testimonials, and Sharing")

As you look at the giving opportunities you have to build long-lasting relationships with your customers, ask yourself:

- Will this help my prospects and customers succeed?
- Will this help my prospects and customers achieve their goals?
- Will this help my prospects and customers solve a problem?
- Will this help my prospects and customers feel smart for choosing to do business with us?
- Will this be memorable?
- Will they be compelled to tell their friends, family, and/or business associates about it?

Think of low-cost and high-value options. Your customers will react the most to gifts or actions that are personalized (see Volume 1, Section 3.6, "Personalization," for more information), meaningful, and useful. You can accomplish those goals without a high price tag.

When you're focused on giving, your customers will often be in the giving mode as well. Plan ahead so you're prepared when your customers want to give you the gift of additional and repeat purchases, referrals, input (dialogue, suggestions, ratings/reviews, etc.), social attention (shares, likes, tweets, videos, photos, etc.), and Fusion/Affiliate Marketing opportunities.

By measuring and tracking a customer's lifetime value as a KPI, you'll know if you're reaching your goals. You can find LTV tools in some of the services you may already be using, such as your accounting system, CRM system, or services such as:

- Google Analytics
- Hubspot

The more robust the tool is that you use, the more encompassing and accurate your calculations will be. Capturing purchases, repeat purchases, re-occurring revenue, and referrals will give you the revenue component. The better you can capture the associated expenses, the more valuable the measurement is for your business and your long-term success.

There are other valuable components that are difficult to capture in your financial analysis, such as the value of your customers' shares, likes, five-star ratings, glowing reviews, etc. Guerrilla marketers never lose sight of the power of relationship-building with their customers. It not only makes being in business far more rewarding, but it also makes your business stand out because it's something that very few businesses do, even though it's one of the most powerful facets of marketing.

Fortunately, Guerrilla marketers value relationships. Therefore, it's easy to remember that LTV provides two valuable pieces to your success puzzle: one, which customers should be handled with the greatest care and, two, which customers you want to "clone" (e.g., demographics, psychographics, etc.) and attract more of as they are your ideal customers (see Section 8.50, "Ideal Customers"). Alternately, it will help you see which customers you don't want to clone.

8.45 * THE POWER OF COLOR

Guerrilla marketers tend to the tiny, supercharged details that can generate big profits. Recognizing the power of visual appeal is one of those tiny, supercharged details that can generate big profits. Appealing to your prospects and customers with the use of color is a free and easy way to increase your success. Consider that consumers will pay more for products in colors that appeal to them.

At the same time, businesses can be easily identified by a dominant color. For example, when you think of Target, what dominant color do they use? When you think of Walmart, what dominant color do they use? When you think of Barnes & Noble, what dominant color do they use?

The appeal and identification of color can help to set your business apart. After all, colors elicit moods and feelings that can be persuasive. However, it's important to know that there are many factors that influence the appeal of colors, including:

- Cultural influences
- Nationality
- Gender
- Experiences

The appeal of colors for your prospects and customers is influenced by simple factors, such as the color of the flag for their country or even the school colors they cherished (e.g., their school colors) and loathed (e.g., the school colors of their archrival). With that in mind, there is some interesting research to be aware of when it comes to the impact of color and your marketing efforts. Shutterstock has shared the characteristics of powerful colors, which include:

- "Red: exciting, passionate, sometimes aggressive
- Orange: friendly, adventurous, casual
- Yellow: cheerful, warm, serene
- Blue: peaceful, trustworthy, honest
- Green: natural, safe, permissive
- Purple: mystical, mysterious, regal
- Black: luxurious, elegant, powerful"

Therefore, you can see which colors could best suit your business, product(s), and service(s) and, thereby, increase the effectiveness of your marketing. Alternately, you can see how a small combination of colors can broaden the appeal of your marketing. Experimenting with the shades of particular colors can introduce those characteristics without being dominant. For example, a lighter or darker shade of purple can add some mysterious characteristics without it being a dominant characteristic.

The effectiveness of color is improved when you use strong contrast. According to *Psychology Today*, "Research clearly shows that participants are able to recognize and recall an item far better (be it text or an image) when it blatantly sticks out from its surroundings." You can create that valuable contrast with a white background and a single color for the information or areas that you want to stand out (e.g., your logo, headlines, products, links, buy buttons, etc.).

How do you determine which colors will be consistently powerful for your prospects and customers? How do you determine if there is a particular color (or colors) that your prospects and customers dislike or do not respond to? Testing is the answer (see Section 2.16, "Testing," for more information). There are several ways you can test with colors, such as:

- Split test with the only variable being color
- If you sell products in a variety of colors, look at your sales data to see if there is a strong color preference
- Survey your customers
- Share information about color with your prospects and observe the responses

With a powerful CRM platform, you don't need to be concerned with selecting one color from your carefully selected color palette (see Volume 1, Section 8.7, "Color Palette, Typeface, and Fonts"). Instead, you can tag the responses of your customers and prospects and segment them by their color preferences. In doing so, you can communicate the same information but customize it according to their color preferences. As a result, your business makes your marketing far more appealing and motivating.

Keep in mind that what works in your marketing (e.g., your website, retail location, email marketing, etc.) may have a different response with your advertising efforts. For example, the surrounding, accent, background, and contrasting colors on a website that you're advertising on can impact your results (e.g., clicks, views, etc.). If the background and accent colors in your advertising match the website/platform your advertising appears on, your advertising may blend in and go unnoticed. While that might work with your discovery ads (see Volume 2, Section 4.56, "Discovery Ads"), it can easily work against your other advertising efforts. Therefore, you may need to change the colors for greater contrast and noticeability. Paying attention to those tiny, supercharged details can generate big profits.

For more information, refer to these related sections:
- Section 1.13, "Consumer Decision-Making"
- Section 2.16, "Testing"
- Section 4.61, "Customer Relationship Management Platforms (CRMs)"
- Volume 1, Section 8.7, "Color Palette, Typeface, and Fonts"
- Volume 1, Section 8.32, "Subliminal Marketing"

8.46 * APPEAL TO THE SENSES

Just as color is a free way to pay attention to the details and make your marketing more appealing, expanding to include all of the senses is also a tiny, supercharged detail that can generate big profits.

For example, Tommy Bahama—if you're not familiar—is a casual and tropical resort-oriented lifestyle brand that ranges from restaurants to spirits, furniture, décor, apparel, and accessories. If you've had the chance to shop at their retail locations, you know you enter and feel the immediate sensation of being at a tropical resort. How do they create that sensation?

The answer is simple; they utilize a full sensory experience to achieve that sensation. For the sake of clarity, let's review the basic senses that your business wants to appeal to:
- Sight
- Touch
- Smell
- Taste
- Hearing

For Tommy Bahama, they utilize every surface (e.g., the ceiling, walls, floor, fixtures, etc.) to create a sensory experience to appeal to the visual (e.g., tropical colors) and touch senses (e.g., soft clothing) of their prospects and customers. They also appeal to their sense of smell by filling their locations with appealing tropical scents, which they sell in the form of candles, colognes, etc. At the same time, tropical music is playing to appeal to their prospects' and customers' sense of hearing and, in their restaurants, they also appeal to their sense of taste with tropical dishes on the menu.

The senses are a Guerrilla marketer's opportunity to create an enjoyable, sharable, compelling, and motivating experience that increases sales and profits. It's important to consider the appropriate level of your sensory appeal. For example, low lighting creates a more relaxed environment than bright lights. A strong scent needs to be widely appealing to avoid repelling some prospects and customers.

Starbucks is another example of a retailer that appeals to the senses to create an appealing experience. They appeal to all of the senses in their locations. From lighting to music, they create a calming environment while selling an energizing product.

A consumer recently shared their experience of walking into their local Starbucks and seeing an unexpected product that compelled them to make an unexpected additional purchase. This individual shared their compelling description of waiting in line, seeing a product on display with a spotlight shining directly on it, and feeling as if the store knew what would appeal to them—before they even knew themselves. The consumer felt compelled to purchase this product, which they previously had never considered buying, and enjoyed telling the story while utilizing the product and raving about the product and the experience with Starbucks with approximately ten nearby people, most of whom were not known to this particular customer.

Why did the consumer enjoy sharing their story? Because it was a rich experience that appealed to their senses (the smell of coffee, the sound of enjoyable music, the targeted lighting, etc.). Therefore, the experience was far more compelling, motivating, emotional, and memorable—all of which motivate sharing and inspire loyalty to a business. Guerrilla marketers look for every opportunity to make the ordinary . . . extraordinary by appealing to the senses. Let's look at a few more examples:

- Cinnabon: for those who are familiar with their products, the mere mention of their name will make most consumers immediately recall the smell of freshly baked cinnamon rolls, which wafts from their storefronts
- Anthropologie: appeals to the senses throughout the store with simple yet intentional decisions, such as their music, the use of fragrant candles (which they sell) to appeal to your sense of smell, the creation of an environment that is a visual feast with a variety of items offered, including featuring plush items that invite touching, and lighting to spotlight products

Whether your business is offline or online (or both), it's easy to be ordinary. It takes a little effort and some Guerrilla Creativity (see Volume 1, Section 1.2, "Guerrilla Creativity) to be unconventional, memorable, emotional, and extraordinary. By appealing to the senses of your prospects and customers, you can make your business compelling, memorable, and sharable for your customers who are motivated to be loyal to your business over the long term.

Also refer to:
- Volume 1, Section 3.1, "Interior Design and Signage," for more ideas for your physical retail location
- Volume 2, Section 6.22, "Be Stickie and Compelling"

8.47 * AI BUSINESS OPTIMIZATION

As your business grows in volume and complexity, you begin to see the need for optimization. Starting and growing a business can be "messy business." The bigger it gets, the messier it can become—unless you make optimization an ongoing activity. Fortunately for Guerrilla businesses, you have a wide variety of optimization options that are increasingly powered by AI. These options seek to reduce cost, increase efficiency, and improve operational excellence.

When looking for optimization opportunities, you'll first look to create efficiencies. Where in your business are there bottlenecks? Where are the complaints? In which area of your business are people (e.g., employees, customers, prospects, etc.) struggling or complaining about process breakdowns, complications, and/or inefficiencies?

You can step linearly through your business to optimize it at each step. In each of these areas, there are platforms and tools that utilize AI to improve workflow and efficiency while improving accuracy and your use of capital:
- Marketing
- Sales
- Customer/Client support
- Fulfillment
- Operations
- Finance

- Innovation

Marketing and Sales

AI and machine learning are rapidly changing and improving the way marketing and sales function. From platforms that automate the purchasing and optimizing of advertising to platforms that generate creativity and analyze performance—and also the tools to handle email replies automatically, chatbots, automated follow-ups, sales training, and scripting—the ability to be efficient and improve your performance and create greater personalization is infinite.

Refer to Section IV:
- 4.65, "Artificial Intelligence (AI) Overview"
- 4.66, "AI Marketing Copy and Content"
- 4.67, "AI Audio and Video"
- 4.68, "AI and Marketing Performance"
- 4.69, "AI Creativity"
- Volume 4, Section 4.74, "AI Selling"

Support

With advancements in automation, AI and machine learning are giving businesses more efficient, and in many ways more effective, ways to delight their prospects and customers. According to Hubspot, "76% of companies in 2021 report using automation." Of those companies, the top uses are task management, content automation and chatbots."

Message bots (see Volume 2, Section 4.47, "Message Bots") can provide engaging support for your prospects and customers with quick and always available (i.e., 24/7) responses to service and sales inquiries that require lower expertise. By doing so, your business can utilize your highly-skilled support resources (people/employees) for inquiries and issues that require more expertise. At the same time, many message bots feature automated scoring models. When handing an inquiry to your support resources (people/employees), the scoring model indicates (to your support resources), for example, an elevated likelihood of a customer leaving your business (i.e., churn) or an indication of an increased revenue opportunity.

Message bots powered by AI and machine learning can also help your business increase revenue with upsells and cross-sells. The growing ability of bots to detect purchase intention indications can exceed that of support resources, who can be distracted with multi-tasking and/or who are not skilled salespeople. At the same time, bots can increase your revenue with consistent, compelling, and accurate cross-selling suggestions.

Fulfillment

From finding the least costly routing of shipments to workflow optimization, automated routing of workers, mapping, routing of drivers and robotic process automation, your ability to get your product(s) or service(s) quickly, flawlessly, and efficiently to your customer is rapidly improving.

Operations and Finance

AI and machine learning are making the process involved from recruiting to hiring job candidates more efficient. From resumes to screening candidates, your ability is enhanced with, for example, automating high-volume tasks to help your business efficiently narrow candidates and reduce biases. Your business can also have better insight regarding the talent you already have in your business that could be inadvertently overlooked.

Throughout the operations of your business, AI and machine learning are enhancing and automating workflows, quality assurance processes, standard operating procedures (SOPs), communication, collaboration, and scheduling. In doing so, they can be made more efficient and improved. Additionally, dashboard tools with AI-powered analysis show areas to focus on in the business.

AI-powered financial reporting systems, decision management platforms and tools, and AI-powered loan platforms are also ways to improve your business and its cash flow.

Innovation

AI-optimized hardware is changing how people function in their lives. From Siri to Alexa and Google Assistant, consumers are finding the power and convenience of using their voice to control devices (e.g., voice remotes, assistant devices, appliances, home automation, etc.).

At the same time, advances in voice to text, robotic automation, analysis of images, and/or video and biometrics are creating AI and machine learning products, services, and conveniences that consumers are increasingly reliant on. Guerrilla marketers seek to innovate and disrupt businesses every day. Innovations with AI can help your business breakthrough and be disruptive.

Conclusion

In Section 2.18, "Optimization," we outlined the purpose of optimizing your marketing and advertising. The purpose of optimizing your business operations is similar:

- Improve or remove what's not working
- Identify and do more of what is working
- Identify new tools and innovations to add, based on what's working

Fortunately, AI and machine learning are available to help your business get more done with less effort. Whether you're seeking to scale your business, remove bottlenecks and complexities, or improve your relationships with your prospects and customers, a continual focus on optimizing your business will help your long-term success.

Just as with any new technology, there is hype and misrepresentation regarding the uses of AI. Therefore, Guerrilla marketers use knowledge to help them sort through the options to find the right tools to optimize their business.

See Section XI, 125+ Free Tools for resources—many of which incorporate AI and machine learning—you can experiment with and evaluate those tools and resources, based on your business needs, to determine if they are worth your investment.

8.48 * BALANCING ACT

Finding balance, when you have your own business, is a challenge. It's easy as an entrepreneur and/or business owner to fall into a cycle of being focused on your work 24/7. In Volume 2, Section 1.8, "Crucial Skills for Effectively Using Guerrilla Marketing," we touched on the importance of creating balance. As we noted, a balance between work and life makes you more creative and innovative, both of which help your business thrive.

The balance that helps you be more creative and innovative also helps you easily find answers, opportunities, resources, and solutions. In turn, you'll find it easier to build valuable relationships (see Section 9.29, "Relationship Builder," for more information) that help your business thrive, and it will show.

It's easily said but how do you successfully perform the balancing act? Here are some ideas to consider:

- Guerrillas spend time enjoying activities they love, ones that are not work-related. Those activities could be sports, reading a great book, meditation, exercise, or any other activity that gives you valuable and pleasurable time away from your business
- Mentoring or being mentored is a great way to spend time working on yourself. See Volume 2, Section 9.22, "Mentoring," for more information
- Being community-minded gives you the opportunity to spend valuable time giving back and expanding your focus and your network beyond your business. See Volume 2, Section 9.18, "Community-Minded," for more information
- Grow your expertise and learn a new skill. Whether it's a workshop, online course, or formal continuing education, stretching your expertise—related or unrelated to your business—will provide valuable new perspectives

Your time and focus away from your business helps you gain a remarkable level of appreciation, gratitude, and freedom from work-related stress. Equally, as we noted, when you take time away from the challenges of your business, you'll easily find answers, opportunities, resources, and solutions. Your lateral thinking skills (see Volume 2, "Lateral Thinking") will also be improved.

If you find it difficult to take time away, start with a small amount of time. Even fifteen minutes is a valuable place to start carving out time for yourself and find your balance. As you expand that amount of time, you'll find it easier as you enjoy the benefits of more balance.

8.49 * PERCEPTION AND REALITY

Perception is defined, in part, by Merriam-Webster as "result of perceiving: observation" and "a mental image: concept." Your business can believe it is doing everything right and still find itself fighting one or many perceptions. Those perceptions can be rooted in many factors, such as:
- Review comments
- Language or cultural differences
- Consumer mindset (see Volume 2, Section 6.17, "Consumer Mindset")

- Cognitive biases (explained by SimplyPsychology as, "unconscious errors in thinking that arise from problems related to memory, attention, and other mental mistakes")
- Inconsistent marketing (see Volume 2, Section 1.9, "Guerrilla Marketing Consistency")
- Misinformation
- Marketing efforts that didn't yield the anticipated results

Consider The General Insurance, which is investing in marketing and advertising efforts to change the perception their prospects have of their business. They are seeking to re-brand their business because according to The General Insurance, ". . . when we at The General realized there was a perception that our insurance lacks quality based upon our commercials, we knew we couldn't ignore it."

When perception and reality is not perfectly aligned for your business, it's a red flag that should not be ignored. Guerrilla marketers know this is the time to take measured action to control the narrative. It's time to evaluate the situation and determine if it's time to act, just as The General Insurance did when they decided it was time to re-brand and tell a different story to take control of the narrative and change the perception of their prospects to make their business more appealing.

It's important to not overact so your business can take measured action. By determining and evaluating the source of the perception, you may find that it's just one marketing or advertising effort that needs to be altered.

By interacting with those prospects and/or customers who share the negative perception, you can get to the root of the issue. Often, credible experts (e.g., the business owner, an industry expert, an influencer) can help shift those perceptions to match the reality.

8.50 * IDEAL CUSTOMERS

Guerrilla marketers set their businesses apart because they know that not all customers are equal. By knowing your ideal customer(s) (often referred to as a customer avatar), you'll reap profitable rewards.

It's very easy to get caught up in the appeal of large numbers. Often, in business, you can get trapped into chasing vanity metrics. Vanity metrics are ones that make the business seem or feel successful, but they don't necessarily drive profits. Guerrilla marketers know that focusing on quality can make a business far more profitable. Therefore, they take the time and put in the effort to understand and identify their ideal customers.

There are many factors to consider when your business defines the characteristics of your ideal customers, such as:

- How much revenue do they generate?
- How much profit do they generate?
- How many referrals do they generate?
- Do they regularly make repeat and additional purchases?
- Do they remain your customers for the long term? That length of time is valuable for all businesses but especially impactful for membership and subscription businesses (see Volume 2, Section, 5.16, "Subscriptions")
- Do they purchase specific products that are relevant (e.g., highly profitable, innovative, re-occurring revenue, etc.)?
- Are they influential (e.g., social media, community leadership, industry expert, media contributor, etc.)?

To successfully define the characteristics of your ideal customers requires, first, the ability to segment your customers (see Section 8.54, "Customer Segmentation") and then the ability to look at the data from many angles. For example, if you decide to solely focus on the highest revenue-generating customers, you may be including some that are unprofitable due to factors, such as:

- The amount of marketing (including the sales costs) it took to attract them
- The amount of time they spend with customer service
- Returns and exchanges
- Reviews and ratings
- The length of time they remain your customer

Your goal is not to be narrowly focused and pick one characteristic. Your goal is to identify as many ideal characteristics as possible. There are many tools and calculations you can incorporate to identify and track your ideal customers, such as:

- Customer lifetime value (see Section 8.44, "Customer Lifetime Value (CLV or LTV)")
- Your financials
- Your referrals (see Volume 1, Section 8.25, "Referral Programs")

- Your robust CRM system (see Volume 3, Section 4.61 "Customer Relationship Management Platforms (CRMs)")
- Attribution (see Section 2.17, "Attribution," and Section 4.62, "Digital Attribution")
- Your marketing and sales funnels (see Section 4.57, "Marketing and Sales Funnels")
- Lead scoring (Section 8.55, "Lead Scoring")

Taking the time to identify the characteristics of your ideal customers allows your business to then work backward. How do you work backward? It's easier than you think:

- Identify their demographics, psychographics, etc.
- Identify your motivating marketing tactics
- Identify your marketing messages and the pain points and pleasure points they respond to
- Identify your motivating call to action and messages (e.g., pain points, coupons, sales, free trials, downloads, etc.)
- Identify motivating images
- Identify what motivates them to share and like
- Identify which of your product(s) and/or service(s) are most appealing to your ideal customers
- Identify color preferences (see Section 8.45, "The Power of Color")

You'll find some of that information in your CRM, and you can supplement it with surveys, hosting Meetups (see Volume 1, Section 7.1, "Organizing and Hosting Meetups"), and your customer interactions (see Volume 1, Section 6.15, "Connection and Interaction").

As you identify the characteristics of your ideal customers and what motivates them, you'll also be identifying the characteristics of your least desirable customers. That means you have the opportunity to identify particular marketing tactics that you're investing in and attract customers that your business is better off without (i.e., they are not profitable).

By reducing or eliminating marketing tactics that are attracting your least desirable customers, you can increase your profits multi-fold. For example, you might find that a particular marketing tactic attracts only customers that use the free version of your service (and they never upgrade to a paid service) or a tactic that attracts customers that have a high propensity to return products. By reducing or eliminating that marketing tactic, your business not only saves the marketing investment, but your business also reduces or eliminates the costs associated with their use of your free service (e.g., systems, customers services, etc.) or returned merchandised that may be unsellable (e.g., customer service, hard costs for merchandise, shipping, repackaging, or reselling the product).

It may sound counterintuitive, but Guerrilla marketers understand that, in this case, less truly is more. Non-Guerrilla businesses focus on their customer count and revenue instead of profits and customer loyalty. Guerrilla marketers focus on ideal customers and how they can offer additional products and services that offer greater expertise, capabilities, and conveniences to them (see Volume 4, Section 8.59, "Upselling").

Your focus on your ideal customers helps your business create long-term mutually satisfying relationships that result in delighted customers and precious referrals of their friends, family, and associates.

8.51 * INTERNATIONAL EXPANSION

What once was a foreboding and gigantic world now grows more accessible by the day. Shopify predicts that global ecommerce will swell to over $3.4 trillion dollars by 2024. If your business is doing well in one county, can your business do well in other countries?

There are many considerations, such as:
- Language support
- Customer support
- Shipping and returns (including importing and exporting)
- Payments (e.g., exchange rates, options, fees, etc.)
- Marketing
- Laws and regulations
- Taxes
- Cultural differences (e.g., holidays, customs, etc.)

According to Hubspot, the top challenges that businesses are facing with international marketing are exchange rates, cultural differences, tariff barriers, legal constraints, place constraints, and localization (translation).

Fortunately, Guerrilla marketers know that when they only have a portion of the resources they need, they first look for opportunities to collaborate. That's the ideal strategy considering how many opportunities there are to collaborate and accomplish your international expansion. Being familiar with these options will help you navigate international opportunities successfully.

The Guerrilla Marketers' Approach

Guerrilla marketers approach international expansion as an opportunity to walk before they run. Your top priority is to ensure your business gets it right for your prospects and customers and that your business is delivering a personalized and localized experience.

Therefore, begin with one (or a small number of) priority country first and take what you learn (e.g., the success and the challenges) to fuel greater growth. Social media engagement and surveys provide great information for identifying your top international markets.

When it comes to evaluating your international opportunities, an important KPI is ROI (return on investment). What might appear to be your top market based on sales potential may easily drop far from the top slot based on your projected returns. Shipping costs, shipping logistics, tax compliance, and return rates are significant considerations for your ROI. A simple oversight (or lack of understanding) of how your product will land at your international customers' doors is the difference between absolute customer satisfaction and devastating dissatisfaction, perhaps due to fees, tariffs, and taxes due.

Never lose sight of your maximum opportunity for success with international growth, which requires your business to adapt to your chosen market. If you take the approach that your prospects need to adapt to your business, you'll minimize your success.

Services

Guerrilla marketers are always eager to look for opportunities to collaborate. When it comes to the international expansion of your service business, collaborating with a like-minded business is a great option. Look for collaboration opportunities with:

- Industry associations
- B2B or B2C professional selling organization (e.g., manufacturer representatives)

- Referral networks, such as BNI, which has thousands of global chapters
- Leverage joint ventures to enter new markets while mitigating costs and risks

Collaborating with like-minded businesses with established relationships with your prospects can give your service business a tremendous advantage.

Products

Once you've determined your top international markets, utilizing trusted third-party selling platforms can help your business break through the skepticism and doubt that often keeps consumers from making an international purchase. As we noted earlier, a Guerrilla marketer ensures that every aspect of their marketing is accurate and consistent to compete on those platforms and win customers.

Your enhanced images and descriptions (see Volume 2, Section 4.46, "Enhanced Images and Descriptions") will help ensure that your customers receive what they're anticipating and are delighted with your business.

Third-Party Selling Platforms That Support International Sales

In Volume 2, Section 7.23, "Expanded Distribution," we addressed the pros and cons of third-party sellers. Third-party selling platforms take on the responsibility for the technology and security that's required to run the site. These platforms give your business a great chance to test your products in international markets before investing in a custom, international-capable ecommerce website.

However, a Guerrilla marketer, as we noted earlier, ensures that every aspect of their marketing is accurate and consistent to compete on those platforms and win customers. The level of support third-party selling platforms offer for international sales varies. Examples of third-party selling platforms that support international selling include:
- Shopify Plus: allows your business to sell internationally from one store or to create expansion stores for a localized and personalized experience, including in multiple languages. With Shopify Payments, they take the challenge out of currency differences and allow your customers local payment options. They also have Shopify Plus Partners that can help fill in any gaps you have

- Big Commerce: provides multiple languages and allows payments in any currency. They also support international shipping and integrations to assist with collecting taxes
- WooCommerce: provides extensions that give you the ability to create individual stores to serve multiple languages. They also offer extensions to support multiple currencies for easy payment options for your prospects and customers
- eBay: supports international shipping and payments. They also offer a number of international sites to list your products and increase your appeal in those markets

Other third-party selling platforms, such as Amazon Seller Central and Etsy, support international shipping.

In Section 8.52, we'll dive deeper into "International Fulfillment and Shipping" information and options.

8.52 * INTERNATIONAL FULFILLMENT AND SHIPPING

An important consideration for a Guerrilla marketer is how your business will flawlessly get your products into the hands of your customers. Delivering your products to your international customers is not without its challenges. You'll want to consider:

- Packaging that is sturdy and durable and items that are well-packed to deliver your product in perfect condition
- The weight and size of your packages, which determines the shipping costs that you want to factor into your pricing strategy to avoid high cart abandonment rates due to high shipping costs
- Insurance
- Tracking
- Country-specific rules and regulations, which lead to other considerations. For example, country-specific rules and regulations can prohibit your products from being imported. Additionally, those rules and regulations govern if your product meets their legal standards

- Duties and taxes
- Required documents (e.g., purchase receipts, packing lists, customs forms, etc.)
- Shipping service options that allow your customers to, for example, choose a quicker delivery service
- Address verifications in the ordering process
- Communicating the status of an order and the shipping process with your customers
- Returns

Fortunately, Guerrilla marketers know they do not have to go it alone. There are a number of options your business can consider to bring much-needed expertise to the process. Here are some options to consider, whether you want to do the shipping yourself or a more robust collaboration with a fulfillment service.

Shipping

From doing it yourself to leaving it to the experts, there are several options to be familiar with. Your business can ship internationally directly with major carriers, such as UPS, FedEx, and DHL, which provide particular advantages for freight shipping. Alternately, there are other services available that offer valuable features worth being familiar with. Examples include:

- ShipStation: offers services from inventory management to integrations with third-party selling platforms and, of course, shipping with most major carriers along with the ability to compare prices. They enable international shipping and assist with the additional paperwork (e.g., customs declarations) that is required
- Endicia: offers integrations with third-party selling platforms and shipping with USPS and GlobalPost for international shipping. They offer global address verification, electronic customs, insurance options, priority shipping options, and more

Fulfillment

Fulfillment services take care of the logistics involved between the time your customer places an order and getting your product to your customer's door. A good fulfillment business stores your products, and the inventory data is connected to your sales system. When an order is placed, they pick, pack, and ship the product and upload the shipping and tracking information to keep your

customers informed. It's ideal if they also process your customers' returns. As you consider international expansion, it's a good idea to look for in-market, third-party logistics/fulfillment partners to eliminate the cross-border shipping challenges. Examples include:
- ShipBob: offers robust fulfillment services and numerous shipping carriers that facilitate international shipping. They have several locations, domestically and internationally, which can reduce delivery time and shipping costs. They support subscription-based, recurring orders (see Volume 2, Section 5.16, "Subscriptions") and returns processing. They also support customized packaging to help your marketing shine
- Shipfusion: offers robust fulfillment services and domestic and international shipping. They have several temperature-controlled locations, which can reduce delivery time and shipping costs. According to Shipfusion, they support cold-chain transportation, FDA-compliant chain processes, and food-grade storage for supplements and nutraceuticals. They also support subscription services and returns processing

Conclusion

Expanding your business to include international markets is a great way for your business to grow when done correctly. It's a necessary practice to map out the entire process to ensure that you're addressing every step in the process to flawlessly move a customer's order from your business to their door. Keeping impeccable records is also a necessary practice.

8.53 * LONGEVITY

Guerrilla marketers build their business with longevity in mind. You may want to hand down your business to future generations or you may simply want the ability to successfully sell your business; either way, longevity is key. At this point, in Volume 3 of the all-new series of *Guerrilla Marketing* books, you have many tools, tactics, and examples at your fingertips that will build a long-lasting business.

At their core, businesses with longevity consistently utilize the tactics of Guerrilla Marketing. They begin with a strong business foundation (see Section 1.14, "Business Foundation") and a strong foundation for Guerrilla Marketing success (see Section I, in each of the volumes of the all-new series of *Guerrilla Marketing* books. Additionally, those businesses are:

- Identifiable: Refer to:
  - Volume 1, Section 8.1, "Brand"
  - Volume 1, Section 8.2, "Name"
  - Volume 1, Section 8.3, "Identity"
  - Volume 1, Section 8.4, "Logo"
  - Volume 1, Section 8.5, "Memes and Jingles"
  - Volume 1, Section 8.6, "Tagline"
  - Volume 1, Section 8.7, "Color Palette, Typeface, and Fonts"
  - Volume 2, Section 1.9, "Guerrilla Marketing Consistency"
  - Volume 2, Section 1.10, "Guerrilla Marketing Repetition"
- Relevant: Refer to:
  - Volume 1, Section 1.3, "Unique Selling Proposition (USP)"
  - Volume 1, Section 8.8, "Intelligent Positioning"
  - Volume 1, Section 8.9, "What Your Business Stands For"
- Credible: Refer to:
  - Volume 1, Section 8.10, "How Your Business Delivers"
  - Volume 1, Section 8.11, "Innovation"
  - Volume 1, Section 8.12, "Quality"
  - Volume 1, Section 8.13, "Efficiency"
  - Volume 1, Section 8.14, "Credibility"
  - Volume 1, Section 8.20, "Testimonials, Reviews, and Ratings"
- Customer-focused: Refer to Section 8.44, "Customer Lifetime Value (CLV or LTV)" and to:
  - Volume 1, Section 8.15, "Special Orders"
  - Volume 1, Section 8.20, "Testimonials, Reviews, and Ratings"
  - Volume 1, Section 8.21, "Convenience"
  - Volume 1, Section 8.22, "Service"
  - Volume 1, Section 8.23, "Selection and Cross-Selling"
  - Volume 1, Section 8.24, "Price and Upgrade Opportunities"
  - Volume 1, Section 8.25, "Referral Programs"
  - Volume 2, Section 6.18, "Five-Star"

- o   Volume 2, Section 8.34, "Conflict Resolution"
- o   Section 8.50, "Ideal Customers"
- o   Section 8.56, "Ideal Employees"
- Memorable: Refer to:
  - o   Volume 2, Section, 6.22, "Be Stickie and Compelling"
  - o   Section 7.24, "Exclusive Experiences"
  - o   Section 8.43, "Being Memorable"

We could go on and on and on . . . but hopefully, we've made the point that the tactics of Guerrilla Marketing help you build a business with longevity in mind, which includes loyal, long-term, and engaged employees and customers.

Guerrilla Marketing is a series of moving parts that when they work together, create a business that stands the test of time for the owner, employees, suppliers, customers, etc. Guerrilla Marketing is a 360-degree, consistent methodology that weaves through every aspect of your business. By being intentional and consistent, you're creating a business with longevity, and we salute your success.

8.54 * CUSTOMER SEGMENTATION

Guerrilla marketers know the power of making connections with their prospects and customers. Before they make that connection—and, once they do, the more appealing they are—the more rewards they reap.

Customer segmentation gives your business a greater opportunity to say the right thing to the right prospects and customers. The value of customer segmentation is:

- Personalized marketing (see Volume 1, Section 3.6, "Personalization")
- The ability to appeal to their emotions (see Section 6.23, "Appealing to Emotions")
- The ability to appeal to their needs (see Section 6.25, "Appealing to Needs")
- Maximized referrals (see Volume 1, Section 8.25, "Referral Programs")
- Customer retention (see Volume 2, Section 7.18, "Customer Loyalty")
- The ability to determine your ideal customers (see Section 8.50, "Ideal Customers") and lead scoring (see Section 8.55, "Lead Scoring")

Here are some important data points to be aware of:
- According to MailChimp, regarding email campaigns, "On average, segmented campaigns result in 23% higher open rates and 49% higher click through rates than unsegmented campaigns."
- According to Instapage, "74% of customers feel frustrated when website content is not personalized." Also, "87% of consumers surveyed say that personally relevant branded content positively influences how they feel about a brand." Lastly, "75% of consumers are more likely to buy from a retailer that recognizes them by name, recommends options based on past purchases, OR knows their purchase history."
- According to Salesforce, "66% of customers expect companies to understand their unique needs and expectations, yet 66% say they're generally treated like numbers."

Given the value of customer segmentation, for the satisfaction of your prospects and customers, where do you begin? Your robust CRM system, marketing automation platform, or email marketing platform will provide the tools (e.g., tags, fixed or customizable data fields, etc.) for segmentation options. By utilizing data fields and tags, your business can apply your research and knowing (see Volume 1, Section 1.1, "Research and Knowing") in an ongoing manner, including:
- Demographics
- Psychographics
- Firmographics and Technographics for B2B
- Observation
- Surveys
- Marketing responses (e.g., email opens, clicks on your website or emails, etc.)
- Buying behavior (e.g., quantity of purchase, types of purchases, frequency of purchases, etc.)
- Preferences (see Section 8.45, "The Power of Color")
- Purchased leads data (see Volume 1, Section 8.33, "Lead Buying")
- Lifetime value (see Section 8.44, "Customer Lifetime Value (CLV or LTV)")
- Data appending services

Quality data appending services can help your business fill in your data gaps when it comes to valuable information about your customers and prospects. Each data appending service has its own process. For example, your business may upload your customer list and the service will match the records and provide its data elements.

The data may include everything from attribute information to online and offline behavior. It's imperative, that you only work with highly credible data appending services because the success or failure of your business relies on it. The security of the information you provide and the quality of the information you receive are critical for your success.

The options regarding the customer segments you can create are limitless. For example, in Volume 4, Section 8.59, "Upselling," we'll address ideas for marketing products and services that deliver more convenience, expertise, capabilities, and more to your customers.

The importance of segments also changes over time. Therefore, it's important to limit the number of segments to what your business can effectively manage and ensure each segment is large enough.

Be sure to refer to Section IV, "Guerrilla E-Media Marketing," for additional tactics and resources.

8.55 * LEAD SCORING

Guerrilla marketers are in the business of attracting leads and converting them into customers. Leads are prospects that are a result of lead buying (see Volume 1, Section 8.33, "Lead Buying") and/or those prospects that have interacted (organically or as a result of your marketing) with your business.

In general terms, there are three types of leads:
- Cold leads are prospects that are not familiar with your business. It's your job to warm those leads and interest them in your product(s) or service(s) by giving them a compelling desire to purchase your product(s) or service(s) and become your customer
- Medium leads are prospects that you are marketing to as a part of a marketing arrangement with Fusion/Affiliate Marketing partners. These prospects have a relationship with your Fusion/Affiliate Marketing partner, who is recommending or endorsing your business, product, or service

- Hot leads are prospects that have been referred by your customers, a referral site, etc. They could also be prospects that opted into your quiz or survey, downloaded your ebook or white paper, or requested your updates/newsletter and, therefore, have provided their information. Hot leads have a high propensity to buy

By scoring and categorizing your leads, your business can focus on those that are of the highest quality (see Section 8.50, "Ideal Customers"). Therefore, to be effective, your business must develop a scoring and classification system.

Marketo suggests using explicit and implicit information to determine your lead scoring system. According to Marketo, "*Explicit scoring* is based on information the prospect provides or tells you directly, such as age, gender, geography, job title, or company role. *Implicit scoring* is based on information that you observe or infer about the prospect, such as their online behaviors."

As we referenced in Section 8.54, "Customer Segmentation," your business can utilize a highly credible, quality data appending service to help your business fill in your data gaps.

You'll want to utilize the capabilities of your robust CRM system, marketing automation platform, or email marketing platform to capture behavioral activity in your implicit scoring. With your determination of how your business defines the highest quality leads and the capabilities of your system or platform, you can assign ascending point levels to associated activities and attributes. You can also deduct points, as necessary.

The purpose of lead scoring is similar to segmenting your customers. Your goal is to apply specialized and focused marketing tactics, based on the lead score, to each prospect/lead to move them through the sales journey and turn them into customers. Guerrilla marketers do not make the mistake that many businesses do, which is to focus only on the high-scoring leads and ignore the rest.

Doing so is choosing to ignore a great deal of opportunity, and it's choosing to ignore, first, pin effects (i.e., one action that causes another action). You never know what the relationship could be between a high-scoring lead and a low-scoring lead and what the pin effect could be on a high-scoring lead by choosing to ignore a particular low-scoring lead. Second, doing so ignores potential by-product opportunities (see Volume 1, Section 5.3, "By-Product"), such as those referenced in Section 7.28, "Cycling." After all, low-scoring leads may have a high propensity to buy when you market the right product(s) or service(s) to them.

8.56 * IDEAL EMPLOYEES

In Section 8.50, "Ideal Customers," we addressed the value of taking the time to identify your ideal customers. You'll recall that as you identify the characteristics of your ideal customers and what motivates them, you'll also be identifying the characteristics of your least desirable customers.

The same principle applies to your employees. When you identify the characteristics of your ideal employees, you have the opportunity to identify the characteristics of employees your business is better off without. It seems simple enough, but many businesses choose to rely on "gut instinct" when it comes to selecting employee candidates instead of taking the time to identify the ideal characteristics.

Where do you begin when you're identifying characteristics of your ideal employees? It's simpler than you think; look at the characteristics of your ideal customers. At the end of the day, the goal of everyone in your business is to attract, delight, and retain your ideal customers. Therefore, your ideal employees need to possess the characteristics that are magnetic for your prospects and customers now and into the future.

The Ritz Carlton has a well-known employee promise that exemplifies the importance of determining the characteristics of your ideal employees to attract, delight, and retain your ideal customers. Their motto is, "We are Ladies and Gentlemen serving Ladies and Gentlemen." Their employee promise is:

> *At The Ritz-Carlton, our Ladies and Gentlemen are the most important resource in our service commitment to our guests.*
>
> *By applying the principles of trust, honesty, respect, integrity, and commitment, we nurture and maximize talent to the benefit of each individual and the company.*
>
> *The Ritz-Carlton fosters a work environment where diversity is valued, quality of life is enhanced, individual aspirations are fulfilled, and The Ritz-Carlton Mystique is strengthened.*

Their employee promise makes the characteristics of their ideal employees jump out. When you look at the characteristics of your ideal customers, along with understanding each of your marketing efforts—this includes all interactions with your employees—which are more powerful when they're consistent and aligned with your Attributes (see Section VIII, "Guerrilla Company Attributes" in each volume) and Attitudes (see Section IX, "Guerrilla Company Attitudes" in each volume), it's much easier to identify the characteristics of your ideal employees. After all, those candidates that don't possess those ideal characteristics will find greater success with another business.

The skills and characteristics that your ideal employees possess relate to their ability to attract, delight, and retain your ideal customers for your business, which fuels everyone's success. After all, an SMB's labor is both an investment (i.e., cost) and a source of revenue generation.

Payroll percentage is a KPI for every SMB to factor in and monitor. It's a KPI that will help you focus on your ongoing success by measuring the results of your investment in your employees. It will also help you identify opportunities to reward their success and inspire their loyalty.

According to Netsuite, payroll percentage is calculated as:

(Total payroll expenses/gross revenue) x 100

For example, if your payroll expense is $325,000, and your gross revenue is $900,000, your payroll percentage is 36 percent.

To accurately capture total payroll expenses, you want to include everything from commissions and bonuses to vacation pay, benefits, taxes, insurance, owner draws, auto allowances, etc. According to the SBA, "There's a rule of thumb that the cost is typically 1.25 to 1.4 times the salary. . ."

While factoring in revenue, be sure to remove "any charges that you collect and pass through without a markup, such as sales taxes and freight charges." For the benefit of comparison, Netsuite offers "examples of typical payroll percentages by industry:

- Retail: 10% to 20%
- Manufacturing: 12%
- Construction: 20%
- Hospitality: 30%
- Restaurants: 30%
- Professional, scientific and technical services: 39%
- Health care and social assistance: 41%

- Beauty salons and barber shops [sic]: 44%"

By identifying, hiring, and retaining your ideal employees, you're equipping your business for success. Just as your ideal customers—and their loyalty and referrals of additional ideal customers—is the fuel for your long-term success, so are your ideal employees and their loyalty and referrals of additional ideal employees.

8.57 * DISRUPTION

Guerrilla marketers seek to disrupt and innovate (see Volume 1, Section 8.11, "Innovation") every day as they pave their path to profits. From tiny improvements to technological advancements, your Guerrilla Creativity (see Volume 1, Section 1.2, "Guerrilla Creativity) and skilled thinking (see Section 9.28, "Skilled Thinking") will help you step outside of the box and see new opportunities.

Your opportunities for disruption are ever-growing with advancements, such as:
- Blockchain, NFTs, smart contracts, and cryptocurrency (see Section 7.29, "Blockchain Solutions")
- AI, machine learning, and natural language processing (see Section 8.47, "AI Business Optimization," and Sections 4.65 through 4.69)
- AR and VR (see Section 3.32, "Experiential Marketing")
- Systems and automation (see Volume 1, Section 8.31, "Systems and Automation")

However, disruption does not rely solely on technological advancements. Disruption can occur with simple tactics, such as:
- Convenience (see Volume 1, Section 8.21, "Convenience)
- Quality content (see Section 5.21 "Creating Sellable Content")
- Purpose (see Volume 1, Section 8.9, "What Your Business Stands For," and Volume 2, "Purpose Minded")
- Like-minded collaboration (see Volume 1, Section 7.6, "Fusion/Affiliate Marketing and Collaboration")
- Expertise (see Volume 1, Section 6.3, "Your Expertise and Credibility")

Your skilled thinking (see Section 9.28, "Skilled Thinking") can help you look at what is and find an entirely new opportunity for what could be.

In our series of Guerrilla Marketing Case Studies, found in each volume of this all-new series of *Guerrilla Marketing* books, you'll find a variety of disruptions, from personalized hair care products to cupcake ATMs, that helped businesses breakthrough and succeed.

- Volume 1
  - Guerrilla Marketing Case Study 1 – Nike
  - Guerrilla Marketing Case Study 2 – Whole Foods Market
  - Guerrilla Marketing Case Study 3 – Function of Beauty
  - Guerrilla Marketing Case Study 4 – Red Bull
- Volume 2
  - Guerrilla Marketing Case Study 5 – Sprinkles
  - Guerrilla Marketing Case Study 6 – Barnes & Noble
  - Guerrilla Marketing Case Study 7 – Ace Hardware
  - Guerrilla Marketing Case Study 8 – Brooks Brothers
- Volume 3
  - Guerrilla Marketing Case Study 9 – Starbucks
  - Guerrilla Marketing Case Study 10 – URBN Brands
  - Guerrilla Marketing Case Study 11 – Forbes
  - Guerrilla Marketing Case Study 12 – Tommy Bahama

The moment you stop innovating and asking the important questions of yourself and your customers and prospects, your business becomes less disruptive and compelling. When your business is less disruptive and compelling, your business needs to spend more on marketing—oftentimes, while you're getting fewer results. In Volume 4, Section 8.58, "Hidden Opportunities," we'll dive deeper into optimizing your business.

SECTION IX

Guerrilla Company Attitudes

GUERRILLA COMPANY ATTITUDES

Your Guerrilla Company Attitudes are where the rubber meets the road for your customers and prospects. You can do everything right with your marketing and advertising efforts and attract prospects who want to become customers. However, if you forget, for even a second, that your company attitudes are a critical part of your marketing, your business can turn that hot prospect into a negative review or social post faster than you can say, "Social media."

Prospects and customers expect, consciously and subconsciously, consistency in everything your business does. If you're marketing and advertising the friendly and fast service of your business, you must consistently deliver the friendly and fast service that meets and exceeds your prospects' and customers' expectations.

When your Guerrilla Company Attitudes are consistent with all of your marketing and advertising efforts, your business is turning prospects into customers. It's also turning customers into repeat buyers and precious referrers of new prospects to your business.

When your company attitudes are inconsistent with your marketing, your business will need a lot more prospects because many will not become customers. Those who do become customers are not likely to be repeat customers, and your ratings and reviews will show it.

You don't need to look very far to find a rating or review that is directly tied to the attitudes of the business. Equally, you'll find a five-star review that says even though they had a problem with the product or service, they were delighted with the fantastic customer service they received. Customers will forgive a problem, but they won't forgive inconsistency.

Your Guerrilla Company Attitudes are on display at all times, so pay attention to the details and be intentional. It's as simple as the greeting your business offers when prospects and customers enter your business. From that point, everything they see, feel, and hear conveys the attitude of your business.

On the other hand, if your prospects and customers enter your business via your website, your company attitudes are also conveyed. If they are met with pop-ups, advertisements, auto-play videos, and slow to load content, you're conveying the attitudes of your business.

As we detailed in Volume 1, in the book *Guerrilla Marketing*, Jay Conrad Levinson pointed out some of the important unconscious factors that your

prospects and customers process when it comes to doing business with you, which include:
- Speed
- Neatness
- Telephone demeanor
- Value
- Flexibility

Jay Conrad Levinson's observation of these important unconscious factors remains true today. Guerrilla Marketing's success spans decades because it focuses on the details that most businesses ignore. Guerrilla marketers tend to those tiny, supercharged details that can generate big profits.

It's simple and inexpensive to understand your Guerrilla Company Attitudes. It's worth a reminder that when those attitudes are consistent with all of your marketing and advertising efforts, your business is turning prospects into customers. It's also turning customers into repeat buyers and precious referrers of new prospects to your business.

Managing your Guerrilla Company Attitudes will put your business far ahead of most other businesses, including your competition. Think about businesses that you enjoy doing business with.

Take some time and dissect that business (or multiple businesses) that you enjoy doing business with. What are their company attitudes? Are their company attitudes consistent with their marketing and advertising? As you break down their marketing, it becomes easy to see that your business is marketing with every interaction, so be intentional about it and utilize every aspect of Guerrilla Marketing to your advantage.

In Volume 1, we addressed:

9.1	Passion and Enthusiasm
9.2	Easy to Do Business With
9.3	Technology Friendly
9.4	Your Employees' Voices
9.5	Responsive and Attentive
9.6	Honest Interest in People
9.7	Self-Confidence and Intention
9.8	Aggressiveness and Competitiveness
9.9	High Energy and Take Action
9.10	Focused

9.11 Consistency
9.12 Generosity

In Volume 2, we addressed:
9.13 Guerrilla Agile Mind
9.14 Inspire
9.15 Open Door
9.16 Authenticity
9.17 Purpose-Minded
9.18 Community-Minded
9.19 Demeanor
9.20 Curiosity
9.21 Make Goods
9.22 Mentoring
9.23 Lateral Thinking
9.24 Attention to Detail
9.25 Owner Mindset
9.26 Resilience

Now, we'll pick up where we left off. These factors and many more make up the Guerrilla Company Attitudes of your business, so let's dig a bit deeper.

9.27 * UNCONVENTIONAL

In Volume 2, Section 1.8, "Crucial Skills for Effectively Using Guerrilla Marketing," we addressed the importance of being unconventional. Guerrilla marketers thrive on the nontraditional, and they do the unconventional if the conventional is nonsensical.

It can be easy to think, "I'll do everything that's the opposite of my competition" and that will make your business unconventional, but that thinking can quickly take you off target. Being nontraditional and unconventional does not necessarily mean always being the opposite. Instead, it simply means making your business more appealing to your prospects and customers, and many times, that can be accomplished with simple changes.

What are the characteristics of a traditional (non-Guerrilla business)? Here are a few examples of how the characteristics of a *traditional business* compare to those of a *Guerrilla business*:

- Non-flexible *instead of* meeting their prospects and customers where they are (see Volume 2, Section 6.16, "Meet Prospects and Customers Where They Are")
- Rules-based *instead of* being easy (see Volume 1, Section 9.2, "Easy to Do Business With")
- Slow to respond and behind the counter *instead of* being accessible and moving about their physical-based locations to meet and talk to their prospects and customers (see Volume 1, Section 9.5, "Responsive and Attentive")
- Transaction-oriented *instead of* focusing on building relationships (see Section 9.29, "Relationship Builder") and a customer's lifetime value (see Section 8.44, "Customer Lifetime Value (CLV or LTV)")
- Outdated *instead of* being curious (see Volume 2, Section 9.20, "Curiosity") and technology-friendly (see Volume 1, Section 9.3, "Technology Friendly")
- Hierarchy-focused *instead of* being open (see Volume 1, Section 9.4, "Your Employees' Voices," and Volume 2, Section 9.15, "Open Door")
- Inconsistent *instead of* using the power of consistency, all the way down to the tiny, supercharged details that can generate big profits (see Volume 1, Section 9.11, "Consistency," and Volume 2, Section 9.24, "Attention to Detail")

A Guerrilla business owner seeks conventional goals, such as profits and joy, but achieves them using unconventional and creative means. In part, their Guerrilla Company Attitudes reflect their unconventional and creative focus.

Those unconventional means are fueled by knowledge, time, energy, and imagination, and they compel your prospects to notice your business. Once they do, your call to action must then motivate them to take a desired action (e.g., download an ebook, make a purchase, etc.). Your existing customers also need to be motivated to make repeat purchases and precious referrals of their friends, family, and associates.

If you're looking for effective ways for your unconventional means to shine, the answers are with your customers. Often, they are right in front of your business—in your reviews and ratings and those of your competitors. Prospects and customers are typically happy to share their opinions, which is the fuel you need. At the same time, your business's online groups, customer service, salespeople, survey data, and customer relationships are also valuable sources. When you combine the information you have with your desire to take action (see Volume 1, Section 9.9, "High Energy and Take Action"), you'll find a fountain of unconventional and creative ideas.

9.28 * SKILLED THINKING

Guerrilla marketers embrace thinking as a skill. We've already addressed the value of lateral thinking (see Volume 2, Section 9.23, "Lateral Thinking," for more information). In this section, we'll address more options to help improve your ability to successfully solve problems, be innovative, and be creative.

Keep in mind: there are countless books and research available to help you dive deeply into skilled thinking. Our goal is to give you an overview and stimulate your current processes.

Research

It's easy to fall into a pattern of doing things the way you've always done them. When you choose to research a challenge or problem without bias and before taking action, you'll find new, innovative, and creative options. Research is your gateway for new thinking, and it's at your fingertips.

The greatest challenge to effective research is being able to set aside the answers you already know so your research is unbiased. According to Indeed, "A strong critical thinker will only analyze a problem based on the context and facts collected after conducting thorough and impartial research."

When you utilize effective and unbiased research and encourage the same for your employees, you'll change the focus of your business. You'll move your business from a stolid environment to a growth-focused and innovative environment.

Your research may find the way you're currently solving your challenge or problem is the best way to do so, and that's a fantastic validation. However, in the process of effectively researching, you'll likely have found other valuable information that you will put to great use to help your business thrive.

Confirmation Bias

It's human nature to seek knowledge to confirm the thoughts or facts you already believe. However, that bias limits your thinking. The American Psychological Association defines confirmation bias as, "the tendency to gather evidence that confirms preexisting expectations, typically by emphasizing or pursuing supporting evidence while dismissing or failing to seek contradictory evidence."

Confirmation bias often takes place in the subconscious mind. Therefore, you must apply skilled thinking and remain aware of confirmation bias.

If, for example, you want to research a new point-of-sale system, confirmation bias may influence your research. Perhaps, you subconsciously don't want to go through the hassle of changing systems, even though you consciously know different functionality is needed and can help your business. Confirmation bias can make you (subconsciously) more receptive to research that supports or confirms your bias (i.e., not wanting to go through the hassle of changing systems).

To avoid confirmation bias, you want to apply skilled thinking by starting your research, problem solving, creativity, etc., with a clean sheet of paper. It's easier said than done.

Metacognition

Vanderbilt University offers a great explanation of metacognition. "Metacognition is, put simply, thinking about one's thinking. More precisely, it refers to the processes used to plan, monitor, and assess one's understanding and performance. Metacognition includes a critical awareness of a) one's thinking and learning and b) oneself as a thinker and learner."

The American Psychological Association defines metacognition as "awareness of one's own cognitive processes, often involving a conscious attempt to control them. The tip-of-the-tongue phenomenon, in which one struggles to retrieve something that one knows, provides an interesting and common example of metacognition."

Simply stated, metacognition is understanding how you think, which helps you identify your current strengths and weaknesses. Why is that information valuable? When you understand your thinking and learning, you'll better understand when to collaborate and how effective collaboration can expand your thinking and, therefore, the success of your business.

Learning

In Volume 2, Section 5.14, "Variety and Modality," we addressed the various learning styles and why it's important when presenting information to your prospects and customers. It's worth repeating those styles. According to Inspire Education, there are seven learning styles:

1. Visual (spatial)
2. Aural (auditory-musical)
3. Verbal (linguistic)
4. Physical (kinesthetic)
5. Logical (mathematical)
6. Social (interpersonal)
7. Solitary (intrapersonal)

When you take the time to understand your learning style(s) and that of your employees, you'll be more effective. For example, when you're training your employees, the information is better accepted and understood when it's presented in a way that's compatible with their learning style(s), which may be different than yours.

At the same time, when you seek to expand your knowledge and expertise, you'll be far more effective when you seek information in the style(s) in which you learn information with greater ease. If you're not currently aware of your strongest learning styles, take the time to find out and reap the rewards of your enhanced leaning.

Critical Thinking

The Foundation for Critical Thinking offers a valuable definition: "Critical thinking is that mode of thinking—about any subject, content, or problem—in which the thinker improves the quality of his or her thinking by skillfully analyzing, assessing, and reconstructing it." They go on to explain, "It entails effective communication and problem-solving abilities, as well as a commitment to overcome our native egocentrism and sociocentrism."

There are many schools of thought related to the process of critical thinking. The Harvard Business Review offers: "Three simple things that you can do to improve your critical thinking skills:
1. Question assumptions
2. Reason through logic
3. Diversify thought"

The more deliberate you are about critical thinking, the greater your results will be. Critical thinking is an ongoing and ever-evolving form of skilled thinking. Your goal is to continually challenge yourself to improve your critical thinking and, thereby, produce superior results.

Creative Thinking

Creative thinking is, in part, the process of deconstructing an idea, process, product, service, etc. and determine how it can be put back together differently for a better outcome. As we addressed in Volume 1, Section 1.2, "Guerrilla Creativity," creating thinking is a component of "The Strong Foundation of Guerrilla Marketing Success" (see Section I in each volume of this series).

The Association of American Colleges & Universities offers a valuable definition of creative thinking, which is: "Creative thinking is both the capacity to combine or synthesize existing ideas, images, or expertise in original ways and the experience of thinking, reacting, and working in an imaginative way characterized by a high degree of innovation, divergent thinking, and risk taking."

Just as it's effective to apply creativity to your marketing, it's also effective to apply creativity to your thinking. Guerrilla marketers, know the value of uniqueness (see Volume 2, Section 8.39, "Uniqueness"), and your ability to think creatively helps you identify ways to differentiate your business from the perspectives of your prospects and customers in valuable ways.

Convergent Thinking

The process of convergent thinking helps you find the best solution for the challenge you are facing. Convergent thinking is defined by the American Psychological Association as, "critical thinking in which an individual uses linear, logical steps to analyze a number of already formulated solutions to a problem to determine the correct one or the one that is most likely to be successful."

Indeed offers key principles to guide you. In summary, they are:

1. "Using affirmative judgment means focusing on the positives of an idea rather than the negatives."
2. "Keep creativity alive . . . Instead of immediately discarding high-risk or unusual ideas, focus first on the positive aspects and then consider how to minimize any risks."
3. "You must be unwavering about the choices ahead of you, analyzing the gamut of possible solutions fairly and then testing selected options thoroughly."
4. "As you work through possible solutions to a problem, periodically check your objectives to ensure that your focus is where it needs to be."

When there are numerous possible solutions to your challenge or problem, convergent thinking can help you find the best possible solutions to fit your business and your resources.

Debate Yourself or Others

Skilled thinking requires skilled debating—with yourself and with others. To get to the right solution—and successfully apply that solution—you must, in part, be able to:

- Effectively communicate ideas
- Clearly hear objections
- Discuss objections without bias
- Weigh new ideas and options without bias
- Remain curious and creative

Snap judgments, biases, negativity, etc. are the enemies of effective debating. To the contrary, for Guerrilla marketers, an honest interest in people (see Volume 1, Section 9.6, "Honest Interest in People") enhances their debating skills.

Conclusion

There are many more methods of skilled thinking that you can explore to improve your ability to utilize important skills, such as successful problem-solving (see Volume 1, Section 6.4, "Be the Solution"), innovation (see Volume 1, Section 8.11, "Innovation), disruption (see Section 8.57, "Disruption), and creativity (see Volume 1, Section 1.2, "Guerrilla Creativity"). Skilled thinking helps you keep your business from falling into a rut by continually challenging the status quo. It can also help you identify valuable by-products (see Volume

1, Section 5.3, "By-Product") that can be the fuel for you and your business to advance and thrive.

A great way to ensure that your ideas and solutions are as effective as possible is to inspect what you expect (See Volume 2, Section 8.37, "Inspect What You Expect"). The most skilled thinking can generate ideas and solutions that fall flat due to poor execution. Therefore, Guerrilla marketers appreciate the importance of inspecting their expectations.

9.29 * RELATIONSHIP BUILDER

Relationship-building skills are critical to the success of an SMB. In Volume 2, Section 1.8, "Crucial Skills for Effectively Using Guerrilla Marketing," we addressed that relationship-building skills are also critical for your marketing success. As we stated, people want relationships, and your relationship-building skills set you apart.

Guerrillas do everything they can to establish long-term, profitable relationships and nurture a bond between themselves and:
- Prospects and customers
- Industry experts
- Networking contacts
- Media contacts and community leaders
- Other business owners with whom they have similar prospects and customers and compatible Guerrilla Company Attributes (see Section VIII) and Guerrilla Company Attitudes (see Section IX)
- Fusion/Affiliate marketing partners (see Volume 1, Section 7.6, "Fusion/Affiliate Marketing and Collaboration") with whom they create win-win opportunities
- Influencers (see Volume 1, Section 4.6, "Influencer Marketing")
- Suppliers
- Employees
- Investors

Your relationship-building skills help you to be successful with negotiations, problem-solving, collaboration, creativity, innovation, employee retention, customer retention, and attracting valuable referrals that are the fuel for the long-term success of your business.

FastCompany offers valuable relationship-building habits that include:
1. "Become a great listener"
2. "Ask the right questions"
3. "Pay attention to the whole person"
4. "Remember things that are important to others"
5. "Be consistent and manage emotions"
6. "Be open and share when the time is right"
7. "Be genuine, confident, humble, trustworthy, positive and fun"

Guerrilla marketers are naturally curious (see Volume 2, Section 9.20, "Curiosity") and have an interest in and appreciation of people (see Volume 1, Section 9.6, "Honest Interest in People"), and they are also problem solvers. Those valuable attributes lend to building strong and long-lasting relationships.

Take some time to think of businesses that you enjoy doing business with because of their relationship-building skills. By taking account of their actions, you'll find opportunities to improve your relationship-building skills. Perhaps, it's the bakery that knows your name (and those of your family members) and your favorite items, and they offer samples that are catered to your likes.

In Section 4.63, "Online B2B Networking," you'll find opportunities to expand your network and put your relationship-building skills to greater use. In Volume 4, Section 9.36, "Enhanced Customer Service," we'll address opportunities to take your relationship with your customers to the next level.

9.30 * A SUPERB LISTENER

Just as being a superb listener improves you relationship-building skills, in Volume 2, Section 1.8, "Crucial Skills for Effectively Using Guerrilla Marketing," we also addressed its importance to your marketing success.

It's easy to get caught in the trap of doing more *talking* than listening. When you're in selling mode, it's particularly easy to get caught in the trap of *selling* and not listening. During those times, we have to remind ourselves that we listen with our ears and not with our mouths.

The people in and around your business, are eager to share valuable information that can help your business. Those people include your prospects, customers, suppliers, employees, industry experts, media contacts, etc. As a Guerrilla marketer with superb listening skills, you'll learn valuable information about:
- Your competitive advantages and your disadvantages
- New product or service opportunities
- Possible innovations (see Volume 1, Section 8.11, "Innovation")
- Referrals
- By-product possibilities (see Volume 1, Section 5.3, "By-Product")
- Information about your customers (e.g., demographics, psychographics, etc.) and their behavior (see Volume 1, Section 6.9, "Consumer Behavior") that can help you attract more prospects and customers
- Industry trends
- Fusion/Affiliate marketing and collaboration opportunities (see Volume 1, Section 7.6, "Fusion/Affiliate Marketing and Collaboration")

Given the valuable information that you can gain with your superb listening skills, it's time to turn the attention to effective listening skills.
- Be accessible
    - Schedule listening sessions
    - Keep your door open (see Volume 2, Section 9.15, "Open Door")
    - Host Meetups to talk to people at your physical business location or outside of your business (see Volume 1, Section 7.1, "Organizing and Hosting Meetups")
- Be aware of your facial expressions and actions (e.g., looking at your phone or other devices instead of making eye contact), which are signaling if you're interested or not
- Echo back what you've heard and confirm understanding
- Ask questions and let your natural curiosity shine
- Make recommendations, if appropriate, and without disrupting or taking over the conversation
- Express your appreciation
- Take the time to consider what you've heard and how it fits with the goals, attitudes, and attributes of your business
- If appropriate, take action (see Volume 1, Section 9.9, "High Energy and Take Action")

- Inspect what you expect (see Volume 2, Section 8.37, "Inspect What You Expect")

Quite often, the information you need to increase the success of your business is available; you just have to be ready and willing to hear it. However, it's important to keep in mind that not everything you hear is good for your business.

For example, certainly you've heard the adage, "The customer is always right." While the customer is always right about what will satisfy them, it's important to keep in mind that it may not be what is best for your business. Regardless, what your customers have to say is always valuable, and you want to hear it.

9.31 * FOCUSED ON SUCCESS

Guerrilla businesses achieve their goals, in part, due to their focus on their success. That seems simple, and sometimes, it is—but sometimes it's not. At the end of an exhausting day that was full of unexpected challenges, it's easy for your focus on success to get out of focus.

When that happens, unproductive thoughts, actions, and words can creep in and undermine your focus on success, including:

- Focusing on what you don't want instead of what you do want
- Focusing on your fears instead of your dreams
- Focusing on what's "wrong" instead of focusing on everything that's right
- Not clearly outlining your goals
- Making assumptions
- Failing to inspect what you expect
- Choosing the first thought that comes to mind instead of utilizing skilled thinking

Fortunately, Guerrilla marketers focus on their valuable skills and attitudes to stay focused on success. Some of those valuable skills that we've addressed include:

- Self-confidence (see Volume 1, Section 9.7, "Self-Confidence and Intention")

- Competitiveness (see Volume 1, Section 9.8, "Aggressiveness and Competitiveness")
- Productive energy (see Volume 1, Section 9.9, "High Energy and Take Action")
- Focused (see Volume 1, Section, 9.10, "Focused")
- Follow-through (see Volume 2, Section 8.37, "Inspect What You Expect")
- Authenticity (see Volume 2, Section 9.16, "Authenticity")
- Mindset (see Volume 2, Section, 9.25, "Owner Mindset")
- Resilience (see Volume 2, Section, 9.26, "Resilience")
- Skilled thinking (see Section 9.28, "Skilled Thinking," and Volume 2, Section 9.23, "Lateral Thinking")

Beyond those valuable skills and attitudes, Guerrilla marketers can also lean on their confidence that they have built a business with a strong foundation (see Section I, "The Strong Foundation of Guerrilla Marketing Success," in each volume).

If, at any time, you find yourself a bit off focus, invest the time to look back at those sections to regain your focus on success. After all, Guerrilla marketers understand that this is their dream and they will never settle. What do you plan to do with this precious dream and this precious opportunity?

Quite often, the simple difference between success and failure of SMBs is their uniqueness and focus. In many industries, there are competing businesses that are selling the same product(s) and/or service(s). Those businesses compete (whether they realize it or not) based on the uniqueness (see Volume 2, Section 8.39, "Uniqueness") of their business and their focus on success.

9.32 * MYSTERY SHOPPING

Guerrilla marketers know that what they want to happen in their business, may not be happening in their business. Therefore, they understand the purpose and benefit of self-evaluation. In Volume 2, Section 8.37, "Inspect What You Expect," we addressed the mindset of getting to the "why." With mystery shopping, you're first getting to the "what is."

Mystery shopping is the skill of experiencing the journey through your business from being a prospect to becoming your customer. The purpose is to help your business find opportunities where your business is not performing to your expectations. It could be:

- Customer service standards and effectiveness
- Loss prevention (i.e., inventory leaving your business without being sold)
- The experience and effectiveness in the sales journey
- Consistency in your marketing (e.g., retail displays, signage, greetings, etc.)

Whether it's dining at your restaurant, placing an order on your website (perhaps with the assistance of customer service), or the delivery of your product or service, there are countless mystery shopping services available to your business.

While these mystery shopping businesses are valuable, keep in mind that you're seeking unbiased input to get to the "what is." What does that mean? Simply put, the evaluations can still be influenced by the evaluator and their:

- Consumer mindset (see Volume 2, Section 6.17, "Consumer Mindset")
- Cultural influences
- Brand preferences
- Cognitive biases

As we referenced in Section 8.49, "Perception and Reality," cognitive biases are explained by SimplyPsychology as, "unconscious errors in thinking that arise from problems related to memory, attention, and other mental mistakes." That means there can be gaps in the accuracy of what the mystery shopper recalls at the time they document their experience.

Therefore, it's important to make sure your mystery shoppers share the attributes and attitudes of your ideal customers (see Section 8.50, "Ideal Customers"). Equally, it's important that you choose a mystery shopping business with a robust platform that allows your business to easily access the shopping experiences and find measurable results and trends in the data.

Another simple and powerful approach is to engage a friend or loved one that is not known to your employees or representatives. You can ask them to call your business on speaker phone and make a typical inquiry. Listen to how your employee performs and provide any pertinent feedback to your team. You can also ask your friend (or loved one) to send an email or initiate an online chat and share the dialogue with you.

Additional areas of the business can be mystery evaluated, from shipping and fulfillment to vendor inquiries or returns processing. Each of these critical "moments of truth" in your business should be evaluated and can be completed by someone you know or a paid service.

9.33 * THIRST FOR KNOWLEDGE

Guerrilla marketers have a natural thirst for knowledge, and they seek to collaborate with others who share their thirst for knowledge. From marketing collaborations (see Volume 1, Section 7.6, "Fusion/Affiliate Marketing and Collaboration") to employees, fostering and enabling a culture of learning is a benefit for your business.

There are numerous options to consider. For example, creating a customer resource library or knowledge base that is accurate and up-to-date and includes your employees' contributions is a great way to foster a culture of learning.

The result is confident and knowledgeable employees that offer consistent and correct answers, solutions, and marketing messages to your prospects and customers. Your customer knowledge base must be easy to use, consistent with your Guerrilla Company Attributes (see Section VIII) and Guerrilla Company Attitudes (see Section IX), and can include:

- Product(s) or service(s) specifications
- Your USP, elevator pitch, the story of your business, etc.
- Common problems and pain points that your prospects and customers have and how your product(s) and/or service(s) addresses and resolves them
- Troubleshooting
- FAQs
- Promotional offers and all of the supporting details to successfully implement those promotions
- A guide to your advertising and marketing efforts
- Trivia and gamified learning information

By regularly measuring the use and effectiveness of your knowledge base, you'll continually refine and improve it. You'll also be able to utilize the knowledge for your chatbots (see Volume 2, Section 4.47, "Message Bots").

There are numerous software tools to help you create a strong knowledge base, such as:

- Zendesk
- Zoho Desk
- HubSpot Knowledge Base Software

Beyond a knowledge base, there are many other options to consider for fostering and enabling a culture of learning in your business including:

- Mentoring (see Volume 2, Section 9.22, "Mentoring")
- Workshops and demonstrations
- A resource center for learning that can include links to valuable free or paid courses on EdX
- Relationship tips and exercises

The options are limitless for fostering and enabling a culture of learning. The benefit to your business is that you can turn downtime (e.g., slow times) into up-times that work for your business by motivating, engaging, and inspiring your employees to delight your prospects and customers and remain loyal to your business.

9.34 * RIGHT PEOPLE, RIGHT PLACES

A poignant example of the value of having the right people in the right places came to light recently. During a visit to a restaurant, a bartender was working hard to create a large batch of a house-made drink mixer. After multiple trips to the kitchen for various tools and ingredients, approximately one hour passed with the bartender's sole focus on the task of completing the task (while the other bartender covered the bar).

The adage "aces in their places" came to mind. The same task performed by their talented and experienced kitchen prep staff would have been accomplished in a fraction of the time. At the same time, efficiency came to mind. Placing tools and ingredients a great distance from the location where they are needed was creating significant inefficiencies. See Volume 1, Section 8.13, "Efficiency," for more information to help your business get maximum results with minimal effort.

In a small business, it's natural to have people and employees doing all kinds of tasks that may not be within their expertise. On one hand, that provides learning and growth opportunities, but on the other hand, it can mean sacrificing valuable time, quality, and capability.

To ensure that your business is operating with the right people in the right places, turn your attention to your process. As you evaluate your processes, are there opportunities for improvement? Consider:

- Innovation (see Volume 1, Section 8.11, "Innovation")
- Automation (see Volume 1, Section 8.31, "Systems and Automation")
- Skilled thinking to redesign processes (see Section 9.28, "Skilled Thinking," and Volume 2, Section 9.23, "Lateral Thinking")

Sometimes, more resources are the answer, and fortunately, Guerrilla businesses know they have options, such as:

- Collaborating with vendors or fellow business owners
- Part-time skilled labor and/or outsourcing for tasks that require expertise and can be performed quickly and succinctly, which minimizes the cost

Regardless of what approach you take, monitoring your operations and inspecting what you expect (see Volume 2, Section 8.37, "Inspect What You Expect") will help you ensure that you're utilizing the right skilled talent to perform the right skilled work to produce maximum results.

9.35 * CUSTOMER FIRST

Guerrilla marketers have complete clarity that customers come first in their business. Have you ever been to a business where you're standing in line and watching numerous employees performing tasks that seem less important than helping you (and every other customer in the line)? Have you ever been to a business where you're standing in line and watching a manager observe the line and doing nothing to make it move faster (e.g., calling for more cashiers, jumping on a register themselves, deploying employees with handheld checkout capabilities, etc.)? Have you ever been to a business where you're standing in line and either you—or another customer—decide to put your purchase back on the shelf and leave the business instead of waiting in the line?

Guerrilla marketers do not operate their business that way. Whether your business is online or has physical business locations, everyone in your business clearly understands that customers come first. It's easy to state that as a policy in your business, but Guerrilla marketers think through their processes to ensure that their employees understand the procedures for making customers first.

Therefore, a Guerrilla marketer provides clear procedures to their employees to ensure they understand:

- The importance of monitoring customer activity
- What their role is if a bottleneck happens with their customers (e.g., customers on phone hold, customers in line, etc.)
- Specific procedures for them to move from their current roles to roles that help remove the bottleneck of customers, including the necessary training to perform those roles
- Specific procedures for them to return to their roles after the bottleneck is removed

Customers are forgiving of waiting if they are confident that the business is putting them first and doing everything to value and respect them as a customer, including respecting their time and asking about their satisfaction.

If your business is online, it's important to continually monitor check-out activity and abandoned carts. It's also important to include a simple question (e.g., "Let us know if you found checking out easy") with a quick rating scale (e.g., "unsatisfactory, satisfactory, delighted") and an opportunity for them to leave comments.

Saying customers are first is great, but a Guerrilla marketer takes the time to ensure that customers are first. Beyond creating the procedures, they also inspect their expectations (see Volume 2, Section 8.37, "Inspect What You Expect") to ensure the procedures are being followed. They also go the extra mile to ensure their procedures are effective for making customers first . . . and their customers agree as evidenced by their feedback and quickly-returned surveys and/or ratings.

In Volume 4, Section 9.36, "Enhanced Customer Service," we'll address opportunities to take your relationship with your customers to the next level.

Section X

Guerrilla Marketing Case Studies

INTRODUCTION

As you are now aware, Guerrilla Marketing is a 360-degree, consistent methodology that weaves through every aspect of your business. Guerrilla Marketing is intelligent marketing that utilizes a strategy and a plan that is supported with knowledge and low-cost, unconventional, creative tactics to convey and promote a compelling product(s) or idea(s).

Guerrilla Marketing succeeds as it makes the truth fascinating and compelling. It also helps your business identify and market your USP so your prospects and customers take notice of what makes your business unique.

In the following four Guerrilla Marketing Case Studies, we'll look at some well-known companies and outline how Guerrilla Marketing tactics can take an idea and turn it into limitless success. The companies we'll cover are:

- Starbucks
- URBN Brands
- Forbes
- Tommy Bahama

You'll see that many successful businesses utilize these tactics, and they combine them with the values of clarity, focus, and consistency.

These businesses began where every business begins—with an idea and a dream. That idea and dream are precious and so is the opportunity to turn that idea and/or dream into a small business. With Guerrilla Marketing, they turn knowledge, time, energy, and imagination into profits, and you can do the same with your idea, dream, and/or business.

With compelling messages and tactics, along with an authentic and consistent identity, small businesses grow. By consistently repeating and improving upon the compelling messages and winning tactics, businesses turn their prospects into customers. Their success grows as their growing customer base makes repeat purchases and provides precious referrals, which is the fuel for the long-term success of the business.

Guerrilla marketers understand how marketing works, and they constantly put that knowledge and their creativity to work . . . along with the power of consistency, tracking, analysis, and repetition. The simple act of repeating what's working and improving or eliminating what's not can set their success apart. Let's take a look at Guerrilla Marketing in action!

GUERRILLA MARKETING CASE STUDY 9
Starbucks

Starbucks began in 1971 with a single store in the Pike Place Market in Seattle. According to Starbucks, they were "offering fresh-roasted coffee beans, tea and spices from around the world for our customers to take home. Our name was inspired by the classic tale, 'Moby-Dick,' [sic] evoking the seafaring tradition of the early coffee traders."

In 1982, Howard Schultz joined the business as the director of retail operations and marketing, and they began providing coffee to restaurants and espresso bars. In 1983, a trip to Milan inspired Schultz to bring the Italian coffeehouse artistry and culture to the US.

Realizing that his vision of coffeehouses differed from the founder's vision for Starbucks, Schultz left the business in 1985 to launch a business offering brewed coffee and espresso beverages from the Starbucks beans. In 1987, with the success of the new business, it acquired Starbucks's assets and took on their name. At the time, there were seventeen locations.

By 1988, they grew to thirty-three locations and showed their focus on employees by offering full health benefits to eligible employees. By 1991, they expanded their benefits to become the ". . . first privately owned U.S. company to offer a stock option program that includes part-time employees," as their locations had grown to one hundred sixteen in number. A year later, with one hundred sixty-five locations, they went public.

In 1994, they opened their first drive-thru location. A year later, they began serving blended beverages along with debuting their first album, "Blue Note Blend." In 1996, with over a thousand locations, they started selling bottled beverages and began their expansion outside of the US.

In 1998, they expanded their distribution into grocery channels and launched their website. In 1999, they partnered with Conservation International ". . . to promote sustainable coffee growing practices" and in 2001, the partnership included ". . . ethical coffee-sourcing guidelines." In 2002, they launched wi-fi in their stores.

In 2004, Starbucks launched their Coffee Master Program, which is an education program for their employees (whom they call partners). The program includes coursework to learn more about their coffees and "acknowledges their knowledge and skill with the special designation of the black apron after they pass written and taste tests." In 2014, they launched the Starbucks College Achievement Plan that offers qualified partners (i.e., employees) the opportunity to complete a college degree.

In 2008, they entered the world of social media. In 2009, they launched their rewards loyalty program and their first iPhone app that included mobile payment. In 2014, they began offering mobile ordering and payment.

Today, with over thirty-two thousand locations around the globe, their mission is "to inspire and nurture the human spirit – one person, one cup, and one neighborhood at a time." When it comes to their partners (i.e., employees), "We like to say that we are not in the coffee business serving people, but in the people business serving coffee."

Taking the ordinary and making it extraordinary is exactly what Guerrilla Marketing helps you do. Is your idea, business, product(s), or service(s) ready to break through the ordinary and become extraordinary?

The list of evident Guerrilla Marketing tactics at play with Starbucks is long. Let's outline some of the most successful Guerrilla Marketing tactics at play:

- Innovation (see Volume 1, Section 8.11)
- Convenience (see Volume 1, Section 8.21)
- Easy to Do Business With (see Volume 1, Section 9.2)
- Customer Loyalty (see Volume 2, Section 7.18)
- Fusion/Affiliate Marketing and Collaboration (see Volume 1, Section 7.6)
- Retail Location Selection (see Volume 2, Section 3.27)
- Name (see Volume 1, Section 8.2)
- Identity (see Volume 1, Section 8.3)
- Brand (see Volume 1, Section 8.1)
- Power of Color (see Section 8.45)
- Business Attire and Uniforms (see Volume 1, Section 6.2)
- Consistency (see Section 1.9 and Volume 1, Sections 2.8 and 9.11)
- Repetition (see Section 1.10 and Volume 1, Section 2.8)
- Passion and Enthusiasm (see Volume 1, Section 9.1)
- Selection and Cross-Selling (see Volume 1, Section 8.23)
- Guerrilla Creativity (see Volume 1, Section 1.2)
- Intelligent Positioning (see Volume 1, Section 8.8)

- Product Displays/Experiences (see Volume 1, Section 3.1)
- Appeal to the Senses (see Section 8.46)
- By-Product (see Volume 1, Section 5.3)
- Purpose-Minded (see Section 9.17)
- Honest Interest in People (see Volume 1, Section 9.6)
- Your Employees and Representatives (see Volume 1, Section 6.1)

Let's dive a bit deeper into some of these Guerrilla Marketing tactics as they relate to Starbucks. For those tactics that you decide are well-suited for your prospects and customers, and therefore, you want to incorporate them into your Guerrilla Marketing Plan, be sure to take the time re-review the details of each tactic.

Innovation, Convenience, Easy to Do Business With, Customer Loyalty, Fusion/Affiliate Marketing and Collaboration, and Retail Location Selection

Starbucks has been committed to being easy and convenient for their customers. From convenient payment options to app ordering and wi-fi at their locations, they strive for convenience. The ease and convenience, in part, encourages customer loyalty, which they reward with a loyalty program.

With over thirty-two thousand locations around the globe, they know the importance of being where their customers are, especially when they're thirsty. By collaborating with others, they began distributing bottled beverages and then expanded their distribution into grocery channels to make it even more convenient for their customers to purchase their products.

Name, Identity, Brand, Power of Color, Business Attire and Uniforms, Consistency, and Repetition

Starbucks reaps the benefits from utilizing a consistent name, logo, color palette, design, etc. in their marketing and advertising. That consistency flows through their packaging and retail operations, including with their interior and exterior design and signage. At the same time, Starbucks's signature aprons (i.e., uniforms) make their partners (i.e., employees) easy to distinguish.

Their consistency and repetition make their locations and products easily identifiable, even to those who are not their customers.

Passion and Enthusiasm, Selection and Cross-Selling, Guerrilla Creativity, Product Displays/Experiences, Appeal to the Senses, and By-Product

From food to take-home products, music, coffee-making, and coffee-enjoying accessories, Starbucks utilizes numerous cross-selling options for their prospects and customers. Those products are well-suited to expand their sales and appeal to non-coffee drinkers and people seeking gifts for their favorite coffee drinkers.

In their retail locations, they use creative lighting, music, and the aroma of fresh ground and brewed coffee to appeal to the senses of their prospects and customers.

Purpose-Minded, Honest Interest in People, and Your Employees and Representatives

Starbucks has made their commitment to people, the planet, and their growers, widely known. In 2006, Starbucks launched "the industry's first paper beverage cup containing post-consumer recycled fiber." They are also committed to sustainable coffee-growing practices, ethical coffee-sourcing, and "giving back more than we take from the planet."

As they state it, "As it has been from the beginning, our purpose goes far beyond profit. We believe Starbucks can, and should, have a positive impact on the communities we serve."

They strive to be "people positive," and they support their partners (i.e., employees) with benefits that include educational opportunities to learn and grow. They also use creative and engaging titles for their employees by calling them partners instead of employees and then using titles, such as Barista, Coffee Master, etc.

Conclusion

Remember, Guerrilla marketers seek to disrupt and innovate every day as they pave their paths to profits. The moment you stop innovating and asking the important questions of yourself and your customers and prospects, your business becomes less compelling. When your business is less compelling, your business needs to spend more on marketing—often, while you're getting less results.

GUERRILLA MARKETING CASE STUDY 10
URBN Brands

URBN Brands, according to the parent company itself, got its start in 1970 by three people, one of whom was searching for a topic for an entrepreneurial class. The first store was called Free People, and it was a second-hand clothing, furniture, jewelry, and home décor store in West Philadelphia.

URBN Brands collaborates with major retailers to market some of their store brands. Alternately, they also sell directly to consumers.

They "strive to connect with (their) customers through unique products and engaging store design." For example, they choose to create their retail design around the features of the space instead of a cookie-cutter, templated retail design. Their creative atmospheres make each store an experience that is filled with curated products.

URBN Brands operates multiple store brands, each with its own unique marketing strategy and approach to retail and selling. Many of their brands match different lifestyles and stages in life. Their brands include:

- Urban Outfitters: "A lifestyle retailer dedicated to inspiring customers through a unique combination of product, creativity and cultural understanding."
- Anthropologie: "Together, we tell stories – of products thoughtfully designed, crafted, and curated, and of a collaborative, inventive community."
- Free People: "A unique and unwavering bond with our customers sits at the heart of our lifestyle community, where we encourage self-confidence and self-expression."
- Nuuly: ". . . a curated destination for anyone who loves fashion and is exploring how to wear, buy and sell it in ways that are gentler on the planet—and their bank accounts."
- Terain: ". . . a garden, home and outdoor lifestyle brand deeply rooted in nature and plant life."
- BHLDN: ". . . (pronounced "beholden") offers a carefully edited assortment of wedding gowns, bridesmaid dresses, accessories, and décor that caters to the bride in search of unusually beautiful things."

- Menus & Venues: "Deeply rooted in the communities we serve; we strive to connect with our customers and become their favorite destination no matter what the occasion."

Their brands meet their prospects and customers where they are with physical retail locations and robust e-commerce options. Guerrilla marketers know the importance of growing their business by utilizing their by-product and creating spin-off businesses that focus on the unique needs of different segments of their prospects and customers.

The list of evident Guerrilla Marketing tactics at play with URBN Brands is long. Let's outline some of the most successful Guerrilla Marketing tactics at play:

- Name (see Volume 1, Section 8.2)
- Identity (see Volume 1, Section 8.3)
- Brand (see Volume 1, Section 8.1)
- Consistency (see Section 1.9 and Volume 1, Sections 2.8 and 9.11)
- Uniqueness (see Volume 2, Section 8.39)
- Passion and Enthusiasm (see Volume 1, Section 9.1)
- Selection and Cross-Selling (see Volume 1, Section 8.23)
- Product Displays/Experiences (see Volume 1, Section 3.1)
- Guerrilla Creativity (see Volume 1, Section 1.2)
- Retail Location Selection (see Volume 2, Section 3.27)
- The Power of Color (see Section 8.45)
- Appeal to the Senses (see Section 8.46)
- Unconventional (see Section 9.27)
- By-Product (see Volume 1, Section 5.3)
- Spin-Off (see Volume 2, Section 8.41)
- Cycling (see Section 7.28)
- Meet Prospects and Customers Where They Are (see Volume 2, Section 6.16)
- Collaboration (see Volume 1, Section 7.6)
- Convenience (see Volume 1, Section 8.21)

Let's dive a bit deeper into some of these Guerrilla Marketing tactics as they relate to URBN Brands. For those tactics that you decide are well-suited for your prospects and customers, and therefore, you want to incorporate them into your Guerrilla Marketing Plan, be sure to take the time re-review the details of each tactic.

Name, Identity, Brand, Consistency, Uniqueness, Passion and Enthusiasm

URBN Brands reap the benefits of utilizing consistent identities for each of their store brands. The brands are often lifestyle-focused, and, therefore, their marketing consistently appeals to that lifestyle.

Their passion for distinctive design creates the perfect combination of uniqueness that is wrapped in a consistent and polished identity in their marketing and advertising. Their uniqueness and consistency also flow through their retail operations, including within their interior and exterior design and signage, which makes their retail stores, though unique, easily identifiable.

It's not easy to balance creativity and maintaining a consistent brand. Oftentimes, the creativity will override (i.e., overpower and drown out) the brand. When that happens, your prospects and customers remember a creative store, but they don't easily recall the name of the business. Therefore, the experience might be top-of-mind, but the business is not. When they share their experiences, they say things, such as, "It's that really creative store—oh, I can't remember the name, but I'm sure your know which one I'm talking about."

Selection and Cross-Selling, Product Displays/Experiences, Guerrilla Creativity, Retail Location Selection, The Power of Color, Appeal to the Senses, and Unconventional

In their retail locations, URBN Brands choose to be consistently inconsistent. While that might sound contradictory with the principles of Guerrilla Marketing, in reality, it's the perfect combination of unconventional, creativity, and consistency.

A signature aspect of URBN Brands is its retail locations, which are feasts for the eyes with the powerful use of color. Additionally, as we conveyed in Section 8.46, "Appeal to the Senses," Anthropologie, for example, also appeals to the senses throughout the store with simple additions, such as lighting the fragrant candles they sell to appeal to your sense of smell. In combination with music and featuring plush items that invite touching, they appeal to many of the senses of their prospects and customers.

It's not always easy to create memorable experiences in physical business locations. URBN Brands excels at creating compelling atmospheres with their creativity and a wide and varied selection of interesting and engaging products.

By-Product, Spin-Off, Cycling, Meet Prospects and Customers Where They Are, Convenience, and Collaboration

URBN Brands collaborate with major retailers to market some of their brands. Alternately, they sell directly to consumers through retail stores and e-commerce. The combination allows them to meet their prospects and customers where they are and offer convenience.

Of the URBN brands, Nuuly is a fascinating example of cycling, by-product, and a spin-off, which are effective Guerrilla Marketing tactics. Nuuly has two programs: Nuuly Rent is a subscription clothing rental program that includes clothing from other URBN brands (e.g., Anthropologie, Free People, Urban Outfitters, etc.). Nuuly Thrift is a resale platform that enables consumers to buy and sell clothing and accessories. The URBN brands, such as Anthropologie, then resell gently-used items in conjunction with Nuuly.

Conclusion

Whether you're starting your business or you've been in business for decades, how can you rethink your business from the customer's point of view? If you're not constantly thinking creatively and focusing on the needs of your prospects and customers and their lifestyles, be aware that someone else is. That someone else could be your competition or a start-up business with its sights set on your customers because they think it's possible to compete with and win against your business.

Guerrilla marketers seek to be unconventional and disrupt traditional businesses every day. Your Guerrilla Creativity is always a strength for you to draw upon. Never stop asking questions and challenging yourself and your business. In your weekly or daily meetings, be sure that you're asking questions to improve your success, such as:

- Can we be more creative and maintain and build our identity?
- Can purchasing be made easier?
- Can our business, product(s), or service(s) be more convenient?
- How can we make our selection so compelling that our customers want to buy more products?
- Can we offer an experience (or experiences) that results in greater customer satisfaction, higher ratings, positive reviews, sales, and profits?
- How can we be more irresistible to our prospects?

- If employees were more satisfied in their jobs, what would be the positive impact on the business?
- How can we improve our ratings and reviews?
- Can we do more while spending less?
- What can be done to make our customers love us more?
- What other problems/pain points do our prospects and customers have that we can solve?
- Are we using Guerrilla Creativity to our full advantage?
- Are we using the power of consistency in our marketing?

While change for the sake of change is rarely a good use of your resources; change for the sake of progress is a good use of your resources. The moment you stop asking the important questions, your business becomes less innovative, convenient, and compelling to your customers and prospects, which means your business is spending more on marketing and getting less results.

GUERRILLA MARKETING CASE STUDY 11
Forbes

Content marketing is widely used by businesses of all sizes. According to HubSpot, in 2021, marketers are focused on content, and "82% report actively using content marketing." Forbes has a long history in content marketing. In fact, *Forbes* magazine began in 1917 by B.C. Forbes.

In the first issue, B.C. Forbes expressed his viewpoint, "Business was originated to produce happiness, not to pile up millions." In 1928, he turned down an offer to be acquired by William Randolph Hearst. By 1932, the depression had hit, and his business was devastated. Fortunately, he had focused on multiple revenue streams, and he had freelance earnings to his advantage.

In the mid 1940s, the company began hiring full-time editorial staffers to improve their product. They launched a new product, "The Forbes Investor," a weekly subscription newsletter, which they sold for more than eight times the subscription price of the magazine.

In January 1949, they launched their ". . . annual report card on industries and companies. . ." They chose the month of January because it was typically a slow advertising month, and their annual issue was the innovation that was needed to change that trend. In 1950, they launched another innovation with their coverage of the mutual fund industry and annually giving mutual funds ". . . a letter grade for long-term performance in up markets and another in down markets." In 1982, they added another annual issue, which ranked the 400 richest Americans. Their annual issue success has continued and also includes "Forbes 30 Under 30."

When they launched online in 1996, they focused on creating unique and original content, which was different from their competitors—who were simply putting their print copy online. The convergence of print and digital was a significant challenge. They adopted a contributor model to bring more expert content to light. As they did so, they "boldly instituted what's called native advertising."

They earned a reputation "for hard-hitting stories that evaluate companies the way critics critique a stage play. What made these pieces ring true was our growing sophistication in digging into corporate balance sheets in a way that no other publication did."

They have relied on customer entertainment and experiences to woo advertisers. From yachts to hot-air balloons and properties around the world, they focused on intentional marketing and unique experiences. According to Steve Forbes, "To some outsiders, all of this looked like wasteful extravagance. It was the opposite: It created a global image for Forbes that is as powerful today as it was decades ago. Many businesspeople and entertainers regard landing on the cover of *Forbes* as the ultimate proof of their achievements."

The list of evident Guerrilla Marketing tactics at play with Forbes is long. Let's outline some of the most successful Guerrilla Marketing tactics at play:

- Collaboration (see Volume 1, Section 7.6)
- Subscriptions (see Volume 2, Section 5.16)
- Creating Sharable Content (see Section 5.19)
- Creating Sellable Content (see Section 5.21)
- Writing, Copy, and Headlines (see Volume 1, Section 8.17)
- Your Expertise and Credibility (see Volume 1, Section 6.3)
- Convenience (see Volume 1, Section 8.21)
- Name (see Volume 1, Section 8.2)
- Identity (see Volume 1, Section 8.3)
- Brand (see Volume 1, Section 8.1)
- Intelligent Positioning (see Volume 1, Section 8.8)
- Guerrilla Creativity (see Volume 1, Section 1.2)
- Consistency (see Section 1.9 and Volume 1, Sections 2.8 and 9.11)
- Repetition (see Section 1.10 and Volume 1, Section 2.8)
- Meet Prospects and Customers Where They Are (see Volume 2, Section 6.16)
- Revenue Streams and Channels of Revenue (see Volume 1, Section 4.24)
- Innovation (see Volume 1, Section 8.11)
- Resilience (see Volume 2, Section 9.26)
- Customer Entertainment (see Volume 2, Section 7.21)
- Exclusive Experiences (see Section 7.24)

Let's dive a bit deeper into some of these Guerrilla Marketing tactics as they relate to Forbes. For those tactics that you decide are well-suited for your prospects and customers, and therefore, you want to incorporate them into your Guerrilla Marketing Plan, be sure to take the time re-review the details of each tactic.

Collaboration, Subscriptions, Creating Sharable Content, Creating Sellable Content, Writing, Copy, and Headlines, Your Expertise and Credibility, and Convenience

When it comes to sellable content, utilizing the power of collaboration is a great way to add to your expertise and credibility while broadening your appeal with different writing styles and varied content—written and contributed to with expertise. At the same time, utilizing contributors helps to expand your reach as each contributor shares their content with their social networks.

Name, Identity, Brand, Intelligent Positioning, Guerrilla Creativity, Consistency, Repetition, and Meet Prospects and Customers Where They Are

Since 1917, Forbes has been consistently building their brand. By intentionally and consistently marketing with every interaction you have, you're building a brand that is aligned with your attitudes and attributes. Prospects and customers are drawn to authentic, engaging, and appealing businesses. Your prospects and customers want to know, like, and trust your business.

Customer Entertainment and Exclusive Experiences

Forbes's effective use of customer entertainment and exclusive experiences is legendary. As we noted from Steve Forbes, "It created a global image for Forbes that is as powerful today as it was decades ago. Many businesspeople and entertainers regard landing on the cover of *Forbes* as the ultimate proof of their achievements."

They utilized their entertainment skills with business leaders, world leaders, celebrities, advertisers, etc. They created "see and be seen" experiences that motivated people to want to be featured in their content, which attracts advertisers and readers alike.

Revenue Streams and Channels of Revenue, Innovation, and Resilience

Forbes has seen the best of times and worst of times, and they have continually innovated with content and delivery to attract powerful audiences that want to be associated with their business. Their ability to navigate through challenges (from the Depression to the conversion to digital) took resilience and innovation.

From the list of the richest people to the list of the "up and comers," they strategically created innovative content to appeal to their customers, prospects, and advertisers. At the same time, they amassed a following of people that covet the opportunity to be featured in their content.

Conclusion

When it comes to content marketing, the competition is immense and breaking through is no easy task. A combination of consistency and innovation help to keep your business and your content recognizable, relevant, and compelling. It's very easy for content to become separated from the business it came from, which makes it important to ensure that your brand and business are so appealing that people want to keep it tied together.

Your goal is to have your customers sharing, "Check this out from [insert your business name]!" Anything less means you have work to do to motivate your customers' desire to keep your content and business tied together. Guerrilla marketers know they are marketing with every interaction they have, and that is especially important with online content.

GUERRILLA MARKETING CASE STUDY 12
Tommy Bahama

In the world of fast fashion and constantly changing trends, Tommy Bahama has set itself apart. Tommy Bahama, if you're not familiar, is a casual and tropical-island-resort-oriented lifestyle brand that ranges from restaurants to spirits and furniture, décor, apparel, and accessories.

In the 1980s, two couples imagined what life would be like if they never had to leave the beach. That's a common thought of everyone who enjoys a great beach vacation. They let their imaginations run free, and according to the company, their imagined life at the beach, "led to the invention of a character named Tommy Bahama. By asking 'What would Tommy wear?' and imagining the details of his life, they unwittingly created the springboard for a new brand and the Tommy Bahama Group, Inc."

In 1991, a collaboration was formed and they "launched a collection of menswear that transported people to an island state of mind and celebrated the best part of the week - the weekend." From the beginning and through today, Tommy Bahama embraces the "island lifestyle" in collections that include "men's and women's clothing and accessories, food, cocktails, home furnishings, beach gear and more."

To secure their growth, they again turned to collaboration and according to the company, "Since 2003, the Tommy Bahama Group has been wholly owned by Oxford Industries, Inc., an international apparel design, sourcing and marketing company. Oxford's acquisition of Tommy Bahama gave the brand more exposure and the secure financial backing to grow. They share our values and respect our desire to maintain our unique culture."

Their viewpoint is, "Long Live The Island Life. Through artistry, craftsmanship, and exceptional hospitality, our people and products embody the island life and all that it has to offer."

They also focus on sustainability and according to the company, "The only footprints we want to leave are in the sand. We're working every day to reduce our environmental impact, bringing you the best of the Island Life while caring for the world that sustains it."

"We are uncompromising in our commitment to reduce emissions, improve our energy efficiency, and minimize the amount of waste we produce."

The list of evident Guerrilla Marketing tactics at play with Tommy Bahama is long. Let's outline some of the most successful Guerrilla Marketing tactics at play:

- Guerrilla Creativity (see Volume 1, Section 1.2)
- Name (see Volume 1, Section 8.2)
- Identity (see Volume 1, Section 8.3)
- Brand (see Volume 1, Section 8.1)
- Consistency (see Section 1.9 and Volume 1, Sections 2.8 and 9.11)
- Uniqueness (see Volume 2, Section 8.39)
- Passion and Enthusiasm (see Volume 1, Section 9.1)
- Selection and Cross-Selling (see Volume 1, Section 8.23)
- By-Product (see Volume 1, Section 5.3)
- Product Displays/Experiences (see Volume 1, Section 3.1)
- The Power of Color (see Section 8.45)
- Appeal to the Senses (see Section 8.46)
- Selection and Cross-Selling (see Volume 1. Section, 8.23)
- Collaboration (see Volume 1, Section 7.6)
- Purpose-Minded (see Volume 2, Section 9.17)

Let's dive a bit deeper into some of these Guerrilla Marketing tactics as they relate to Tommy Bahama. For those tactics that you decide are well-suited for your prospects and customers, and therefore, you want to incorporate them into your Guerrilla Marketing Plan, be sure to take the time re-review the details of each tactic.

Guerrilla Creativity, Uniqueness, Name, Identity, Brand, Consistency, Passion, and Enthusiasm

Tommy Bahama embodies creativity and uniqueness. By taking a relatable, appealing, and desirable island lifestyle, the founders created a unique story. That story, and the resulting products, engage their prospects and customers who share their passion and enthusiasm to live the island lifestyle.

With consistent and repeated use of their name and identity, they turned successful products into a comprehensive lifestyle brand.

Selection and Cross-Selling, By-Product, Product Displays/Experiences, Guerrilla Creativity, The Power of Color, and Appeal to the Senses

When you enter their retail locations, you feel the immediate sensation of being at a tropical resort. How do they create that sensation? The answer is simple: They utilize a full sensory experience.

They use every surface (e.g., the ceiling, walls, floor, fixtures, etc.) to create a sensory experience that appeals to the visual (e.g., tropical colors) and touch senses (e.g., soft clothing) of their prospects and customers. They also appeal to their sense of smell by filling their locations with appealing tropical scents, which they sell in the form of candles, colognes, etc. At the same time, tropical music is playing to appeal to their prospects and customers sense of hearing, and in their restaurants, they also appeal to their sense of taste with tropical dishes on the menu.

Their by-product has created and opportunity for an expansive and robust selection and cross-selling options with products that range from restaurants to spirits and furniture, décor, apparel, and accessories.

Collaboration

From the beginning, Tommy Bahama has used the power of collaboration. From the formation of the business to its collaboration in 2003 to give "the brand more exposure and the secure financial backing to grow," they show how like-minded businesses can accomplish more together.

Purpose-Minded

With a charitable focus and a commitment to sustainability, they have created a business focused with specific purposes in mind. They also provide community support through hosting events with their retails stores and restaurants.

Conclusion

For a retail business to create a unique brand and grow it into a robust lifestyle brand, the power of consistency is required. From the beginning, Tommy Bahama has focused on an "island lifestyle" that makes them unique.

Now that you've seen four more great examples of Guerrilla Marketing success (also see Volume 1, Case Studies 1–4 and Volume 2, Case Studies 5–8), it's time to develop and execute your Guerrilla Marketing plan and Guerrilla Creative and Advertising Strategy and overachieve the success of these businesses. Guerrilla marketers understand that this is their dream, and they will never settle. What do you plan to do with your precious dream and the opportunities you have?

SECTION XI

125+ Free Tools

125+ FREE TOOLS TO PROPEL YOUR GUERRILLA MARKETING SUCCESS INTO PROFITS

Refer to gMarketing.com/Club for convenient links.

Business Operations Resources and Tools

From accounting to communications, customer relations, HR, project management, data analytics, and more, there are high-quality tools at your fingertips, which a Guerrilla marketer can use to put their business on the path to profitable growth. Note: Any offers or services shown are subject to change by that business.

Refer to gMarketing.com/Club for convenient links.

Agiloft	"Agiloft, Inc. is a trusted provider of agile software for contract and commerce lifecycle management. Our unique platform enables our pre-built and custom modules to be tailored to your exact needs without writing custom code, so deployment times and costs are a fraction of those required for other systems."
	Get started with the free Agiloft edition, which is designed to meet the needs of growing organizations. You'll be able to select the functions you need and their robust options (paid) are ready to grow with your business.
Avast	"We believe everyone has the right to be safe online, which is why we offer our award-winning free antivirus to millions of people around the world. Using real-time intelligence from over 400 million Avast users, we prevent more than 66 million threats every day."
	Get started for free with Avast and add (paid) features and services to meet the needs of your business.
BlogTalk Radio	"Effortless Broadcasting. Why make things harder than they need to be? That's the thinking behind our comprehensive studio, which makes managing multiple elements simultaneously child's play."
	BlogTalkRadio allows you to get started for free to create your radio broadcasts anywhere in the world. As your needs grow, they will help you scale with paid options with more callers, hours, storage, and live studio sessions.

BP Simulator	"Free business process simulation modeling software . . ."
	With BP Simulator, you can map out your business process to ensure that your goals and plans are aligned to give you the results you're expecting. It's a great way to develop new business processes or improve existing processes to create efficiency, improved customer experiences, and cost reductions.
ClickUp	"One app to replace them all. All your work in one place: Tasks, docs, chat, goals, & more." "Automatically import your stuff from other 'productivity' apps in minutes and instantly bring your team together."
	If you're tired of wasting time with multiple productivity apps, this is your opportunity to reclaim your time. ClickUp offers a "free forever" plan to get started. You can then upgrade (paid) to unlock more valuable features to increase your productivity.
Diagrams	"Diagram with anyone, anywhere. Diagrams is open source, online, desktop and container deployable diagramming software."
	With Diagrams, you can create professional diagrams for free that work with your existing tools, such as G Suite, Google Drive, Dropbox, Github, OneDrive, Office 365, and more.
DocuSign	"We pioneered the development of e-signature technology, and today DocuSign helps organizations connect and automate how they prepare, sign, act on, and manage agreements."
	Start with their free edition to sign documents, and then add (paid) features and services to meet your growing needs.
EdX	"Access 2500+ online courses from 140 institutions."
	Guerrilla marketers are curious and thrive with knowledge. With thousands of courses to choose from, EdX provides the opportunity to learn from institutions, such as Harvard University, Massachusetts Institute of Technology (MIT), Princeton University, and many more. The courses (free and paid) are offered individually or in a series for those that want to gain in-depth knowledge about a subject.
Evernote	"Evernote helps people focus on what matters most to them. It's where ideas become answers, where individuals organize their daily lives, and where teams come to create and share work together."
	Turn your "To-do" chaos into streamlined productivity. With the free Evernote Basic program, you can get started with organizing your notetaking, lists, reminders, and ideas with notebooks, tags, and searching and sharing capabilities. With robust features, you can upgrade (paid) to add more features to help you become streamlined and productive.

Evernote Scannable	"Scannable - Scanner app for documents. Scannable captures the paper in your life quickly and beautifully, transforming it into high-quality scans ready to save or share. Whether on the go or at the office, send paper on its way and move on." Evernote Scannable is a convenient way to scan documents, receipts, business cards, and more while you're on the go with your mobile device. With easy editing features, you'll be ready to share your document via email, text, or exported as a PDF or JPG.
Free-Conference-Call	"FreeConferenceCall.com, an award-winning conferencing solution, is everything you want it to be—from phone conferencing service with international teleconferences to free video conferencing and free screen sharing." It may sound too good to be true, but it's true. Started in 2001, FreeConferenceCall helps businesses around the globe. With robust features and offerings, these free tools will help your business function like a top-tier company.
Genius Scan	"Genius Scan is a scanner in your pocket. It helps users digitize millions of documents on the go every day. Discover how it will help you too!" With Genius Scan, your phone camera becomes your scanner. Simply use Genius Scan to automatically detect your document using your camera. Your scan is turned into a PDF file that you can edit, keep, or share (email, cloud storage services, social media, etc.) with just a few clicks. Enhanced features are available in the paid edition.
GitHub	"GitHub is a development platform inspired by the way you work. From open source to business, you can host and review code, manage projects, and build software alongside 50 million developers." Get started for free with public/private repositories, storage, collaborators, community support, and more. As your collaboration and the needs of your team grow, GitHub is ready to grow (paid) with you.
Gmail	Gmail, provided by Google, is a staple for SMBs. Gmail is free and you can easily and affordably upgrade to a G Suite account to access valuable features, such as a professional email address with your domain, chat, video and voice conferencing, storage, and many other tools to make your business productive.

Google Account	Your free Google account includes a number of productivity tools that can save you a lot of money. Here are a few: **Google Drive**: Google offers a set number of GBs for free, and that storage is used by Google Drive, Gmail, and Google Photos. You can upgrade to Google One to increase your capacity. Your Google Drive files are private, but you can choose to share them with an invitation. A shared file allows others to view, comment, and edit any file or folder you choose, making online collaboration easy. **Google Docs, Sheets, and Slides**: Google provides you with tools to create documents, spreadsheets, and presentations to move your business forward. **Google Forms**: put together a form in minutes to conduct a survey or offer an online form. The collected data is accumulated in a spreadsheet to give you the answers and the data that you need. **Google Drawings**: create easy diagrams and flow charts for your documents or to embed them on your website. **Google Apps**: choose from the numerous productivity, collaboration, and creativity apps in the Google Drive collection in the Chrome Web Store.
Klipfolio	"The first and only analytics tool you need." "We help people succeed with data. With the power of business intelligence, you can transform the way you use data to make confident, data-driven decisions." Bring your cloud applications together on a dynamic platform for the analysis you need to make business decisions. Get started for free with power metrics, which includes unlimited metrics, dashboards, and viewer users. As your business grows, upgrade (paid) to expand your data history, data services, and more.
Lucidspark	"Where teamwork and ideas ignite. The virtual whiteboard that connects teams so they can bring their best ideas to life." "As the future of work changes, Lucid will be right there with you, providing the visual collaboration platform to help your teams dream, plan, and build in real time." Collaboration is the path to enhancing your success. Get started with their free plan with editable boards, collaboration, and integrations. As your team and needs grow, you can upgrade (paid) and benefit from tools to help your business organize, facilitate, and manage collaboration.

Microsoft Power BI Desktop	"Bring your data to life with Power BI Desktop." "Dig deeper into data and find patterns you may have otherwise missed that lead to actionable insights." "Explore your data, automatically find patterns, understand what your data means, and predict future outcomes to drive business results."

Let Microsoft help do the heavy lifting when it comes to visualizing and analyzing your business data. With Power BI Desktop, free from Microsoft, you can pull your data (from hundreds of supported services) and easily prep and model your data to find patterns and insights to drive your business forward. Microsoft Power BI Pro (paid service) is available as you grow your business. |
| Miro | "Where . . . teams get work done. The online collaborative whiteboard platform to bring teams together, anytime, anywhere."

Get started for free with editable boards and unlimited team members. Miro is integrated with Slack, Microsoft One Drive and Teams, Google Drive, Dropbox, and more to give you the ease you need and the productivity and creativity you desire. |
| MURAL | "MURAL is space for your team to collaborate visually and problem-solve faster with an easy-to-use digital canvas. No ordinary online whiteboard, MURAL has powerful facilitation features, guided methods, and the deep expertise organizations need to transform teamwork."

Unleash the power of creativity and collaboration. Their free plan lets you get started with AI visual collaboration and facilitation features, a template library, and more. As your collaboration needs grow, you'll add (paid) valuable features, such as privacy controls, integrations, capacity, and more. |
| PandaDoc | "Take the work out of your document workflow. Finally, enable your fast-moving teams with a simple, sophisticated all-in-one solution to easily manage the creation, editing, and signing of documents."

PandaDoc helps businesses simplify processes, such as proposals, quotes, contracts, forms, and e-signatures. With their free plan, you can begin with e-signatures. You can then upgrade with valuable features, such as templates, tracking, CRM integration, workflow approvals, etc. |
| Podbean | "Podbean is an easy and powerful way to start a podcast. Everything you need for a successful podcast. No difficult technology to learn."

Get started for free, and Podbean will scale (paid) with your business to include more storage space, monetization, video, etc. |

Proposify	"Discover the proposal software that gives control and insight into the most important stage of your sales process. From design to sign-off, get the confidence and consistency to dominate your deals." Proposify helps businesses that rely on proposals thrive. With consistent, accurate, and powerful content, your proposals will stand out. With popular integrations, your prospects will find it easy to become your customers while your business has key insights along the way. While their free plan is ideal for solo deals, they offer (paid) solutions for all levels.
Slack	"Work more easily with everyone. Stay on the same page and make decisions faster by bringing all of your work communication into one place." Slack offers an innovative channels system that will help your business stay organized and focused with your conversations, files, and tools. Collaboration is made easy, even with voice and video calls, and workflows become automated for routine actions. Slack provides a scalable framework to grow with your business. You can get started for free with a limited plan and move into a paid plan as your business grows.
Trello	"Trello lets you work more collaboratively and get more done. Trello's boards, lists, and cards enable you to organize and prioritize your projects in a fun, flexible, and rewarding way." Forget boring spreadsheets and make productivity, organization, and teamwork a snap. With Trello you get an easy interface and automation tools; you'll get more done with ease. You can get started with a free plan, and Trello is then ready to help your business soar with the additional tools offered with their paid plans.
Ultradox	"Automate Your Business . . . With Ultradox you can automate tedious tasks and create your own enterprise apps without hiring a team of developers. The unique combination of workflow and template engine allows you to merge, send and print documents, generate websites or send out responsive emails as part of your process." Stop allowing your business to be slowed down by repetitive tasks. You can get started with a free Ultradox plan and add (paid) automation features as your needs grow. If you use G Suite, you'll enjoy additional benefits.
Watson Speech to Text (IBM)	"Watson Speech to Text. Convert speech into text using AI-powered speech recognition and transcription" Get started for free with the Lite plan of Watson Speech to Text from IBM, which provides an allotment of minutes each month. Upgrade (paid) for more minutes and enhancements.

Wave Apps	"Wave is an award-winning financial management software company that is changing how entrepreneurs make money, move money and track money. Wave provides solutions that empower small business owners to simplify their finances while giving them more confidence to run their businesses." Wave offers free accounting software to help you with income and expense tracking, invoicing, sales tax tracking, financial statements, reporting, integrations, a performance dashboard, and more. Get started with their free program, and as your needs grow, they will grow with your business (with a paid service).
Webex	"One app for everything. And everyone. Calling, meetings, and messaging in the cloud for teams of all sizes." Their free plan allows you to get started with calls, scheduling, screen sharing, recordings, chat, polling, and more. You can then upgrade (paid) to unlock more meeting capacity and advanced features, such as transcriptions, alternate host, in-meeting file transfers, and much more.
Wrike	"Project management is easy and efficient with Wrike. All-in-one collaboration software for leading productive, happy teams." Get started for free with features that every business needs, including task management, file sharing, storage space, activity streams, desktop and mobile apps, and more. As your business grows, Wrike can grow with your business and offer additional (paid) features to keep your productivity soaring.
Yahoo Mail	"Show the world you mean business." Yahoo offers free email with improved organization and helpful tools to allow you to be more productive and efficient. With their subscriptions tab, you can easily unsubscribe from unwanted lists. For a low monthly fee, a Guerrilla marketer will get a business email address that matches their domain to enhance their professional image and build trust with their prospects and customers.
ZipBooks	"Simple accounting software that makes you even smarter. Simple, beautiful, and powerful, ZipBooks gives you the tools and intelligence to take your business to the next level." With ZipBooks, you can send custom quotes, estimates, and invoices and get paid with major credit cards or PayPal. With auto-billing and automated payment reminders, you can take the heavy lifting out of your recurring invoicing while providing a polished experience for your customers. ZipBooks offers a variety of additional features to make your bookkeeping easier with their free service. As your business grows, upgrade to a paid version and benefit from even more productivity features.

Zoho Desk	"Put customer service at the heart of your company. Zoho Desk is the industry's first context-aware help desk software that helps businesses focus on the customer."
	Get your important customer service activities organized and working for your customers with email ticketing, customer management, a knowledge base to ensure consistency, a help center, a mobile app, and more with the free version of Zoho Desk. As your business and customer needs grow, Zoho Desk offers a robust set of (paid) features, from integrations to AI, to help you grow and excel at customer service.
Zoho Docs	"Online file management for teams and individuals. Bring your team to a secure and collaborative workspace where everything is available to everyone in real time. Create, collaborate, and get work done, securely."
	Have the documents you need at your fingertips wherever you go. Start with a free Zoho Docs account for a small team and expand into a paid service as your data needs and team size grow.
Zoho Recruit	"An ATS (or applicant tracking system) is a software that manages your entire hiring and recruitment process. It helps you to speed up candidate management and significantly reduce time-to-fill. From posting the job online to making the job offer an ATS keeps track of all the activity that takes place in the recruiting department."
	Zoho Recruit lets you get started for free with a basic program to test out the process with your job opening. They then grow with you (with paid services) as you need to add more positions.
Zoom	"One consistent enterprise experience for all use cases. Engineered & optimized to work reliably." "Easy-to-use, buy & scale. Most affordable, straightforward pricing."
	Whether you need online meetings, video webinars, virtual conference rooms, phone systems, or cross-platform messaging and file sharing, Zoom makes it easy. Get started for free, and upgrade (paid) to meet the needs of your growing business.

Marketing Resources and Tools

From PR to surveys, search, content, social media, email marketing, and more, there are high-quality tools at your fingertips. A Guerrilla marketer can put these to use to ensure their marketing is on the path to profitable growth for their business. Note: Any offers or services shown are subject to change by that business.

Refer to gMarketing.com/Club for convenient links.

Agile CRM	"All-in-One CRM. Automate your sales, marketing, and service in one platform. Avoid data leaks and enable consistent messaging."
	Get started with their free plan and a limited number of contacts to try features, such as lead scoring, appointment scheduling, deal milestones, email campaigns, forms, landing page builders, and more. You can then upgrade (paid) as your contacts increase and benefit from more features, such as marketing automation, social monitoring, mobile marketing, and more.
Agorapulse Facebook Barometer	"The Barometer will determine how many fans this page has and will compare it to thousands of other pages with a similar fan range. You will see how your last 50 Facebook posts compare in terms of: Facebook Reach…Facebook Engagement…Facebook Click-through rate."
	This free tool is to help you gauge your performance and to understand which pages you need to work on to improve your score.
Agorapulse AdsReport	"Getting important statistics and data regarding your Facebook campaigns and accounts can be exhausting and a drain on your workday. The format on Facebook itself is confusing and not as streamlined and efficient as it can be. Enter AdsReport, Agorapulse's free tool for helping social media managers and agencies easily and efficiently get the analytics they need regarding their Facebook Ad accounts and ad campaigns."
	This free tool helps you analyze your spend, conversions, reach, impressions, clicks, CTR, CPC, and CPM. Guerrilla marketers know their careful analysis helps them do more of what's working and less of what's not, which helps pave their path to profits.
Agorapulse Twitter Report Card	"Do you perform better than your competitors on Twitter? Compare Twitter accounts with each other and gain new insights into your Twitter performance."
	This free tool provides a report card to help you understand how you compare to the accounts you choose. You'll be able to examine your audience quality, brand engagement, and content performance.

Airtable	"Orchestrate powerful business solutions with a single source of truth. The only limit is your imagination." "Get started in a snap. From day one, your team will love the familiarity of a spreadsheet, and the power of a database." Airtable is a strong planning and performance tool to help your marketing succeed. See and track all your marketing efforts and collaborate, all in one place. With numerous available integrations, you can get more out of the tools you're already using. Get started with their free plan and grow your capabilities with their advanced (paid) options.
AnswerThe-Public	"Discover an untapped goldmine of content ideas. AnswerThePublic listens into autocomplete data from search engines like Google then quickly cranks out every useful phrase and question people are asking around your keyword. It's a goldmine of consumer insight you can use to create fresh, ultra-useful content, products, and services. The kind your customers really want." AnswerThePublic will tell you every question people are asking on a given topic, which is invaluable for building your business. For example, if you simply type in "dog grooming," they will generate hundreds of questions that people are asking related to dog grooming across numerous search engines.
Apptivo	"Connect to your favorite services. Everything you need in one cloud solution: CRM, Project Management, Invoicing & more." Apptivo is customizable and flexible to provide the apps that are necessary for your business. Small businesses can get started for free with their Starter package, which includes sales automation and business management, data management, and analytics tools. Their (paid) services grow with you as you move from a small business to an enterprise business.
BenchmarkOne	"All-in-one CRM software that saves you time. Spending too much time on sales and marketing, instead of your business? We can change that." Start for free with their basic program for sending newsletters and growing your audience, including marketing automation. Upgrade (paid) to unlock advanced productivity pages, such as dashboards and live activity feeds.
BuzzStream	"Use our free tools to find link opportunities, conduct link research or automate link building tasks." From email research tools to link-building query generators and extraction tools, you'll find numerous free tools on BuzzStream to increase your productivity.

Canva	"Canva, your secret weapon for stunning design. Design anything in minutes with thousands of beautiful templates and images." Canva offers a basic program to get started for free. Canva Basic includes free templates, photos, elements, fonts, design types, and storage. When your business is ready to take it to the next level, you can move to a paid plan that provides even more of what's included in the basic program, along with more storage, a brand-building kit, priority support, and more.
Canvy	"In its core, Canvy is built for painters and poster designers – if you are creating art for walls, chances are good that you will love using Canvy in your everyday life." From images to showcase your artwork to building a website, Canvy offers numerous tools. Get started for free with a limited number of rooms and daily downloads. Canvy offers paid plans to unlock even more rooms and resources.
Coupon Sites	Along with social media, these coupon sites—that feature online coupon codes and printable coupons—give your business added exposure and are worth getting to know: • Groupon • RetailMeNot • Coupons • Shop Savvy • Smart Source • Sunday Saver • Coupon Cactus • Extrabux • Rakuten—formerly Ebates Some of these sites require an account and a fee to post your coupons, and others do not, so be sure to do your homework to find the right fit for your business and its customers and prospects.
Crowdfire	"Social media management, simplified. Crowdfire helps you discover and schedule content and manage all your social accounts from one place." "Crowdfire is a powerful social media tool used by businesses and individuals all over the world to drive social media engagement and growth." Get started for free with select supported social networks. You'll be able to schedule posts and benefit from content curation tools and analytics tools. As your needs grow, so do their (paid) capabilities to help your business succeed.

DearDiary	Give your creativity a boost with the help of AI. Type anything (e.g., feelings, thoughts, goals, stories, etc.) and transform it into music as you type. The music that you've created can then be shared with a link.
Deep Dream Generator	"Deep Dream Generator is a set of tools which make it possible to explore different AI algorithms. We focus on creative tools for visual content generation like those for merging image styles and content or such as Deep Dream which explores the insight of a deep neural network." Deep Dream Generator is a great opportunity to explore the combination of creativity and AI. Get started for free and upgrade (paid) to unlock more power and higher resolution capabilities.
Email Copy Checker	"This is a free email spam checking tool, which looks at your email copy or your entire email sequence to ensure you aren't triggering any spam words or spam keywords." Email Copy Checker is a great free tool to check your email copy and receive guidance that helps you improve your deliverability rate.
EngageBay	"Market better. Sell faster. Support smarter. One platform for all your Marketing, Sales, and Support teams" Begin with their free plan to begin using valuable features, such as email marketing, autoresponders, email broadcast, sequences, lead grabbers, landing pages, CRM, live chat, and more.
Fanpage Karma	"With Fanpage Karma you have everything you need for professional social media management: analyzing, publishing, communicating, researching and presenting. Everything in one tool." Fanpage Karma is a social media analytics and monitoring tool. They support Facebook, Instagram, Twitter, LinkedIn, YouTube, and more. The performance knowledge you'll gain will help you determine the most valuable posts/content. You can get started with a free account that lets you analyze Facebook and upgrade (paid) from there.
Feedly	"Goodbye information overload. Keep up with the topics and trends you care about, without the overwhelm." "Organize all your trusted sources in one place." Feedly gives you the control to organize and prioritize what matters to you. Feedly offers a free plan on the web and mobile to help you follow a select number of sources and organize them into feeds. You can then upgrade (paid) to include more sources, notes, highlights, organized and curated team sharing, and so much more.

Flowcode	"Create a free, customer QR code in 60 seconds."
	Begin with three free Flowcodes, which last forever, allow for unlimited scans, and offer free analytics. You can then choose a (paid) plan that fits the needs of your growing business.
Follower-wonk	"Followerwonk is a social analytics mega-tool that digs through Twitter data. Use it to track your follower gains and losses, compare Twitter accounts, do global searches in Twitter bios, and analyze any account's followers!"
	Get started for free with this analytics and discovery tool for Twitter and optimize one profile. You can then increase (paid) the number of profiles as needed.
Fotor	"Free online photo editor for everyone. Free to edit photos with Fotor's photo editor in just a few clicks. It covers all online photo editing tools, so you can crop images, resize images, add text to photos, even make photo collages, and create graphic designs easily."
	Get started with Fotor Basic for free and complete your basic photo editing needs with touch ups, effects, and collage layouts with ease. You can then upgrade (paid) to add advanced editing features, stock photos. templates, and more.

Free Business Profiles	Being listed in as many directories as possible helps your business build credibility. When your prospects reach the point of researching your business, you can build trust by being everywhere they look, or you can create doubt with your absence. Guerrillas tend to the small details, which build valuable trust. Be sure to build out your profiles with: • Google My Business • Bing Places for Business • Foursquare • Yahoo! • Apple Maps • MapQuest • Yelp • Angie's List (Angi) • Home Advisor • Nextdoor • Manta • Trip Advisor • Better Business Bureau • LinkedIn • Facebook • HubSpot • Superpages and Yellow Pages • Yellowbook • Thumbtack • MerchantCircle
Free Classified Ads/ Listings	These online services provide an opportunity to increase the reach of those businesses that are selling products or services: • Classified Ads • Craigslist • Oodle • Global-free-classified-ads • Letgo • Facebook Shops

GetResponse	"Powerful, simplified tool to send emails, create pages, and automate your marketing." Get started with their "free-forever" plan that includes email marketing, a website builder, limited contacts, landing pages, and forms. As your needs grow, you can upgrade (paid) to add valuable features, such as sales funnels, autoresponders, ecommerce features, and more.
Guerrilla Marketing	Your source for ever-expanding Guerrilla Marketing tactics, tools, and tips. Be connected to all the latest information to help you continually grow your profits and success. Join us at gMarketing.com/Club.
Google Alerts	"Monitor the web for interesting new content." A great tool to keep you in the know is at your fingertips, and it's free. You can get email alerts for any topic you choose using Google Alerts. Google searches news, blogs, the web, videos, books, discussions, and finance information to bring you the alerts you need about a particular topic (e.g., your business, products and services, your competitors, your industry, etc.).
Google Analytics	Google Analytics requires a simple snippet of code that you will add to your website. That snippet of code tracks all the visitors to your website and, thereby, provides you with a wealth of valuable information. The information is provided in Google Analytics to help you understand how to turn more prospects into customers and how to compel customers to make repeat purchases.
Google Analytics - Social Interactions	"You can use social interaction analytics to measure the number of times users click on social buttons embedded in webpages. For example, you might measure a Facebook 'Like' or a Twitter 'Tweet.'" Extend the benefit of Google Analytics by utilizing this free tool to measure and analyze your important social shares/interactions.
Google Analytics - App/Screen Measurement	"Screens in Google Analytics represent content users are viewing within an app." "Measuring screen views allows you to see which content is being viewed most by your users, and how are they are navigating between different pieces of content." If your business is using an app, this valuable and free tool will help you analyze how your prospects and customers are moving through and interacting with your app.

Google for Small Business	"Get help for your business with simple steps and free resources. Help people find you online, know that you're open, and stay connected to customers with simple steps and free resources." Google for Small Business offers tools, such as the Digital Toolkit. With the Digital Toolkit, you can create surveys, explore new markets for your business, test your websites speeds, receive insights and recommendations for improvement, and even create a personalized marketing kit with content from your business profile on Google.
Google My Business	"Engage with customers on Google for free. With a Google My Business account, you get more than a business listing. Your free Business Profile lets you easily connect with customers across Google Search and Maps." Actively managing and leveraging all the benefits of your Google Business Profile is "must-do" marketing every Guerrilla business utilizes to its full benefit. You can set your business hours and phone number and add photos of your products, as well as include Q&As. If your business takes appointments or reservations, you can take your convenience to the next level by linking those services.
Google Optimize	"Whether it's a custom-tailored message at checkout or a completely revamped homepage, Optimize shows you which site experiences engage and delight your customers, and gives you the solutions you need to deliver them." Google Optimize uses your existing Google Analytics data to help you target areas of your site to improve. Model your experiments with statistical methods to get more accurate results that lead to the right experience for your customers and prospects.
Google Postmaster Tools	"If you send a large volume of emails to Gmail users, you can use Postmaster Tools to see: • If users are marking your emails as spam • How to prevent your emails from being blocked by Gmail • Why your emails might not be delivered • If your emails are being sent securely" Google Postmaster Tools are a great way to improve your email deliverability rate to Gmail users.

Google Search Console	"Search Console tools and reports help you measure your site's Search traffic and performance, fix issues, and make your site shine in Google Search results." Guerrilla marketers embrace tools, such as the Google Search Console, which make it easy to optimize content with search analytics, understand how Google sees pages, and receive alerts when there are issues. Then, it lets Google know when the business has fixed them.
Google Trends	"Google Trends provides access to a largely unfiltered sample of actual search requests made to Google. It's anonymized (no one is personally identified), categorized (determining the topic for a search query) and aggregated (grouped together)." Google Trends allows you to see what the world is searching for by term or topic. With that information, you can be aware of searches related to your business, and you can write about trending topics.
Grammarly	"Great Writing, Simplified. Compose bold, clear, mistake-free writing with Grammarly's AI-powered writing assistant." Grammarly is a free Chrome extension to help you write more clearly and effectively across many of your favorite sites. Get started for free and become familiar with their (paid) business program that can help your team communicate consistently and more quickly to increase satisfaction with your prospects and customers.
H5P	"Create richer html5 content in existing publishing platforms. Share content seamlessly across any H5P capable site. Reuse and modify content in your browser at any time." With a variety of available integrations, H5P is "free and open technology, licensed with the MIT license." Create rich, interactive, and mobile-friendly content to make your website more engaging.
HARO	"HARO connects journalists seeking expertise to include in their content with sources who have that expertise." Similar to ProfNet, Help A Reporter Out (HARO) is a great free resource to boost your content (for journalists and bloggers) and/or boost your public and media relations efforts (for experts and sources). You'll have daily opportunities to respond to requests for experts or to post requests for experts to provide content. HARO offers a free membership that allows you to receive or post requests for media content.

Hootsuite	"Discover what's possible when you unite your social campaigns on one platform. Schedule and publish content to the right channels at the right time, track effectiveness in real time, and crank the volume on your top-performing content." Guerrilla marketers know that consistency is one of the most powerful marketing tools to put to work for their businesses. Hootsuite makes it easy to create consistent marketing messages across multiple social platforms and keep a consistent presence with scheduled posts. Hootsuite offers a limited free plan that lets you get started with a few social profiles and scheduled messages. When you find that Hootsuite is delivering benefits for your business, you can then upgrade to a paid plan to unleash the power of what Hootsuite can do for your business and social presence.
Hotjar	"We help you better understand user behavior so you can make the right changes, improve UX, and grow conversions." With the free personal Basic account, you can begin to understand how your prospects and customers interact with your site. You can create Heatmaps and on-demand, manual reports, get users' feedback, and more.
Hubspot	"Think CRM software is just about contact management? Think again. HubSpot CRM has free tools for everyone on your team, and it's 100% free." "You have a lot on your plate. Make things easier on yourself by tracking your contacts and customers and sending bulk email — all using the same tool. It's easy to use, and completely free." Hubspot offers the tools you need to manage and organize your contacts in one CRM database. You'll benefit from free features, such as lead management and tracking, document tracking, pipeline management, and ticketing. As your business needs advance, they have a robust line-up of (paid) features and tools to help your business grow.
HubSpot Marketing Hub	"With Marketing Hub, all your marketing tools and data are on one easy-to-use, powerful platform. You'll save valuable time and get all the context you need to provide a personalized experience that attracts and converts the right customers at scale." You can begin with free tools, such as forms, email marketing, ad management, live chat, and a reporting dashboard. As your needs grow, they have a wide array of robust tools you can upgrade (paid) to receive and help your business elevate its capacity.

| JotForm | "Easy-to-use online form builder for every business. Create online forms and publish them. Get an email for each response. Collect data."

JotForm is a great resource for simple or advanced forms. With a broad array of templates to choose from—or customized forms with a drag-and-drop interface—they make getting started easy. Their free plan is full of features to start creating online surveys, applications, contact and request forms, and much more. |
|---|---|
| Klaviyo | "Build strong relationships based on customer data. We know personalization can get overwhelming. Don't worry – we've made the most powerful segmentation engine in the industry so intuitive, anyone can use it. See it for yourself."

With tools focused on personalization, segmentation, split testing, automation, analytics, and more, you can build long-lasting relationships with your customers. Begin with their free tier plan to explore their tools with a limited number of email and SMS contacts. |
| Latest | "We automatically collect the links posted by a bunch of the most interesting people on Twitter. You know the people that always tweet the best links - first. We take all the links they tweet and compile a real-time updated list of the 10 most popular links right now. Plus, all links are automatically posted to our Twitter feed too. Pretty useful, right?"

If staying up to date is important for your business, Latest is a great free tool to keep you informed of the latest links from Twitter. |
| Leadfeeder | "Generate more leads by seeing which companies visit your site. Leadfeeder shows you the companies visiting your website, how they found you and what they're interested in."

Take the mystery out of your website traffic and turn that information into valuable leads for your follow-up. Leadfeeder offers a free, "lite" package. Although it offers limited functionality, you can begin by seeing the last three days' worth of leads (with a maximum number of leads provided). As your needs and success grow, they offer a wide array of (paid) features and robust solutions. |

Linktree	"The Only Link You'll Ever Need. Connect audiences to all of your content with just one link" "Take your Linktree wherever your audience is, to help them to discover all your important content."	
	Linktree makes it easy to connect all your content with your audiences. Their free plan offers unlimited links, built-in themes, and the ability to embed video content, collect payments, and track your views and clicks. You can upgrade (paid) to unlock more valuable customizations, integrations, the ability to seamlessly collect contact information, and much more.	
MailChimp	"With Mailchimp, you can promote your business across email, social, landing pages, shoppable landing pages, postcards, and more—all from a single platform."	
	Get started for free with MailChimp with templates, CRM, surveys, and more. As your business grows, you can upgrade (paid) your features to include split testing, retargeting, segmentation, multivariate testing, and much more.	
Mail-Tester	"We needed a cheap, simple and efficient way to quickly test the quality of our own newsletters. We simply built on our own tool. Now we're sharing it for free via our web-interface and enable you to include our tests in your own app and whitelist our service by creating an account. We're geeky email software engineers."	
	With Mail-Tester, you'll send a test email to the email address they generate for you, and you'll then receive a score for your email. You can continue to refine your email to score a perfect ten prior to sending your email to your audience.	
ManyChat	"Turn Conversations Into Conversions. Automate two-way, interactive conversations in Instagram Direct Messages, Facebook Messenger, and SMS to grow your brand."	
	If your business can benefit from connecting with your customers and prospects via chat, take the time to become familiar with ManyChat. You can begin with a free account that accesses Facebook Messenger to help you automate conversations, segment your audience, and more.	
MeetUp	"Discover events for all the things you love." "Starting a Meetup group connects you with passionate people looking to share experiences in real life. It's simple to start a group and schedule events, and we'll help promote your group to interested people who are ready to join you."	
	MeetUp is an essential way for Guerrilla marketers to join and host like-minded individuals who want to collaborate to solve problems and/or grow their businesses. It's also a great way to host your prospects and customers.	

Mentionmapp	"Social Network Analysis & Insights. See what you're missing. Identify critical online relationships and conversations with our network visualization tool." "Mentionmapp collects the last 200 Tweets for any profile or hashtag searched for."
	Mentionmapp will help you, for free, search and find more people and conversations on Twitter.
MockUpPhotos	". . . a[n] online mockup platform for high quality mockup photos, made by independent creatives from all around the world."
	A great resource for images that allow you to place your product in desirable scenarios that compel and motivate your prospects and customers.
MoEngage	"Create deeper, meaningful connections. With MoEngage, you get an insights-led customer engagement platform with robust analytics, AI-powered automation, and optimization capabilities that will enable you to create personalized engagements at scale."
	MoEngage has a pay-as-you-grow structure. Get started with features, such as behavioral segmentation, push notifications, in-app messaging, email and SMS campaigns, web push, campaign analytics, and more.
Moz	"At Moz, we believe there is a better way to do marketing. A more valuable way where customers are earned rather than bought. We're obsessively passionate about it, and our mission is to help people achieve it. We focus on search engine optimization." "Try the best free SEO tools for link building and analysis, keyword research, webpage performance, local listing audits, and more!"
	Select from numerous free tools, including keyword explorer, link explorer, MozBar (to analyze search, social and page metrics), domain analysis, MozCast, and more.
Namecheckr	". . . an online service designed to permit Users to check the availability of domain names and social usernames across multiple networks."
	Namecheckr allows you to check domain and social username availability across multiple networks. With this free tool, you can be sure that you own your identity across countless platforms.

Pixabay	"Stunning free images & royalty free stock. Over 1.8 million+ high quality stock images and videos shared by our talented community." Pixabay is a fantastic resource for otherwise difficult to find, free images, and royalty-free stock. Members of the community freely share their great works in this easy-to-search platform. Pixabay provides an attribution option if you wish to give photo credits. Additionally, you can follow and donate to your favorite contributors in the community. You can learn about the Pixabay license on their website.
Peltarion	"The Peltarion cloud platform makes it easier to get started with, build, and deploy AI for whatever you do." "Our mission is to make AI accessible to as many people as possible by building and integrating features into our platform that help take away some of the expertise required to build, train and evaluate deep learning models." You can get started for free with a hobby project and/or to validate the platform. You can then upgrade (paid) to unlock more features.
Popurls	"Popurls encapsulates headlines from the most popular websites on a single page and is also known as the mother of all news aggregators." Popurls is a trending topic website that's easy to use and provides great insight and information. They aggregate all kinds of pop viral news from the most popular websites. With their data, you can write about current events.
Portent's Content Idea Generator	"Portent's Content Idea Generator lets you create catchy titles for your next blog post, podcast, or video. Simply type in your subject and the Idea Generator will spin up a creative title and advice to take it to the next level." This is a fantastic tool to expand your creativity as you develop compelling titles for your well-crafted content.
ProfNet	"There is a real opportunity for your organization to tap into the news coming out of your industry. When your experts become quotable sources for journalists, not only do they earn your organization a lot of free and often high-profile PR, but they also help you develop relationships with the members of the media you need in your corner." Similar to HARO, ProfNet offers a free membership that allows you to receive regular updates with media opportunities that you can preview and respond to, or you have the ability to request that experts respond and provide their content to your publication or blog.

Referrizer	"Local Business Marketing At Its Finest. With Referrizer, you get an automated marketing system that helps you get new customers, increase repeating purchases and generate long term sustainable results. It's all-in-one communication platform that increases referrals, boosts retention and improves your Google reputation." Begin with their free plan and start benefiting from their tools for lead capture, email marketing, local business partnering and exchange referrals, and more. As your needs and contacts grow, so do their tools and capabilities (paid).
Runway	"Runway is inventing the next generation of creativity tools. We are taking recent advancements in computer graphics and deep learning to push the boundaries of content and in turn, lower the barriers of content creation; unfastening a new wave of storytelling. Runway is reimagining how we create; so we can create impossible things." When you're ready to push the limits of your creativity, Runway offers a starter package to let you reimagine your video content and marketing. You can also experiment with machine learning (paid option) and expand your options with upgraded paid plans as your needs grow.
Segment	"The leading Customer Data Platform. Join 20,000+ businesses that use Segment's software and APIs to collect, clean, and control their customer data." Guerrilla marketers embrace opportunities to better understand their prospects and customers. With Segment, you can get started collecting your data and turning it into powerful experiences for your prospects and customers. You can begin with their free plan and as your business grows, their (paid) plans are designed to scale with your success.
Shareaholic	"Shareaholic provides you with a comprehensive set of marketing tools to engage with your audience, get found across search and social, and grow your following. All for Free. Code-free Customization." Shareaholic offers valuable tools that can be used with multiple platforms to make your content easily shared, compelling, consumable, and revenue-generating with ads and affiliate links.

SharedCount	"Created in 2010, SharedCount was the first API tool capable of giving you holistic engagement data on your website content. From simple use with WordPress, to larger API integrations, SharedCount makes it easy to see what content is connecting, what content is not, and where you should focus your efforts to maximize ROI." SharedCount offers a free account with 500 free API calls per day, to learn about the shares of your website content. For more API calls per day, you can choose from the best (paid) plan to fit your needs.
Social Media Sites and Networks	Take the time to manage your presence on the social media sites/networks that are compatible with your prospects and customers. Social media is your opportunity to connect with your prospects and customers in an environment that they find favorable. Facebook, Instagram, Pinterest, Snapchat, LinkedIn, Twitter, YouTube, and Clubhouse are great places to start, and you can add on with TikTok, Flickr, Tumblr, Medium, MeetUp, and Nextdoor. Be sure to use services such as Namecheckr to make sure your business is well represented within the vast pool of available social media sites and networks.
Sumo	"We've noticed lots of people struggle to collect emails because the tools just aren't available or are too expensive. So, we thought, why not make our tools available for you? Our goal, plain and simple, is to help you grow your website." Sumo can help your business grow your list and communicate with your customers as well as provide analytics. Get started with their free account to grow your business and then upgrade (paid) to benefit from their enhanced features to help grow your relationship with your customers.
SurveyGizmo	"SurveyGizmo provides the best and most affordable tools to connect you with your customers and employees. We also help you identify the actions to take to support them. Now more than ever, staying close to people is critical to the well-being of your company." SurveyGizmo offers a free account to get started with your small and basic survey needs. Perfect for a small or new business with a small number of customers and employees to get started with the benefits of surveying. As your business expands, SurveyGizmo has robust features (paid) to grow with your business.

SurveyLegend	"Create engaging surveys on your tablet or computer with ease. No matter who you are, we make creating a survey as easy as breathing." With SurveyLegend, you choose from designed themes and then customize them to reflect the look and feel of the marketing for your business. You can then share your survey via email, SMS, Facebook, Twitter, blogs, and more. Best of all, you can get started for free, and you can receive unlimited responses. Try a few surveys before you decide if it's the right fit for your business.
SurveyMonkey	"A global leader in survey software. 20 million questions answered daily." SurveyMonkey offers a free basic program with a limited number of responses per survey. It's a great way, if you're getting started, to learn more about what your employees, prospects, or customers are thinking while utilizing the easy templates. As your business succeeds, you can upgrade (paid) for far greater capabilities.
Tableau Public	"Tableau Public is a free service that lets anyone publish interactive data visualizations to the web. Visualizations that have been published to Tableau Public ("vizzes") can be embedded into web pages and blogs, they can be shared via social media or email, and they can be made available for download to other users." For businesses that have broadly appealing data, which they want to present creatively and make public, Tableau Public allows you to create interactive graphs, maps, and dashboards—called a Viz—and share them anywhere on the web. Additionally, if your business needs data, you can search for a Viz created by others to convey the data in an appealing way. Additional paid services are available for businesses needing a robust analytics platform.
Tiny URL	Tiny URL takes your long URLs and shortens them for redirection on your website and for easy linking in emails. This free service helps your business look polished and effortless.
Unsplash	"The internet's source of freely-usable images." "Unsplash is a platform powered by an amazing community that has gifted hundreds of thousands of their own photos to fuel creativity around the world. So, sign up for free, or don't. Either way, you've got access to over a million photos under the Unsplash license—which makes them free to do-whatever-you-want with." Unsplash is a great resource for photos, which you can download for free and use for commercial or non-commercial purposes without needing permission. Image contributors, of course, appreciate your attributions. You can learn about the Unsplash license on their website.

Vimeo	"The world's leading all-in-one video solution." "We enable professional-quality video for all." "Simple tools for you and your team to create, manage and share high-quality videos." You can get started with Vimeo Basic for free. As your needs grow, and you want to store more videos, customize, live stream, and benefit from analytics, you can upgrade (paid) to a plan suited to your success.
Watson Assistant (IBM)	"AI that's more than your average chatbot. Watson is built on deep learning, machine learning, and Natural Language Processing (NLP) models to elevate customer experiences and help customers change an appointment, track a shipment, or check a balance. Watson also uses machine learning algorithms and asks follow-up questions to better understand customers and pass them off to a human agent when needed." Get started with Watson Assistant, from IBM, for free with their Lite plan. Their Lite plan offers a limited number of active users, messages per month, and skills, along with usage analytics. You can then upgrade (paid) to unlock greater capabilities and capacity.
Website Grader	"Grade your website in seconds. Then learn how to improve it for free." This free tool is provided by HubSpot. When you enter your website and email address, you will receive information regarding their relevant content, products, and services, designed to improve your website.
Wistia	"The video host with the most." "One easy-to-use platform that turns your videos and podcasts into marketing machines." Wistia offers a customizable player, lead generation tools, embeddable channels, integrations, analytics, and more to help your videos and podcasts work for your business. You can get started with the free package that offers their standard features and the ability to embed a select number of videos or podcasts and a channel to share. You can then easily upgrade (paid) to enjoy more valuable features.
WordPress	"Beautiful designs, powerful features, and the freedom to build anything you want. WordPress is both free and priceless at the same time." WordPress is indeed priceless, especially for SMBs. It's the open-source software platform that has allowed everyone from bloggers to retailers to thrive online. With countless available plug-ins (free and paid) and a community of developers, content creators, and website owners, you can build a website that fits your needs and your budget now . . . and also grows with you into the future.

Wordtracker	"Our own proprietary data and toolset means you can get 10,000 keywords per search as well as related keywords, so your pages can be optimized more effectively to outrank the competition." Wordtracker allows you to get started with a few free keyword searches before you move into a paid plan.
Wufoo	"Easy-to-Use Online Form Builder For Every Organization. Cloud-based form builder that makes it easy to create registration forms, application forms, surveys, contact forms, payment forms and more." With an easy-to-use, drag-and-drop form builder, you'll be creating beautiful online forms with ease. Get started with a few forms with their free plan and move up (paid) to enjoy more features and conveniences.
Zendo	"An A.I. agent for visual tasks. Teach Zendo to identify & locate objects in images" Zendo, from DeepAI, allows you to experience AI and upload images and teach it to identify and locate objects in the image, which can transform your approach to visual tasks. Their community plan allows you to create unlimited tasks with unlimited collaborators. You can then upgrade (paid) to build things at scale.
Zoho Social	"The easiest way to manage your brands on social media. Schedule unlimited posts, monitor what matters, and create custom-reports to analyze your social media performance with Zoho Social." Zoho Social offers a free edition, with limited features, to help you get started. They also offer numerous (paid) options for growing businesses that can benefit from more robust features.

SMB Resources and Organizations

These resources and organizations are designed for your success. Whether you get to know them as a subscriber or as a member, be sure to know these free resources that drive Guerrilla business success. Note: Any offers or services shown are subject to change by that business.

Refer to gMarketing.com/Club for convenient links.

Better Business Bureau (BBB)	"BBB's Vision: An ethical marketplace where buyers and sellers trust each other." The Better Business Bureau (BBB) offers the National Programs Insights, which outlines best practices to help businesses succeed with information on a variety of helpful topics. For example, they provide Data Protection information covering a wide range of topics. They also offer the Better Business Bureau (BBB) Cybersecurity, which is a resource to help educate SMBs and provide tools and tips to manage their cyber risks, thereby learning best practices.
Federal Trade Commission (FTC)	"Protecting consumers and competition by preventing anticompetitive, deceptive, and unfair business practices through law enforcement, advocacy, and education without unduly burdening legitimate business activity." The FTC business center is an important resource for your business to learn about topics from advertising and marketing to protecting your business and finding legal resources. For example, the FTC offers tips and tools for cybersecurity for small businesses. The Small Biz Cyber Planner will help you create a customized cybersecurity plan. To learn more, visit their website.
Guerrilla Marketing	"We exist for your success. Guerrilla Marketing has been producing results since its introduction in 1984. There is no other source for Guerrilla Marketing success." Visit gMarketing.com/Club for more information. Guerrilla Marketing exists to give you the tactics, tools, and tips you need to succeed beyond your wildest expectations. The simple question is: Will you react and claim your success, or will you fold? We think you're ready to react and claim your success. You've nearly reached the end of the book, so we know you're ready for success.
National Cyber Security Alliance	The vision of the National Cyber Security Alliance is: "Empowering a more secure, interconnected world." The National Cyber Security Alliance focuses on helping SMBs conduct business safely and securely online. They offer free checkups, tools, and education to help your business be secure and manage privacy.

National Federation of Independent Business (NFIB)	"NFIB is the voice of small business, advocating on behalf of America's small and independent business owners, both in Washington, D.C., and in all 50 state capitals. NFIB is nonprofit, nonpartisan, and member-driven. Since our founding in 1943, NFIB has been exclusively dedicated to small and independent businesses, and remains so today." The NFIB has been leading the way for small businesses for decades. They offer countless resources to help small businesses succeed. You can subscribe for free and join as your business grows.
National Retail Federation	"The National Retail Federation has represented retail for over a century. Every day, we passionately stand up for the people, policies and ideas that help retail thrive." The NRF is a membership-based organization that offers valuable insight and research regarding consumers and retail businesses in their blog and podcast. As your business grows, joining the NRF will give you even more valuable information and opportunities, such as research findings and live events.
SCORE	"SCORE, the nation's largest network of volunteer, expert business mentors, is dedicated to helping small businesses get off the ground, grow and achieve their goals." SCORE offers mentoring access to experts in entrepreneurship, webinars, courses on demand, online resources, and local events. Whether you're starting your business or growing your business, SCORE provides invaluable resources and networking opportunities.
Small Business & Entrepreneurship Council (SBE Council)	"The Small Business & Entrepreneurship Council (SBE Council) is an influential voice and advocate for entrepreneurs and small business owners . . . Our network of supporters, including entrepreneurs and small business owners, state and local business organizations, corporate partners and associations work with us to strengthen the environment for entrepreneurship, investment, innovation and quality job creation." The SBE Council is focused on the key issues that matter to small businesses and entrepreneurs. Their news and resources can help you and your business stay ahead of the curve. You can subscribe for free and join as your business grows.

Small Business Administration (SBA)	"Created in 1953, the U.S. Small Business Administration (SBA continues to help small business owners and entrepreneurs pursue the American dream."
	The SBA is a great resource for SMBs . . . from business funding to education and local assistance. Whether you're just starting your business, building your business, or you want to grow your business, the SBA is a great resource. Though it's often only thought of for business funding, there are many more resources available for businesses. Take advantage of the numerous free opportunities to learn all that's available—right at your fingertips.
	For help with staying legally compliant with state and federal business laws, see a list of courses, and more, visit the SBA website.
The International Association of Privacy Professionals (IAPP)	The International Association of Privacy Professionals (IAPP) describes themselves as: "the world's largest and most comprehensive global information privacy community."
	In a world filled with new and constantly changing laws and regulations, you need a source like the IAPP to help keep you on top of the latest developments.

SECTION XII

Guerrilla Marketing Definitions

THE DEFINITIONS

TERM	DEFINITION
80/20 Rule	The Pareto principle, also known as the 80/20 Rule, has been translated into many meanings since it was first introduced in the late 1800s. For Guerrilla businesses, the 80/20 Rule teaches simplicity, and it applies throughout your business, for example: • 20 percent of your marketing generates 80 percent of your sales. • 20 percent of the time you spend working generates 80 percent of what you achieve at work. • 20 percent of a company's products usually account for 80 percent of its sales. • 20 percent of a company's employees contribute to 80 percent of the work that generates profits Therefore, Guerrilla marketers seek to continually prune the 80 percent, and they delegate to people in their business to carry out the necessary workload so they focus on the critical 20 percent that's difficult to delegate.
Advanced TV	Advanced TV, according to Cuebiq, is a term that includes: • Connected TV (CTV), which is an internet-connected television, such as a smart TV • Over-the-top (OTT) devices, such as Roku, Amazon Fire, Apple TV, smartphones, tablets, computers, and media players (e.g., video game consoles) • Subscription video-on-demand services (SVoD), such as Amazon Prime and Netflix, and partially ad-supported services, such as Hulu, CBS All Access, and Amazon's IMDb TV • Addressable TV via network providers (e.g., Comcast, Dish, Direct TV, etc.)
Agencies	The services that an agency provides can vary widely. From full service to niche services, it's important to understand their expertise and match that expertise with your needs. Common agencies are: • Social Media Agencies • Digital Media Agencies • Public Relations Agencies • Branding Agencies • Direct Response or Promotional Agencies • Media Agencies

Agile	A Guerrilla agile mind views their business, product(s), and/or service(s) as ever-evolving and nimble. The lines of communication are wide-open, and they frequently reassess and adapt as needed.
Amazement	Guerrilla marketers make their prospects hear and feel what is amazing, exciting, unique, and compelling about their business, product, or service
Apathy	Apathy is a lack of interest or a sense of indifference. In terms of marketing, a Guerrilla is focused on moving their prospects from apathy to interest and excitement about a purchase.
Attribution	The goal of marketing attribution is to determine which of your marketing tactics are creating sales. It's expected that several of your tactics are working together to create sales, and marketing attribution can help identify how your marketing tactics are working together.
Augmented Reality (AR)	With a smartphone or tablet camera, your prospect or customer can focus on a designated image and turn it into an engaging and interactive product experience. The image can be printed and featured in countless ways, such as in your direct mail, business cards, brochures, vehicle wrap (for events when the vehicle is stationary and on display), etc. Also, your website can feature virtual try-on technology that allows them to experience your product as if they were wearing or seeing it (e.g., eyeglasses, cosmetics, furniture, paint colors, tailoring/clothing, etc.). ARKIT by Apple and ARCore by Google help you develop new augmented reality experiences to transform how your prospects and customers shop and experience your product(s) and service(s).
Awareness	Guerrilla marketers pride themselves on being the "first to know." A business that's informed is a wise business that's utilizing the low-cost opportunities Guerrilla Marketing presents.
B2B	Business-to-business
Bartering	In lieu of money, negotiating the products, services, or capabilities of your business in exchange for something of value, such as advertising, marketing and/or media exposure that increases your success.

Term	Definition
Brand Awareness/Recognition	First, your prospects become aware of your business (i.e., brand awareness) and second, they recognize your business and the product(s) and/or service(s) associated with it (i.e., brand recognition). Once they do, your call to action must then motivate them to take a desired action (e.g., download an ebook, make a purchase, etc.). Your marketing efforts are ideal when they appeal to each aspect (brand awareness, brand recognition, and action) at the same time.
Better Business Bureau (BBB)	The Better Business Bureau (BBB) is a business performance rating service designed to give consumers a trusted resource and a voice related to business performance. The BBB National Programs offer best practices to help businesses succeed with information on a variety of helpful topics.
Blockchain	IBM defines blockchain as: "Blockchain is a shared, immutable ledger that facilitates the process of recording transactions and tracking assets in a business network. An asset can be tangible (a house, car, cash, land) or intangible (intellectual property, patents, copyrights, branding). Virtually anything of value can be tracked and traded on a blockchain network, reducing risk and cutting costs for all involved."
Brand	Your brand is generally recognizable by your visual and graphic representation (e.g., name, logo, tagline, etc.), but all elements of your company attributes and attitudes make up the components of your brand. Your brand is the entirety of your business that you're marketing to your prospects and customers.
Broadcasting	The largest possible audience for your business to share your compelling and engaging information, products, and/or services with (e.g., Advanced TV, social live broadcasts, etc.). When choosing a smaller audience, you're narrowcasting.
Buying Language	Buying language is the collection of words and phrases that motivate and compel your prospects and customers to purchase your product(s) or service(s). Understanding and speaking to their pain points and pleasure points in a way that allows them to visualize how you will solve their problems and the pleasure they will feel with their problems solved is speaking their buying language.
Call to Action (CTA)	Guerrilla marketers use a call to action—a clear and motivating message that tells prospects and customers exactly what you want them to do next (e.g., click here, call before May 1st, shop online before May 1st, enter promo code "ABC" at checkout, etc.).

SECTION XII | 257

Chroma Key	As defined by StudioBinder, "The Chroma key technique is the process by which a specific color is removed from an image, allowing that portion of the image to be replaced. This color can be any solid color, most commonly blue or green." A commonly-used term for the technique is *green screen*.
Click-Through Rates (CTR)	A click-through occurs when your ad or link is clicked. That number is divided by the number of times the ad is seen to determine the click-through rate. The goal of CTR is to understand how many times your ad is seen as compared to how many are compelled to click it. The higher your CTR is, the more compelling, engaging, and effective your ad is.
Cognitive Bias	Cognitive biases are explained by SimplyPsychology as, "unconscious errors in thinking that arise from problems related to memory, attention, and other mental mistakes." "These biases result from our brain's efforts to simplify the incredibly complex world in which we live."
Collaboration	Businesses working together, such as joint ventures, partnerships, mergers, acquisitions, or other arrangements, to share resources and assets and create greater growth together.
Color Palette	A selection of up to six complimentary colors that a business uses consistently and in every bit of its marketing. The chosen colors should be defined in each of the various systems, such as: PMS, CMYK, RGB, HSB, and HEX.
Commitment	Guerrillas learn by doing, imagining, experimenting, being realistic, keeping track, paying attention, improving, and committing to their successful experiments. The simple difference between many successes and failures is a simple marketing plan and a commitment to continue to do what's working.
Compelling	A no-cost tactic for Guerrilla Advertising and marketing that is irresistible, powerful, and motivates prospects to take action.
Competitive Advantages	Guerrilla marketers keep and maintain an ongoing list of their advantages versus their competitors. The list is utilized by everyone in the business to share their advantages (without specifically mentioning a competitor) with prospects, customers, community leaders, public relations contacts, etc.

Complacency	The enemies of Guerrilla Marketing and business success is complacency, rigidity, and sluggishness. When we speak of the importance of consistency, people can mistakenly confuse consistency and complacency. Consistency should not be confused with complacency. "Doing it the way we've always done it" is not the way of Guerrilla Marketing. "Doing it in a way that evolves and builds on what you've already done to continually grow your success" is the way of Guerrilla Marketing.
Confirmation Bias	The American Psychological Association defines confirmation bias as, "the tendency to gather evidence that confirms preexisting expectations, typically by emphasizing or pursuing supporting evidence while dismissing or failing to seek contradictory evidence."
Connections and Interacting	Guerrilla marketers pride themselves on their relationship skills. It's a characteristic that costs zero dollars and when mixed with your energy and imagination, it drives profits.
Consistency, Familiarity and Trust	A no or low-cost way Guerrilla marketers multiply their marketing effectiveness. You're marketing with every bit of contact your company has with anyone. Guerrilla marketers are intentional with that contact, fully utilizing the power of consistency. Consistency builds familiarity; familiarity builds trust, and trust creates sales, repeat purchases, and precious referrals.
Consumer Packaged Goods (CPG)	Consumer packaged goods are products that are packaged to be sold via distribution to retailers for regular and repeat consumption. For example, consumer package goods can be vitamins, toothpaste, deodorant, etc.
Convenience	What is convenient for your prospects and customers is determined by your prospects and customers. Therefore, convenience means being there when and where your prospects need or want your product(s) or service(s).

Conversion Rate Optimization (CRO)	CRO is the art and science of taking the prospects and customers that come to your site and turning them into buyers.
Conversions	The people that view your ad and respond by taking a desired action. This can be measured across your advertising by tracking web clicks, phone calls, and coupon (or other offer) redemptions.
Co-Op Funds	Advertising and marketing funds that your suppliers or vendors offer for mentioning or showcasing their products in your advertising.
Cost-Per-Action (CPA)	Online advertising or Fusion/Affiliate Marketing arrangements are typically structured as CPA, and the action could be a sale, lead (CPL), or click (CPC), as determined by the product owner. A trackable link is provided by the product owner and used by the affiliate partner so the transaction is recorded within the affiliate network. The agreed upon commissions (flat rate or a percentage) is then paid for completed transactions.
Cost-Per-Click (CPC)	Online advertising or Fusion/Affiliate Marketing arrangements may be structured as cost-per-click (CPC). The product owner determines the parameters that constitute a lead, and you want to be aware of those parameters. A trackable link is provided by the product owner and used by the affiliate partner so the transaction is recorded within the affiliate network. The agreed upon commissions (flat rate or a percentage) are then paid for completed transactions.
Cost-Per-Lead (CPL)	Online advertising or Fusion/Affiliate Marketing arrangements may be structured as cost-per-lead (CPL). The product owner determines the parameters that constitute a lead (e.g., filling out form, signing up for a trial, etc.), and you want to be aware of those parameters. A trackable link is provided by the product owner and used by the affiliate partner so the transaction is recorded within the affiliate network. The agreed upon commissions (flat rate or a percentage) are then paid for completed transactions.
Cost-Per-Thousand (CPM) advertising	Cost-per-thousand (CPM) advertising is based on the number of impressions that an ad generates. Guerrilla marketers are wise to focus on viewable impressions to maximize their investment.
Cost-Per-View (CPV) advertising	Cost-per-view (CPV) advertising is for video advertising campaigns. A view is determined by a defined period of time or an action taken, such as clicking the call to action (CTA).
Credibility	Guerrillas should know that two significant factors that influence a purchase decision for your prospects are confidence and trust. An easy way to build confidence and trust is with authentic credibility.

Cross-Selling	Offering compatible and complimentary products to your customers is a way to offer convenience and solutions that your prospects and customers appreciate. Making a cross-selling suggestion in a way that's friendly and engaging can stimulate a valuable conversation for you to learn more about your customers.
Customer	The people that buy your product(s) or service(s). The goal of a Guerrilla marketer is to have highly satisfied customers that make repeat purchases and precious referrals of their friends, family, and associates to their business.
Customer Lifetime Value (CLV) or Lifetime Value (LTV)	Guerrilla marketers understand the power of measuring and tracking a customer's lifetime value as a KPI (key performance indicator). Looking at a customer's lifetime value goes beyond their initial purchase. It accounts for what you deem to be important to the long-term success of your business, such as shares, likes, repeat purchases, referrals, etc. Measuring the value of your customers over their "lifetime" with your business, by accounting for the revenue they generate and the associated costs, gives you two valuable pieces of your success puzzle. One, which customers should be handled with the greatest care and, two, which customers you want to clone (e.g., demographics, psychographics, etc.) and/or attract more of. See Volume 3, Section 8.44, "Customer Lifetime Value (CLV or LTV)," for more information.
Customer Relationship Management (CRM)	Technology systems to manage your business and customer interactions and data (from customer service to marketing and sales). CRM systems are a more robust version of marketing automation systems. CRM tools can range from robust to lighter versions that will help you manage your marketing, customers, and transactions.
Data Appending	Quality data appending services can help your business fill in data gaps when it comes to valuable information about your customers and prospects. The data may include everything from attribute information to online and offline behavior. Each data appending service has its own process. It's imperative that you only work with highly-credible data appending services because the success or failure of your business relies on it. The security of the information you provide and the quality of the information you receive are critical for your success.

Deep Learning	IBM explains, "Deep learning is a subset of machine learning, which is essentially a neural network with three or more layers. These neural networks attempt to simulate the behavior of the human brain—albeit far from matching its ability—allowing it to 'learn' from large amounts of data." They go on to explain that it drives many AI applications and "lies behind everyday products and services (such as digital assistants, voice-enabled TV remotes, and credit card fraud detection) as well as emerging technologies (such as self-driving cars)."
Delegate	Guerrilla marketers engage like-minded experts to shine in the areas of the business that are either not the Guerrilla marketers' strengths or are too time-consuming. A Guerrilla marketer seeks to be true to the 80/20 Rule. Therefore, Guerrilla marketers seek to continually prune the 80 percent, and they delegate to people in their business to carry out the necessary workload so they focus on the critical 20 percent that's difficult to delegate. By doing so, together, they drive the success of the business further than the Guerrilla marketer ever could on their own.
Demographics	As defined by Dictionary.com, demographics are "the statistical data of a population, especially those showing average age, income, education, etc."
Digital Account-Based Marketing	Digital account-based marketing is a B2B marketing strategy that allows your business to target an entire company or the people in a certain division or functional role in a company.
Directories (online)	Online businesses that produce searchable business listings broadly (e.g., Manta, Super Pages, or Yellow Book) or by interest (e.g., Trip Advisor, Yelp, etc.) or by industry (e.g., Angi, Home Advisor, etc.). These businesses typically allow the businesses that are listed to claim and manage their profiles (either for free or for a fee).
Discovery Ads	With Discovery ads, a single ad campaign allows your business to reach your prospects as they interact across the different Google platforms.
Display Advertising	Display advertising, such as banner ads, use photos, videos, graphics, and rich media to promote engagement with your business by placing your business in front of people on targeted websites or social platforms.
Domain Name	Your domain name is the web address for your business.
Dots per inch (DPI)	Web images are usually 72 dpi (i.e., dots per inch) resolution, and images used for print are typically 300 ppi (i.e., pixels per inch) or more.

Ebooks	Ebooks are electronic books that can stand alone or are the electronic version of a printed book. An ebook is extremely easy to create and can be downloaded from your website for free or sold on your website or third-party ebook seller platforms.
Efficiency	For Guerrilla businesses, beyond the traditional definitions, efficiency means increased customer satisfaction and increased profits.
Email Autoresponder Platforms	To send email broadcasts to your prospects and/or customers, you'll need to use a software (email autoresponder) platform. Software platforms offer many advantages for a Guerrilla marketer, such as automation, results tracking, personalization, and customization.
Email Deliverability	Email deliverability is the challenging skill of getting your emails to reach your prospects' or customers' inboxes (rather than bouncing or being delivered to the spam or promotions folder, etc.).
Engagement	A combination of web traffic, ratings/reviews, and social media interactions that determine, in part, your brand favorability and interaction among your prospects and customers.
Engaging	A no-cost tactic for Guerrillas in their advertising and marketing that makes your prospect want to connect and know more.
Ethical Bribes	Ethical bribes mean your business is giving your prospects and customers an ethical incentive to take a particular and ethical action.
Evergreen Content	Your audio and video content that has a useful long-life (e.g., recipes) and will continue to work for your business for years.
Firmographics	Firmographic data helps to segment businesses for B2B marketing. Hubspot breaks down firmographic data into industry type, organizational size, total sales and revenue, current location, ownership framework and growth trends.
Follow-up	Tenacity is a trait that Guerrilla marketers embrace. It makes skills, such as follow-up, a natural part of their business mindset. Relentless follow-up can be the simple difference that turns a prospect into a customer and a customer into a repeat buyer.
Friendly Picketers	Friendly picketers are a Guerrilla Marketing tactic to garner attention and pique the interest of your prospects and customers. Friendly picketers appear to be real picketers, but they are holding clever signs, which promote the business and ask "passer buyers" to honk because they love the business. They may also hand out samples or direct people to a booth at an event.
Fusion/Affiliate Marketing	Businesses working together to create a compelling marketing offer to increase the sales and profits for one or both businesses.

Geofencing	Geofencing is a location-based service. It can work with B2B advertising or with consumers. Geofencing gives you the ability to create a boundary around a physical location and send targeted messages (e.g., alert, advertising, etc.) to your prospects and customers that are within that boundary. It can also be used with your app to send messages to your prospects and customers who have your app and receive notifications.
Google My Business	A powerful Google service that every Guerrilla marketer fully utilizes. Google My Business allows you to be in control (with your Google Business Profile) of the details and services that people see when they Google search or Google Map your business when searching from their phone, tablet, or computer.
Guerrilla Creative and Advertising Strategy	An amazingly simple plan designed to align your advertising efforts to your overall Guerrilla Marketing plan. A Guerrilla Creative and Advertising strategy creates clarity about what you're offering (the benefits), to whom you're making your offer (your target audience, prospects, and customers), and the action you want them to take. See Volume 1, Section 1.6, "Guerrilla Creative and Advertising Strategy Challenge," for more information.
Guerrilla Creativity	The combination of thoughts, ideas, and approaches that create powerful marketing and business ideas. See Volume 1, Section 1.2, "Guerrilla Creativity," for more information.
Guerrilla Marketing	Intelligent marketing that utilizes a plan and strategy along with knowledge, low-cost, unconventional, creative tactics to convey or promote a compelling product or idea. Guerrilla Marketing was introduced to the world in a self-titled book by Jay Conrad Levinson, written in 1984, as an unconventional system of marketing that relies on knowledge, time, energy, imagination, and information rather than a big marketing budget. Visit gMarketing.com/Club for more resources and information.
Guerrilla Marketing Calendar	The way Guerrilla marketers track their efforts and move their successes forward into the next year. Equally, it's the way to ensure they're not continuing to do what is not working. See Volume 1, Section 1.7, "Guerrilla Marketing Calendar," for more information.
Guerrilla Marketing Plan	An amazingly simple plan focused on a core idea that always comes before you engage in any marketing tactics. Your plan makes your Guerrilla Marketing focused, impactful, consistent, compelling, engaging, and profitable. See Volume 1, Section 1.5, "Guerrilla Marketing Plan Challenge," for more information.
Hard Sell	Hard selling is advertising (or one-to-one selling) that attempts to inspire immediate action. For example, the use of price points and a "buy now" button. Soft selling is advertising (or one-to-one selling) that, for example, includes your product and motivates them to go the next step to see your pricing and buying options.

High definition	For videos posted online, it's best to use high definition, 1024x768 or better.
Hot Leads	Prospects that have been referred to your business (e.g., one-on-one, through your referral program, from a referral site, etc.) and have a high propensity to buy. Therefore, a hot lead deserves specialized, consistent, and immediate attention to turn them into a customer.
Identity	Your business identity defines what your business is about and how you go about doing your business.
Impressions	The number of people who have seen (or had the opportunity to see) your advertising, plus how many times they have seen it (e.g., if one person has the opportunity to see your advertising four times, that is four impressions). Guerrilla marketers seek clarity with any advertising partner regarding how they define impressions.
Influencer Marketing	Influencer marketing can be an effective means of paid advertising for Guerrilla marketers. With influencer marketing, you pay (or barter with) an influencer on social media, such as YouTube, Twitter, Instagram, Pinterest, Talk, or other platforms to promote your product(s), service(s) or business.
Innovation	Guerrilla businesses succeed when they focus on desirable innovations—especially those that relate to the pain points of their prospects and customers—and thereby inspire and motivate their customers to make repeat or additional purchases and prospects to make new purchases.
Intelligent Marketing	Guerrilla Marketing is intelligent marketing. A Guerrilla marketer uses knowledge and intentional and intelligent marketing to produce profits, which allows their business to grow, expand, evolve, thrive, and make a difference in their community or the world.
Jingle	Your jingle is an audio trigger for your customers and prospects. This Guerrilla Marketing tactic, with consistent repetition, is designed to help people recognize, remember, and have a favorable view of your business, its name, and, ideally, your condensed USP (i.e., brand awareness and brand recognition). It's ideal when it also motivates them to take a specific action.
Key Performance Indicators (KPIs)	Key performance indicators are the metrics that businesses use to measure their success. Examples, as we've defined in our volumes of the all-new series of *Guerrilla Marketing* books, are ROI, ROAS, CRO, CPA, CPC, CPL, CPM, LTV/CLV, CPV, PPC, NPS, etc.
Lead Buying	Purchasing lists of targeted prospects to market to, as well as marketing to the customers and prospects of other businesses (see Fusion/Affiliate Marketing), are both long-time, proven ways to attract more prospects and customers to your business.

Lead Magnets	Discount or give away something valuable (free trials, an ebook, a free course, an assessment, personalized report, a consultation, etc.) to entice your prospects to buy additional products or services.
Leads	Leads are prospects that are a result of lead buying and/or those prospects that have interacted (organically or as a result of your marketing) with your business. Cold leads are prospects that are not familiar with your business. It's your job to warm those leads and interest them in your product(s) or service(s) by giving them a compelling desire to purchase your product(s) or service(s) and become your customer. Medium leads are prospects that you are marketing to as a part of a marketing arrangement with Fusion/Affiliate Marketing partners. These prospects have a relationship with your Fusion/Affiliate Marketing partner, who is recommending or endorsing your business, product, or service. Hot leads are prospects that have been referred by your customers, a referral site, etc. They could also be prospects that opted into your quiz or survey, downloaded your ebook or white paper, or requested your updates/newsletter and, therefore, have provided their information. Hot leads have a high propensity to buy.
Left Brain	People with left-brain tendencies are motivated by logical and sequential reasoning.
List Building	List building is the art and science of deploying multiple tactics (blogs, lead magnets, etc.) to have people opt-in to connect with your business and receive your email communications.
Logo	A clean and distinct graphic representation of your business name that helps to build recall and familiarity with your prospects and customers.
Machine Learning	The MIT Sloan School of Management explains, "When companies today deploy artificial intelligence programs, they are most likely using machine learning — so much so that the terms are often used interchangeably, and sometimes ambiguously. Machine learning is a subfield of artificial intelligence that gives computers the ability to learn without explicitly being programmed."
Market Research	Guerrillas engage in ongoing marketing research to stay informed of trends, their target audience, advertising options, the competition, the industry, the economy (local and national), and their business and social community.

Marketing and Sales Funnels	Your marketing and sales funnels will map the journey they are on, which consists of: • Awareness (i.e., brand awareness) of your business • Recognizing your business and the product(s) and/or service(s) associated with it (i.e., brand recognition) • Compelling their interest in your product(s) and/or service(s) • Motivating their consideration of your call to action • Taking action
Marketing Automation	These tools allow you to set up your online marketing, from newsletters to promotional mailings, with triggers that allow greater personalization based on the actions your prospects and customers take and/or the information they provide.
Media Contacts	Each reporter, author, blogger, and other public relations contact that you meet and interact with becomes part of your important network of media contacts. Guerrilla marketers realize that building these relationships will help them create more media coverage for their business and, thereby, grow their public relations reach.
Meme	Much like a stop sign or a traffic light, a meme is an instantly recognizable idea without words. In business marketing, it's an image that compliments your name and logo. Your meme is a visual trigger for your customers and prospects. This Guerrilla Marketing tactic, with consistent repetition, is designed to help people recognize, remember, and form a favorable view of your business, its name, and, ideally, your condensed USP (i.e., brand awareness and brand recognition). Examples are: • Pillsbury Doughboy • Michelin Man • The Green Giant • The Energizer Bunny • M&M Characters
Message Bots	Message bots are a form of artificial intelligence (AI). They can boost sales and satisfaction while reducing your costs by providing a variety of services. Message bots can add to your appeal and help your business build and grow relationships with your prospects and customers.
Monadic Design	Two examples of survey designs: • Monadic design is focused on asking multiple questions about one advertising option/design • Sequential monadic design is focused on asking multiple questions about two or more options/designs.

Multivariate Testing	Multivariate testing provides quantitative results to help your businesses understand the preferences of your prospects and customers and maximize your results (e.g., increased conversions, opt-ins, etc.). Multivariate testing is used for most types of advertising to test three or more (as opposed to split testing, which is two) elements (e.g., words, images, products, services, pricing, promotions, etc.) with a group of customers or prospects
Native Advertising	Native ads can be text, display, video, slideshows, or carousel, and they flow with the look, feel, and content of the site or social platform on which they are placed while being marked as "sponsored."
Native and Social Outstream Advertising	According to AdAge: "Social outstream is video ads that autoplay on mute with headlines and formats that match the look and feel of social feeds on Facebook, Instagram, Twitter, etc. Native outstream is the same as social but made to match the look and feel of editorial feeds."
Natural Language Processing	According to the MIT Sloan School of Management, "Natural language processing is a field of machine learning in which machines learn to understand natural language as spoken and written by humans, instead of the data and numbers normally used to program computers. This allows machines to recognize language, understand it, and respond to it, as well as create new text and translate between languages."
Net Promoter Score (NPS)	Simply put, when responding to a survey, it's the score your respondents give when asked, "How likely are you to recommend this business?"
	Given the importance of recommendations and referrals, it's a KPI to carefully monitor and strive to improve.
Neural Networks	Per IBM, "Neural networks reflect the behavior of the human brain, allowing computer programs to recognize patterns and solve common problems in the fields of AI, machine learning, and deep learning."
NFTs	Inc. explains, "A non-fungible token (NFT) is a digital asset that represents an array of virtual and physical things, which cannot be substituted or switched with a fake since they are created on a blockchain that can always be traced back to the original owner or creator. NFTs can be works of art, photos, music, videos, collectibles, memorabilia, contracts, coupons, certificates of authenticity, ID files, health records, and more."
Opt-In	The right opt-in offer enables a Guerrilla marketer to turn curious prospects into customers.
	An opt-in form on your website allows your prospects or customers to enter their information and email addresses to be added to your mailing list and/or take advantage of an offer you have made.

Pain Points	Guerrilla businesses are in the problem-solving business. Your prospects and customers are seeking solutions to their problems. The more effectively your business connects with your prospects and customers by speaking their buying language and relating to their pain points (physically or emotionally), the more likely your business is able to motivate them to buy. Once you've related to their pain points, and you've shown them the pleasure (i.e., pleasure points) they can experience when their problem is solved—and the more they believe you can provide that solution—the more motivated they are to buy. You can think of pain points as their "needs" and pleasure points as their "wants."
Pay-Per-Click (PPC) or Cost-Per-Click (CPC) Advertising	Pay-per-click (PPC) or cost-per-click (CPC) ads are based on the number of clicks on your ad. Therefore, you will pay for each click on your ad.
Personalization	Addressing and connecting with your prospects and customers in a knowledgeable, caring, and attentive manner that makes them feel recognized, noticed, important, and, ultimately, engaged.
Pixels per inch (PPI)	Images used for print are typically 300 ppi (i.e., pixels per inch) or more and web images are usually 72 dpi (i.e., dots per inch) resolution..
Positioning	Your positioning defines what your business, product, or service stands for, its value, and why it should be purchased.
Private Labeling	A product that is typically produced/manufactured and customized exclusively for one retailer. Grocery store chains and drug store chains often utilize private labeling for their branded products.
Programmatic Digital Advertising Buying	Programmatic digital advertising buying as defined by Strategus: ". . . the process of purchasing online advertising impressions through automated platforms, allowing advertisers to aggregate, book, flight, analyze and optimize the ad campaign." The process is less time consuming and more capable of reaching the right prospects and optimizing performance.
Prospect	A target market or segment (people or businesses) that has the demographic, geographic, and/or psychographic characteristics you have identified as being the most likely to purchase your product(s) or service(s) and become a customer. Also referred to as a prospective customer.
Psychographics	As defined by the American Psychological Association, psychographics is, "an extended form of demographic analysis that surveys the values, activities, interests, and opinions of populations or population segments (psychographic segmentation) to predict consumer preferences and behavior."

Public Relations (PR)	Guerrilla public relations (PR) is a low-cost method of garnering high-quality exposure for your business by building strong, collaborative relationships with leading people. Guerrilla PR helps establish the identity of your business (or yourself) and gives you authority and credibility.
Push Notifications	Push notifications are an opportunity to notify your customers with ease. VWO offers, "Push notifications are clickable pop-up messages that appear on your users' browsers irrespective of the device they're using or the browser they're on. They serve as a quick communication channel enabling companies to convey messages, offers, or other information to their customers."
QR Code	A quick response code (QR Code) is a matrix barcode. QR codes (created using a QR code generator) are used in marketing as a convenient and fast way to direct your prospect or customer to a specified URL. When the barcode is scanned, using a QR Code scanner app or a camera on a smartphone or tablet, it directs people to a specified URL that you defined with the QR code generator.
Qualitative and Quantitative	Split testing and opinion polls provide quantitative results (i.e., the numbers). Focus groups, on the other hand, provide more qualitative results (i.e., behavior and observations). Surveys that allow for open comments can provide both quantitative and qualitative results.
Quality	A hallmark of a Guerrilla business. Guerrillas understand that the quality of their product(s) or service(s) is measured by their customers and prospects. The measurement of quality encompasses the entire customer experience. High-quality products and services typically require less marketing investment because positive ratings and reviews, along with customer referrals, attract prospects to your business.
Radio DJ or On-air Personality Endorsements.	Radio personalities can be hired to make direct (scripted or unscripted) endorsements of your product (often referred to as "DJ chatter"). Those endorsements are, ideally, given as an authentically satisfied customer, who's sharing their exceptional experience with their listeners. Keep in mind that those endorsements can be partially or fully paid by bartering (i.e., providing products or services, instead of money, in exchange for paid endorsements.).
Reach	Reach is the number of unique people that are exposed to your marketing and/or advertising.

Referral Programs	Referral programs are a must for a Guerrilla business, as they are the path to profits and a leading indicator that your business is performing well. The referral of a friend, family, or associate to your business, by your customers, is a precious gift that makes Guerrilla marketers extremely grateful and focused on an exceptional experience.
Referral Sites	Referral sites curate compelling content, offers, and solutions for their prospects and customers. They create revenue and profits with a combination of advertising and referral/affiliate commissions. They can be a great source of hot leads and customers for your business.
Referrals	Meaningful endorsements provided by your customers put powerful word-of-mouth marketing to work for your business. Referrals are the precious gift that customers bestow upon grateful Guerrilla marketers. Whether you have a paid (money, credits, or points) or unpaid referral program, the endorsement that your satisfied customers (or affiliate referral partners) provide is one of the most powerful and low-cost methods of marketing your business possesses. Guerrilla marketers maximize the opportunity that a strong referral program provides. Many successful businesses have been built using, primarily, referral marketing.
Relationship Builder	Guerrillas place an emphasis on creating relationships with prospects, customers, employees, other businesses, media contacts, industry leaders, community leaders, etc. Their listening skills and honest interest in people boost their relationship building skills and those relationships are a source of endless knowledge and opportunities. See Volume 3, Section 9.29, "Relationship Builder," for more information.
Repeat Purchases	A powerful opportunity that many businesses do not pay attention to is the repeat purchase. Fortunately, Guerrilla marketers know that when their customers are making additional and repeat purchases, it's an indicator that their customers are happy, and the marketing is working profitably well.
Repetition	Repetition, when done correctly (i.e., with consistency), is at the core of successful Guerrilla Marketing. It's a low-cost method of creating recognition, familiarity, interest, trust, and motivation among your prospects to turn them into customers.
Research	In most cases, great advertising and marketing are preceded by great research. Research helps you identify the demographics and psychographics of your target market, which helps you save time and money (by focusing on prospects that are most likely to buy) and be more personal with your marketing messages.

Retargeting (or Remarketing) Advertising	Retargeting is a tremendously effective Guerrilla Marketing tactic that allows you to target your prospects as they move around the Internet after they've engaged with your brand.

Return on Ad Spend (ROAS)	Return on ad spend (ROAS) is an important metric for determining the success of your advertising spend. The formula is a percentage resulting from:
	
	   Revenue from the transaction
	      - Divided By -
	   The expenses incurred in advertising.
	
	Expenses include creative costs, agency fees, and media spending.
	
	To accurately determine your ROAS, you need appropriate tracking systems. ROAS is a comparison metric to determine advertising efficiency. Successful Guerrilla ROAS is always over 100 percent or expressed as 1.0 ROAS.

Return on Investment (ROI)	Return on investment (ROI) is an important metric for determining the success of your marketing efforts. The formula is:
	
	   Revenue from the transaction
	      - Minus -
	   The expenses incurred to acquire and fulfill the transaction.
	
	Expenses include operations, marketing, sales, and product costs.
	
	To accurately determine your ROI, you need appropriate tracking systems for expenses, production, marketing, and sales. Additionally, if your product is subscription-based, your ROI will account for the increased revenue and expenses over time.

Right Brain	People with right-brain tendencies are motivated by emotional and aesthetic appeal.
Search Engine	Search engines allow you to search the web for answers to whatever query you enter. Search engines can be broad, such as Google, Bing, or Yahoo. Or they can be niche, like travel or entertainment (e.g., Yelp) or maps (e.g., Google Maps or Apple Maps).
Search Engine Keywords	Search engine keywords are the words and phrases your prospects and customers might use in their search for businesses such as yours.
Search Engine Optimization (SEO)	Simply put, SEO is the practice of making sure that your website is optimized for the unpaid results of search engines. Search engines exist for the benefit of their searchers. On-page SEO allows your website to boost its ranking in the search engine results when your site addresses and answers the questions and words that your customers and prospects are searching for with quality information. Off-page SEO is the practice of getting content on other sites to link back to your website in the right context.

Self-Justification	Purchase decisions are made for emotional reasons, and those decisions are justified with logical reasoning. Psychology Today refers to it as self-justification and provides an example: "The person who has bought a luxury item but feels guilty about it may try to alleviate his guilt by coming up with additional reasons to justify his behavior, such as, 'It was on sale, I had to buy it.'"
Service	Your prospects and customers define what is excellent service for them. Excellent service may be defined by your prospects and customers as a seamless experience that's free of resistance and has minimal interaction or it might be a hands-on and high-touch service.
SMBs	Small- and medium-sized (or midsized) businesses
Social Media Monitoring	Social media monitoring is valuable to spot trends, problems, opportunities, and online chatter regarding your business, product(s), service(s), and competitors so you can improve engagement while managing your reputation.
Soft Sell	Soft selling is advertising (or one-to-one selling) that, for example, includes your product and motivates them to go the next step to see your pricing and buying options. Hard selling is advertising (or one-to-one selling) that attempts to inspire immediate action. For example, the use of price points and a "buy now" button.
Solopreneurs	Business owners who are the only person in their business (i.e., they don't have employees, a business partner, etc.).
Solutions and Problems	Guerrilla marketers are in the business of developing and selling solutions to their prospects' and customers' problems.
Split Testing	Split testing provides quantitative results to help your business understand the preferences of your prospects and customers and maximize your results (e.g., increased conversions, opt-ins, etc.). Split testing is used for most types of advertising to test two elements (e.g., words, images, products, services, pricing, promotions, etc.) with a group of customers or prospects
Sponsorships	Providing money, goods, or services to a desirable activity (news broadcasts, targeted information segments, etc.) or event (local events, venues, etc.) in exchange for them promoting your business via advertising, marketing, and/or endorsements.
Squeeze Page	Opt-in forms are placed on squeeze pages, which are a form of a landing page that is dedicated to email opt-ins.
Stories That Sell	Guerrilla marketers sell through storytelling. For example, telling the story of the problem they had that set them on the path to finding a solution. In the process, they turned it into a business, and now they can solve that problem for you.
Strategy	The high-level plan that you create for meeting or exceeding your goals.

Street Teams	Hired promotional teams that are attention-getting and engaging, that attend events and heavy pedestrian traffic areas, handing out samples of your product.
Subconscious or Unconscious Mind	The activity of your mind that you are not aware of (or conscious of) but are impacted or influenced by. In terms of marketing, the subconscious or unconscious mind is taking in all kinds of marketing information. Guerrilla marketers utilize well-crafted marketing and advertising, along with repetition and consistency because they understand the value of the subconscious mind.
Subliminal Marketing	Subliminal marketing is marketing messages, images, and sensations that only the subconscious mind absorbs but the conscious mind is influenced by. Guerrilla marketers focus their attention on the transparent methods of subliminal marketing that influence the purchase decision.
Tactics	The actionable marketing techniques you employ to achieve your strategy.
Tagline	Your tagline expresses your compelling, competitive advantage, company attitude, or USP in just a few powerful words. This Guerrilla Marketing tactic, with consistent repetition, is designed to help people recognize, remember, and form a favorable view of your business (i.e., brand awareness and brand recognition). It's ideal when it also motivates them to take a specific action.
Target Audience or Target Market	The research- and experience-based demographic and psychographic characteristics of your prospects and customers.
Technographics	The technology utilized by a business. The information helps your business segment its B2B prospects to those most likely to become your customers, based on the technology they are currently using.
Testimonials, Endorsements, and Referrals	The precious gift that happy and loyal customers bestow on a Guerrilla business that has met and exceeded their expectations. When customers recommend your business to their friends, family, and associates, you're utilizing one of the lowest-cost and highest-satisfaction methods for generating profits.
Top-of-mind	Being top-of-mind is critical to Guerrilla marketers. For example, when you go to buy a CPG (consumer packaged good), you likely have an idea about the exact product you want to buy. That product is top-of-mind. For example, you likely have a top-of-mind product when you're going to buy toothpaste, deodorant, a beverage, or a sweet treat. Your every marketing effort is to make your business top-of-mind when your prospects and customers are shopping for your product(s) or service(s).
Tracking and Measuring	Guerrilla Marketing evolves and succeeds when the resulting activity (views, sales, and inquiries) is tagged, followed, recorded, and analyzed to determine the value of your investment.

Unconventional	Guerrilla Marketing is a strategy in which knowledge and low-cost unconventional means are utilized to convey or promote a product or an idea. Those unconventional means compel your prospects to notice your business. Once they do, your call to action must then motivate them to take a desired action (e.g., download an ebook, make a purchase, etc.). Your existing customers also need to be motivated to make repeat purchases and precious referrals of their friends, family, and associates.
Unique Selling Proposition (USP)	Your USP represents one of your greatest marketing opportunities, and most businesses neither promote nor have identified theirs. It's your proprietary competitive edge stated clearly and succinctly. See Volume 1, Section 1.3, "Unique Selling Proposition (USP)," for more information.
Upgrade Opportunities	When you design an engaging pricing model you can increase your sales by selling similar products at various prices.
Uniform Resource Locator (URL)	A URL is your web address. It's a good practice, alongside a promotional offer, to use a specific sales page on your website that ties directly to a marketing piece or offer (e.g., direct mail, radio advertisement, social media ad, etc.) to seamlessly continue your message while being able to track the results of that dedicated URL.
Video Advertising	Video ads are immensely powerful and an effective way to market your product(s) or service(s) on platforms, such as YouTube.
Viral Marketing	When stories, images, and/or videos have widespread appeal, people love to share them. When those stories, images, and/or videos hit at just the right moment, and they have broad appeal, the magic begins. As the number of shares grows over a short period of time, the story, image, and/or video reaches critical mass and is considered to have "gone viral."
Webinars	Webinars can be live or recorded. They are your opportunity to host countless people online for the purpose of educating, interacting with, and/or selling your product(s) or service(s).
White Labeling	Allows other businesses to put their name and/or logo (i.e., rebrand) on the product(s) your business manufactures. Equally, online businesses can sell their information products to other businesses, who then market them as their own.

AUTHORS NOTE

When starting the all-new series of *Guerrilla Marketing* books, we had to ask ourselves some important questions:
- Did Jay Conrad Levinson want the world of SMBs to continue to thrive with Guerrilla Marketing?
- Could we build upon his vision and continually evolve the tactics, tools, and tips that SMBs need to thrive?
- Is Guerrilla Marketing as effective today as it was when it was introduced decades ago?
- Could we deliver a complete experience for everyone, regardless of whether they are new to Guerrilla Marketing or have been using it for decades?

When we answered yes to every question, we knew it was time to get to work. It's been no small task, but when you're fueled by a passion for SMBs to succeed, it's a worthy task.

Guerrilla Marketing has always been about you:
- The person with an idea and a dream of being self-employed, their own boss, and/or a business owner
- The SMB that needs help understanding and using intelligent marketing and realizing how it can help them thrive
- The established business that is not meeting its potential and craves support to get it where it knows it can be (or beyond)

We were fortunate to, individually, be born to hard-working parents with tenacity, focus, relentlessness, pride, generosity, and compassion. Those are the foundational energy sources that make SMBs thrive.

As we, individually, grew up with their examples and set out to create our own paths, we intersected at the same Fortune 50 corporate environment. We've never lost the tenacity of our parents' examples, and we've had the good fortune to also engage in large-scale businesses. The contrast was exciting and noteworthy, and it answered several important questions:
- How do start-up companies upend the Goliath of their industries?
- Why does the tiniest decision make or break a business and a dream?
- Does a big budget mean big results?
- Is a large-scale company more capable of driving a higher ROI with their marketing investment than an SMB?

- What are the shared secrets of success that large-scale and SMBs hold?

Ultimately, it's the leveling of the playing field that allows SMBs to take on Goliath and come out victorious. Guerrilla Marketing has always been about not only leveling the playing field but also tilting it in favor of SMBs, and we intend to keep it that way. However, we want your involvement. Don't just read this book—join us. Let's all talk, collaborate, grow, and succeed together. Join us at gMarketing.com/Club.

Know this:
- Collaboration takes an idea and turns it into a movement
- Energy alone is not enough to succeed
- When you continually add knowledge and focused action, you succeed
- Learning is like breathing; it's necessary and exhilarating, and you can't exist without it

We've been fortunate to experience vast backgrounds of success. We, along with you, look forward to helping your ideas and SMBs turn into million-, billion-, or trillion-dollar companies that never forget that Guerrilla Marketing is the path that delivered you there.

GUERRILLA CLUB

THE GUERRILLA CLUB AWAITS YOU WITH FREE TOOLS, EXAMPLES, RESOURCES, AND SO MUCH MORE

Imagine what you'll find to help you succeed!

We know you're ready for success right now, and we're ready to help you make it happen. The best place to start is by building a strong foundation of Guerrilla Marketing. Our FREE companion course will help you build your rock-solid Guerrilla Marketing foundation. Regardless of whether you're currently using Guerrilla Marketing tactics in your business and a great refresher will ensure your foundation is solid, or you're new to Guerrilla Marketing and need a good overview, a few minutes is all you need.

In our FREE companion course, we'll dive in with video tutorials, exercises, and the tools you'll need to build that crucial foundation from which your Guerrilla Marketing success will be born. Remember, businesses that fail have a poor foundation. If you build your castle on a poor foundation, don't be surprised when it collapses into rubble.

Beyond the tools you need to build your strong foundation, our Guerrilla Club members will find a growing list of tools, examples, and resources to help your success going forward.

Scan this QR code with your app or smartphone camera:

Or go to gMarketing.com/Club
We are looking forward to further connecting with you!

WHAT THE GUERRILLA MARKETING BOOK SERIES WILL DO FOR YOU AND YOUR BUSINESS

Guerrilla Marketing, since the original Guerrilla Marketing book was introduced in 1984, has supported and empowered entrepreneurs, small and medium-sized businesses, solopreneurs, and people with ideas they think can be a business to:

- Start and/or build successful Guerrilla businesses
- Understand why and how marketing works and why Guerrilla Marketing is intelligent marketing
- Weave the consistent methodology of Guerrilla Marketing through every aspect of their business
- Create profits for the benefit of themselves, their families, their employees, their community, and the world at large
- Tap into their Guerrilla Creativity to create highly profitable marketing
- Utilize Guerrilla Creative Strategies to ensure their Guerrilla Marketing tactics hit the target

- Create and execute their Guerrilla Marketing plan and Guerrilla Creative and Advertising strategy
- Utilize consistency in their marketing to build familiarity, which, in turn, builds trust; and that trust creates sales, repeat purchases, and precious referrals from their customers
- Define the authentic attitudes of their business and use the power of authenticity in their marketing
- Identify their company attributes and consistently make their prospects and customers aware of them in their marketing and advertising
- Track their marketing to build on their successes and remove their unsuccessful efforts
- Make the truth fascinating
- Thrive with low-cost tactics
- Thrive with unconventional tactics
- Deliver their marketing tactics with creative, low-cost, and unconventional methods
- Upend their competition, big and small
- Sell their successful businesses and start all over again or perfect their favorite pastime as their full-time endeavor
- Win, on purpose

Guerrilla Marketing is a combination of knowledge, unchanging fundamentals and ever-changing ideas, examples, tactics and tools. Our job is to keep you aware of the latest of each of those, to help you succeed.

Your *Guerrilla Marketing* know-how and toolbox are ever-expanding. Be sure to pick up:
Guerrilla Marketing Volume 1
Guerrilla Marketing Volume 2
Guerrilla Marketing Volume 4
**We are hard at work to keep you and your business far ahead of the competition.
Visit gMarketing.com/Club now.**

ABOUT THE AUTHORS

Jason Myers

Chairman, Guerrilla Marketing Global, LLC

My journey into Guerrilla Marketing started while in high school in the 1980s, shortly after Jay published the first book. The timing was perfect, and I embraced the concept immediately. However, I was pretty much always a Guerrilla, perhaps by necessity.

You see, I grew up as a child of parents that were construction workers. They moved us all over the country, from one project to another, and we had times of feast and times of famine. This instability, living in the cycle of being middle-class then dropping into barely scraping by, meant that I had to always be creative, curious, and committed to lifelong learning. I wanted "more," and I knew I could achieve it.

I learned sales and marketing—as many kids did—by reselling candy to my classmates. Often, I would get lunch money on Mondays, with a promise that the lunch money for the rest of the week would come later. To be sure that it did, I would invest my Monday lunch money into a pile of candy, and by Monday at lunchtime, I would have earned the entire week's lunch money. I still remember the first time I told my mom that I didn't need the rest of the week's lunch money. The marketing aspect came in the packaging and positioning. I would try different types of candy and combinations. I would try telling compelling stories of the origin or my adventures acquiring the candy. I learned that people want to buy a story; they would pay more for that than they would for a commodity. I went on to learn to sell many things using these important lessons.

My first business was a Guerrilla fusion marketing experiment. It started when I learned computer programming; I'd buy a computer video game, modify the game, and sell those re-engineered copies to my friends. This led to an intense interest in video games and an introduction to a local amusement company that owned the full-sized coin-operated video games. I inquired about how the business worked for an arcade and before I knew it, I had organized the delivery of a truckload of video games to my new arcade business. We had agreed to split the revenue, and the entire setup cost me nothing to get started. It was a true fusion, joint-venture relationship. As a teenager with an arcade, the next step was to develop my marketing plan. Fortunately, I discovered the first Guerrilla Marketing book and the genius idea that Jay Conrad Levinson brought forward to help small businesses implement intelligent marketing.

My first fifteen minutes of fame came when, inspired by Guerrilla Marketing's concepts, I covered my car with refrigerator magnets for a pizza shop. As I drove around, people stared. When I parked the car, people would "borrow" the magnets. The pizza shop saw an increase in sales. Then, the local newspaper decided to run a small article with a photo of the car covered completely in magnets. The pizza shop was incredibly happy to get the free press, and I became small-town "famous" for a minute. I felt so Guerrilla!

Those early lessons allowed me to start a second business, which grew quickly and had more business activity than I could handle at times. I learned so much from applying the methods and concepts in the first edition of Guerrilla Marketing. Eventually, when that business ran its course, I found my way into a management/leadership position in the telecom industry, and my marketing and sales skills allowed me to stand out in a rapidly growing industry, and I achieved many successes.

As I transitioned back into entrepreneurship, my decades worth of Guerrilla skills—be it marketing, mindset, management, and money-making skills—really paid off. I have started, invested in, grown, and sold dozens of businesses and am often called upon to help others grow their businesses. I'm passionate about mentorship, coaching, and applying Guerrilla techniques.

Since starting to learn and apply Guerrilla Marketing back in the '80s, I've dedicated a chunk of my life to perpetually pursuing knowledge and experience. I think you should, too.

During this journey, I've discovered that anyone who has learned effective sales and marketing skills will never go hungry. These two skills are the most important, self-empowering skills that exist, and they form the foundation for entrepreneurship. I encourage everyone to learn these as early as possible and take control of their financial futures.

I consider Jay to be one of my most significant mentors. His lessons helped form who I am today. To honor him, I have dedicated myself to carrying on his legacy by ensuring that the entire concept of Guerrilla is relevant today and tomorrow for millions more people.

I encourage you to learn as much as you can about Guerrilla Marketing and apply those lessons to your business and share your successes with others. This book is a great next step, and we'll be providing many more steps going forward, to help you and your business grow and succeed—now and long into the future.

I'll see you at the top!

Merrilee Kimble

Chief Creative Officer, Guerrilla Marketing Global, LLC

I had the incredible privilege of being raised in a thriving small-to-medium-sized business success story (from a start-up company that grew into a medium-sized business before being successfully sold), for which I'm very grateful. My father utilized many Guerrilla Marketing tactics, and he combined them with relentless energy. I'm grateful for the experience I had in his business from cleaning the office to sales/customer service and whatever else needed to be done.

My parents insisted that I have a college education, perhaps because they thought it would make my life easier, and what parent doesn't generously want that for their child? I'm also grateful they both wanted me to push myself further. When I graduated college, I had no idea how this was supposed to come together. An entrepreneurial up-bringing, a marketing education, and options of working for large corporations.

Decades later, I not only secured incredibly large corporation experiences under my belt—from managing multi-million-dollar advertising and marketing budgets to executing every aspect of multi-language marketing—but I also earned the priceless experience of my own boot-strapped entrepreneurial endeavors.

I'm excited to share my broad marketing experience with you as we, from here, advance Guerrilla Marketing and your success. There is nothing more satisfying when it comes to work than being your own boss. Guerrilla Marketing is intelligent marketing that can help you stay successful or become successful as your own satisfied boss.

Marketing is getting more complex by the day. Fortunately, Guerrilla Marketing is here for you now and long into the future to reduce the complexity.

We're here to help you build a strong marketing foundation from which you'll be prepared to continually execute fresh marketing tactics with easy-to-use tools.

Guerrilla Marketing helps you turn complicated marketing into the simple and delightful task of knowing, attracting, and connecting with your customers. We're here for, and excited about, your success.

endnotes

Preface
Levinson, J. C. (2007). *Guerrilla Marketing*, 4th Edition. In J. C. Levinson, Guerrilla Marketing, 4th Edition. Houghton Mifflin Harcourt.

Introduction
Levinson, J. C. (2007). *Guerrilla Marketing*, 4th Edition. In J. C. Levinson, Guerrilla Marketing, 4th Edition. Houghton Mifflin Harcourt.

1.13
Heshmat Ph.D., S. (2021, September 2). "10 Factors That Influence Your Purchase Decisions." Retrieved from PsychologyToday.com: https://www.psychologytoday.com/us/blog/science-choice/201712/10-factors-influence-your-purchase-decisions

Levinson, J. C. (2007). *Guerrilla Marketing*, 4th Edition. In J. C. Levinson, Guerrilla Marketing, 4th Edition. Houghton Mifflin Harcourt.

Mahoney, M. (2021, September 2). "The Subconscious Mind of the Consumer (And How To Reach It)." Retrieved from HBSwk.hbs.edu: https://hbswk.hbs.edu/item/the-subconscious-mind-of-the-consumer-and-how-to-reach-it

Parvez, H. (2021, September 2). "8 Characteristics of the Subconscious Mind." Retrieved from PsychMechanics.com: https://www.psychmechanics.com/characteristics-of-subconscious-mind/

1.16
HubSpot. (2021, October 25). "Not Another State of Marketing Report 2021." Retrieved from HubSpot.com: https://www.hubspot.com/state-of-marketing

2.16
Facebook.com/business. (2021, August 23). "Create an A/B Test With Common Scenarios." Retrieved from Facebook.com/business: https://www.facebook.com/business/help/848155685601322

Kearns, S. (2021, August 23). "How to Create an A/B Testing Strategy for Your LinkedIn Ads." Retrieved from Business.Linkedin.com/marketing-solutions/blog/linkedin-sponsored-content: https://business.linkedin.com/marketing-solutions/blog/linkedin-sponsored-content/2017/how-to-create-an-a-b-testing-strategy-for-your-linkedin-ads

Support.Google.com/google-ads. (2021, August 23). "About ad variations." Retrieved from Support.Google.com/google-ads: https://support.google.com/google-ads/answer/7438541?hl=en&ref_topic=3119078

Support.Google.com/google-ads. (2021, August 23). "Apply a campaign experiment." Retrieved from Support.Google.com/google-ads : https://support.google.com/google-ads/answer/7457118?hl=en&ref_topic=6319800

SurveyMonkey.com. (2021, August 20). Ad Testing. Retrieved from SurveyMonkey.com: https://www.surveymonkey.com/mp/ad-testing/

2.17

Raguin, J. (2021, September 18). "Where Marketing Attribution Falls Short—and How to Get it Right." Retrieved from Blog.Marketo.com: https://blog.marketo.com/2019/02/where-marketing-attribution-falls-short-and-how-to-get-it-right.html

2.19

ClearChannelOutdoor.com. (2021, October 27). Digital Billboards. Retrieved from ClearChannelOutdoor.com: https://clearchanneloutdoor.com/products/digital-billboards/

Rollingadz.com. (2021, October 27). Home. Retrieved from Rollingadz.com: https://rollingadz.com/

3.30

Salesforce.com. (2021, September 30). "Small and Medium Business Trends Report." Retrieved from Salesforce.com: https://www.salesforce.com/resources/research-reports/smb-trends/?d=cta-header-1

4.59

Business.Linkedin.com. (2021, October 20). "Measure your sales success with Social Selling Index." Retrieved from Business.Linkedin.com: https://business.linkedin.com/sales-solutions/social-selling/the-social-selling-index-ssi

4.60

Ecwid.com/facebook-commerce. (2021, October 20). Start your Facebook Store in minutes. Retrieved from Ecwid.com/facebook-commerce: https://www.ecwid.com/facebook-commerce

Lipsman, A. (2021, October 20). "Social Commerce 2021." Retrieved from eMarketer.com: https://www.emarketer.com/content/social-commerce-2021

Newsroom.pinterest.com. (2021, October 20). "Pinterest launches Shopify partnership." Retrieved from Newsroom.pinterest.com: https://newsroom.pinterest.com/en/post/pinterest-launches-shopify-app-for-easy-merchant-access-to-catalogs

News.Shopify.com. (2021, October 20)." Scaling social commerce: Shopify introduces new in-app shopping experiences on TikTok." Retrieved from News.Shopify.com: https://news.shopify.com/scaling-social-commerce-shopify-introduces-new-in-app-shopping-experiences-on-tiktok

4.62

Support.Google.com. (2021, October 21). About Attribution. Retrieved from Support.Google.com: https://support.google.com/analytics/answer/9397590?hl=en#zippy=%2Cin-this-article

4.63

Business.Linkedin.com. (2021, October 24). Marketing Solutions. Retrieved from Business.Linkedin.com: https://business.linkedin.com/marketing-solutions

Business.Linkedin.com. (2021, October 20). "Measure your sales success with Social Selling Index." Retrieved from Business.Linkedin.com: https://business.linkedin.com/sales-solutions/social-selling/the-social-selling-index-ssi

4.65

Accenture.com. (2021, October 21). "What is artificial intelligence?" Retrieved from Accenture.com: https://www.accenture.com/us-en/insights/artificial-intelligence-summary-index

Brown, S. (2021, November 1). "Machine learning, explained." Retrieved from mitsloan.mit.edu: https://mitsloan.mit.edu/ideas-made-to-matter/machine-learning-explained

HubSpot. (2021, October 25). "Not Another State of Marketing Report 2021." Retrieved from HubSpot.com: https://www.hubspot.com/state-of-marketing

4.66
OpenAI.com. (2021, October 22). About. Retrieved from OpenAI.com: https://openai.com/about/

4.67
Hope, F. (2021, October 22). "'Embrace the AI Revolution:' The Growing Role of AI in Audio Workflows." Retrieved from ProsoundNetwork.com: https://www.prosoundnetwork.com/international/ai-audio-workflows

Handley, L. (2021, October 22). "The 'world's first' A.I. news anchor has gone live in China." Retrieved from CNBC.com: https://www.cnbc.com/2018/11/09/the-worlds-first-ai-news-anchor-has-gone-live-in-china.html

4.68
Strategus.com. (2021, November 2). "The All-In-One Guide To Programmatic Ad Buying." Retrieved from Strategus.com: https://www.strategus.com/blog/the-all-in-one-guide-to-programmatic-ad-buying

4.69
Magenta.tensorflow.org. (2021, October 22). Studio. Retrieved from Magenta.tensorflow.org: https://magenta.tensorflow.org/studio

4.73
Support.Google.com. (2021, September 2). About responsive search ads. Retrieved from Support.Google.com: https://support.google.com/google-ads/answer/7684791

5.19
New York Times Customer Insight Group. (2011). *The Psychology of Sharing: Why Do People Share Online?* New York: New York Times Customer Insight Group.

Ransaw, R. (2021, August 24). "The Psychology Behind Why We Share on Social Media." Retrieved from Shutterstock.com: https://www.shutterstock.com/blog/the-psychology-behind-why-we-share-on-social-media

5.20
Accenture.com. (2021, November 5). Making It Personal. Retrieved from Accenture.com: https://www.accenture.com/_acnmedia/PDF-77/Accenture-Pulse-Survey.pdf

5.22
Lebow, S. (2021, November 4). "US adults find print and TV ads more trustworthy than social media ads." Retrieved from eMarketer.com: https://www.emarketer.com/content/us-adults-find-traditional-media-advertising-most-trustworthy

6.23
Frontiersin.org. (2021, October 12). "A Model for Basic Emotions Using Observations of Behavior in Drosophila." Retrieved from Frontiersin.org: https://www.frontiersin.org/articles/10.3389/fpsyg.2019.00781/full

Murray, Ph.D., P. N. (2021, October 12). "How Emotions Influence What We Buy." Retrieved from PsychologyToday.com: https://www.psychologytoday.com/us/blog/inside-the-consumer-mind/201302/how-emotions-influence-what-we-buy

6.24
Murray, Ph.D., P. N. (2021, October 12). "How Emotions Influence What We Buy." Retrieved from PsychologyToday.com: https://www.psychologytoday.com/us/blog/inside-the-consumer-mind/201302/how-emotions-influence-what-we-buy

6.25
McLeod, D. (2021, October 12). "Maslow's Hierarchy of Needs." Retrieved from SimplyPsychology.org: https://www.simplypsychology.org/maslow.html

6.26
CampaignMonitor.com. (2021, October 13). "Should You Personalize Your Subject Lines?" Retrieved from CampaignMonitor.com: https://www.campaignmonitor.com/resources/knowledge-base/should-you-personalize-your-subject-lines/

6.29
Stefanski, R. (2021, October 24). "Psychology and Marketing: 8 Concepts to Understand." Retrieved from Pathmatics.com: https://www.pathmatics.com/blog/8-psychological-concepts-to-understand-for-better-marketing

6.30
Epsilon.com. (2021, October 24). New Epsilon research indicates 80% of consumers are more likely to make a purchase when brands offer personalized experiences. Retrieved from Epsilon.com: https://www.epsilon.com/us/about-us/pressroom/new-epsilon-research-indicates-80-of-consumers-are-more-likely-to-make-a-purchase-when-brands-offer-personalized-experiences

7.24
Salesforce.com. (2021, October 12). "What Are Customer Expectations, and How Have They Changed?" Retrieved from Salesforce.com: https://www.salesforce.com/resources/articles/customer-expectations

7.27
Todorov, G. (2021, October 13). "Word of Mouth Marketing: 49 Statistics to Help You Boost Your Bottom Line." Retrieved from Semrush.com/blog: https://www.semrush.com/blog/word-of-mouth-stats/

7.28
BestBuy.com. (2021, October 13). Electronics, Appliances and Fitness Equipment Recycling at Best Buy. Retrieved from BestBuy.com: https://www.bestbuy.com/site/services/recycling/pcmcat149900050025.c?id=pcmcat149900050025

Ikea.com. (2021, October 13). IKEA US helps customers prolong the life of their furniture with launch of Buy Back & Resell service. Retrieved from

Ikea.com: https://www.ikea.com/us/en/newsroom/corporate-news/ikea-us-helps-customers-prolong-the-life-of-their-furniture-with-launch-of-buy-back-and-resell-service-puba9b1f107

Nuuly.com. (2021, October 13). Our Story. Retrieved from Nuuly.com: https://www.nuuly.com/rent/our-story

7.29

Constantino, T. (2021, October 17). "5 Ways NFTs Can Kickstart Your Small Business." Retrieved from Inc.com: https://www.inc.com/tor-constantino/5-ways-nfts-can-kickstart-your-small-business.html

IBM.com. (2021, October 17). Smart Contracts. Retrieved from IBM.com: https://www.ibm.com/topics/smart-contracts

IBM.com. (2021, October 16). What Is Blockchain. Retrieved from IBM.com: https://www.ibm.com/topics/what-is-blockchain

Legalzoom.com. (2021, October 16). "31 Blockchain Ideas to Capitalize on in 2021." Retrieved from Legalzoom.com: https://www.legalzoom.com/articles/31-blockchain-business-ideas-to-capitalize-on-in-2021

8.45

Shutterstock.com/blog. (2021, September 4). "Use Color Meaning to Strengthen Your Brand and Increase Sales." Retrieved from Shutterstock.com/blog: https://www.shutterstock.com/blog/color-meaning-symbolism-branding

Ciotti, G. (2021, September 6). "Color Psychology: How Colors Influence the Mind." Retrieved from PsychologyToday.com: https://www.psychologytoday.com/us/blog/habits-not-hacks/201408/color-psychology-how-colors-influence-the-mind

8.47

HubSpot. (2021, October 25). "Not Another State of Marketing Report 2021." Retrieved from HubSpot.com: https://www.hubspot.com/state-of-marketing

8.49

Merriam-Webster.com. (2021, October 10). Perception. Retrieved from Merriam-Webster.com: https://www.merriam-webster.com/dictionary/perception

Ruhl, C. (2021, October 11). "What Is Cognitive Bias?" Retrieved from SimplyPsychology.org: https://www.simplypsychology.org/cognitive-bias.html

TheGeneral.com. (2021, October 10). The General Insurance Brand. Retrieved from TheGeneral.com: https://www.thegeneral.com/blog/the-general-insurance-brand/

8.51

HubSpot. (2021, October 25). "Not Another State of Marketing Report 2021." Retrieved from HubSpot.com: https://www.hubspot.com/state-of-marketing

Shopify Plus. (2021, October 9). "The Global Ecommerce Playbook." Retrieved from Enterprise.Plus.Shopify.com: https://enterprise.plus.shopify.com/rs/932-KRM-548/images/global-ecommerce-guide.pdf

8.52

Shipfusion.com. (2021, October 10). Shipfusion.com. Retrieved from Shipfusion.com: https://www.shipfusion.com/

8.54

Instapage.com . (2021, October 12). Personalization Statistics. Retrieved from Instapage.com : https://instapage.com/blog/personalization-statistics

MailChimp.com. (2021, October 12). "Send the right campaigns to the right people." Retrieved from MailChimp.com: https://mailchimp.com/features/segmentation

Salesforce.com. (2021, October 12). "What Are Customer Expectations, and How Have They Changed?" Retrieved from Salesforce.com: https://www.salesforce.com/resources/articles/customer-expectations

8.55

Marketo.com. (2021, October 12). "The Definitive Guide to Lead Scoring." Retrieved from Marketo.com: https://www.marketo.com/definitive-guides/lead-scoring/

8.56

Holliday, M. (2021, October 28). "How Much of Sales or Gross Revenue Should go Toward my Small Business Payroll?" Retrieved from Netsuite.

com: https://www.netsuite.com/portal/resource/articles/financial-management/small-business-payroll-percentage.shtml

Weltman, B. (2021, October 28). "How Much Does an Employee Cost You?" Retrieved from SBA.gov: https://www.sba.gov/blog/how-much-does-employee-cost-you

RitzCarlton.com. (2021, November 7). Gold Standards. Retrieved from Ritz-Carlton.com: https://www.ritzcarlton.com/en/about/gold-standards

Section IX

Levinson, J. C. (2007). *Guerrilla Marketing*, 4th Edition. In J. C. Levinson, Guerrilla Marketing, 4th Edition. Houghton Mifflin Harcourt.

9.28

AACU.org. (2021, September 16). "Creative Thinking VALUE Rubric." Retrieved from AACU.org: https://www.aacu.org/value/rubrics/creative-thinking

American Psychological Association. (2021, September 16). APA Dictionary of Psychology. Retrieved from Dictionary.apa.org: https://dictionary.apa.org/confirmation-bias

Bouygues, H. L. (2021, September 16). "3 Simple Habits to Improve Your Critical Thinking." Retrieved from HBR.org: https://hbr.org/2019/05/3-simple-habits-to-improve-your-critical-thinking

Chick, N. (2021, September 16). "Metacognition." Retrieved from cft.Vanderbilt.edu: https://cft.vanderbilt.edu/guides-sub-pages/metacognition/

Indeed Editorial Team. (2021, September 16). "10 Essential Critical Thinking Skills (And How to Improve Them)." Retrieved from Indeed.com: https://www.indeed.com/career-advice/career-development/critical-thinking-skills

Indeed Editorial Team. (2021, September 16). "Convergent Thinking: Definition, Principles and Examples." Retrieved from Indeed.com: https://www.indeed.com/career-advice/career-development/convergent-thinking

Inspire Education. (2021, May 24). "The Seven Learning Styles – How do you learn?" Retrieved from InspireEducation.net: https://www.inspireeducation.net.au/blog/the-seven-learning-styles/

The Foundation for Critical Thinking. (2021, September 16). Our Concept and Definition of Critical Thinking. Retrieved from CriticalThinking.org:

https://www.criticalthinking.org/pages/our-conception-of-critical-thinking/411

9.29
Deutschendorf, H. (2021, September 16). "7 Key Habits For Building Better Relationships." Retrieved from FastCompany.com: https://www.fastcompany.com/3041774/7-key-habits-for-building-better-relationships

9.32
Ruhl, C. (2021, October 11). "What Is Cognitive Bias?" Retrieved from SimplyPsychology.org: https://www.simplypsychology.org/cognitive-bias.html

Guerrilla Marketing Case Study 9
Starbucks.com. (2021, October 25). About Us. Retrieved from Starbucks.com: https://www.starbucks.com/about-us/

Stories.Starbucks.com. (2021, October 25). "Starbucks Coffee Masters Share Passion for Coffee." Retrieved from Stories.Starbucks.com: https://stories.starbucks.com/stories/2015/starbucks-coffee-masters-share-passion-for-coffee/

Guerrilla Marketing Case Study 10
Urbn.com. (2021, October 13). Our Brands. Retrieved from Urbn.com: https://www.urbn.com/our-brands/urban-outfitters

Urbn.com. (2021, October 13). Our History. Retrieved from Urbn.com: https://www.urbn.com/who-we-are/history

Guerrilla Marketing Case Study 11
Forbes, S. (2021, October 25). "Our First 100 Years." Retrieved from Forbes.com: https://www.forbes.com/sites/steveforbes/2017/09/19/our-first-100-years

HubSpot. (2021, October 25). "Not Another State of Marketing Report 2021." Retrieved from HubSpot.com: https://www.hubspot.com/state-of-marketing

Guerrilla Marketing Case Study 12

TommyBahama.com. (2021, November 2). Company Information. Retrieved from TommyBahama.com: https://www.tommybahama.com/guest-services/company-information

TommyBahama.com. (2021, November 2). Sustainability. Retrieved from TommyBahama.com: https://www.tommybahama.com/en/about/sustainability/operations

Definitions

American Psychological Association. (2021, September 16). APA Dictionary of Psychology. Retrieved from Dictionary.apa.org: https://dictionary.apa.org/confirmation-bias

Brown, S. (2021, November 1). "Machine learning, explained." Retrieved from mitsloan.mit.edu: https://mitsloan.mit.edu/ideas-made-to-matter/machine-learning-explained

Constantino, T. (2021, October 17). "5 Ways NFTs Can Kickstart Your Small Business." Retrieved from Inc.com: https://www.inc.com/tor-constantino/5-ways-nfts-can-kickstart-your-small-business.html

Dictionary.apa.org. (2020, April 30). APA Dictionary of Psychology. Retrieved from Dictionary.apa.org: https://dictionary.apa.org/psychographics

Dictionary.com. (2020, April 30). Demographics. Retrieved from Dictionary.com: https://www.dictionary.com/browse/demographics

Falkner, C. (2020, April 04). "Linear vs. Advanced TV: The Current State of Television Advertising." Retrieved from www.cuebiq.com: https://www.cuebiq.com/resource-center/resources/linear-vs-advanced-tv/

Forsey, C. (2021, July 7). "The Complete Guide to Firmographic Data." Retrieved from www.Blog.HubSpot.com: https://blog.hubspot.com/marketing/firmographics

Heshmat Ph.D., S. (2021, September 2). "10 Factors That Influence Your Purchase Decisions." Retrieved from PsychologyToday.com: https://www.psychologytoday.com/us/blog/science-choice/201712/10-factors-influence-your-purchase-decisions

IBM.com. (2021, November 3). Deep Learning. Retrieved from IBM.com: https://www.ibm.com/cloud/learn/deep-learning

IBM.com. (2021, November 3). Neural Networks. Retrieved from IBM.com: https://www.ibm.com/cloud/learn/neural-networks?mhsrc=ibm-search_a&mhq=define%20neural%20network

IBM.com. (2021, October 16). What Is Blockchain. Retrieved from IBM.com: https://www.ibm.com/topics/what-is-blockchain

Levinson, J. C. (2007). Guerrilla Marketing, 4th Edition. In J. C. Levinson, Guerrilla Marketing, 4th Edition. Houghton Mifflin Harcourt.

Maguire, F. (2021, August 6). "Reaching Consumers With Video: The Interruptibility Myth." Retrieved from adage.com: https://adage.com/article/sharethrough/reaching-consumers-video-interruptibility-myth/313945

Ruhl, C. (2021, October 11). "What Is Cognitive Bias?" Retrieved from SimplyPsychology.org: https://www.simplypsychology.org/cognitive-bias.html

Strategus.com. (2021, November 2). "The All-In-One Guide To Programmatic Ad Buying." Retrieved from Strategus.com: https://www.strategus.com/blog/the-all-in-one-guide-to-programmatic-ad-buying

StudioBinder.com. (2021, August 20). "What is Chroma Key Technology." Retrieved from StudioBinder.com: https://www.studiobinder.com/blog/what-is-chroma-key-green-screen/

VWO.com. (2021, June 7). Push Notifications. Retrieved from VWO.com: https://vwo.com/push-notifications/

Back Cover

James, Geoffrey. (2021, May 4). "Top 10 Influential Business Books of All Time." Retrieved from Inc.com: https://www.inc.com/geoffrey-james/top-10-influential-business-books-of-all-time.html

INDEX

360-degree/360 degrees, xiii, xvii, xxi, 3, 19, 21, 113, 148, 172, 202
80/20 Rule, 31, 109, 254, 261
Advanced TV, 8, 254, 256
Advertising keys to success, 27, 28, 31, 33, 36, 57, 123
Advertorials, 103-104
Affiliate, 43, 46-47, 51, 92, 98, 103, 128, 135, 150, 152, 174, 178, 191, 193, 197, 204-205, 244, 259, 262, 264, 265, 270
Agencies, 27, 230, 254
Agile, 83, 184, 222, 230, 255
AI (Artificial intelligence), 67, 74-76, 77-79, 79-80, 80-81, 82, 90, 102, 157-160, 178, 226, 227, 229, 233, 238, 242, 243, 247, 248, 261, 265, 266, 267
AI-generated, 79-80
AI-generated video, 79
Aligned, 19-20, 21-23, 32, 38, 48, 54, 72, 105, 162, 177, 214, 223
Alignment, 21-23, 54, 122
Amazement, 110, 145, 255
Analysis, 9, 27, 31-34, 35, 60, 102, 152, 159, 202, 225, 230, 242, 268
Analytics, 35, 74, 152, 222, 225, 230, 231, 232, 233, 234, 236, 237, 238, 240, 242, 245, 246, 247
Apathy, 12, 22, 122-123, 149, 255

Appeal to the senses, 14, 102, 110, 113, 147, 155-157, 205-206, 208-209, 217-218
Appealing to emotions, 93, 102, 109-112, 113, 129-130, 172
AR (Augmented reality), 49-50, 178, 255
Art and science of marketing, 109
Artificial Intelligence (AI), 67, 74-76, 77-79, 79-80, 80-81, 82, 90, 102, 157-160, 178, 226, 227, 229, 233, 238, 242, 243, 247, 248, 261, 265, 266, 267
Assessment(s), 58-59, 98, 265
Attention to detail, 184, 185
Attribution, 30-34, 35, 68-70, 164, 243, 246, 255
Augmented reality (AR), 49-50, 178, 255
Authenticity, xiv, 92, 139, 148, 184, 195, 267, 279
Automation, 16, 35, 57, 59-60, 66-67, 78, 79, 99, 145, 158-159, 173, 175, 178, 199, 227, 230, 231, 240, 242, 260, 262, 266
Awareness, 10-11, 19-20, 29, 45, 56, 62-63, 110, 112, 122, 144-145, 146, 187, 255, 256, 264, 266, 273
B2B, 12, 32, 52, 70-73, 81, 120, 130, 150-151, 166, 173, 192, 255, 261, 262, 263, 273
Balance, 160-161, 209, 212, 247

Bartering, 27, 255, 269
Be the solution, 104, 109, 147, 150, 190
Benefits and competitive advantages, 77, 128
Better Business Bureau (BBB), 52, 235, 249, 256
Bias/biases, 37, 75, 159, 162, 186-187, 190, 196, 257, 258
Blockchain, 137-139, 178, 256, 267
Body language, 119, 122
Bot, 56, 76, 81, 98, 115, 119-120, 158-159, 198, 247, 266
Bottleneck, 157, 160, 200
Brand, 10-11, 19-20, 29-30, 33, 47, 56-57, 62-63, 65, 74, 95-97, 109-110, 112-113, 114, 122, 125, 135, 137, 145, 146, 155, 162, 171, 173, 179, 196, 202, 204-205, 207-210, 213-215, 216-218, 230, 232, 241, 248, 254, 256, 262, 264, 266, 268, 271, 273, 274
Brand advantage, 29
Brand awareness, 10-11, 19-20, 29, 56, 62-63, 110, 112, 122, 146, 256, 264, 266, 273
Brand favorability, 29, 262
Brand recognition, 10-11, 19-20, 29, 57, 63, 110, 112, 122, 146, 256, 264, 266, 273
Broadcasting, 8, 73, 93, 103, 146, 222, 256
Browsing behavior, 98
Browsing intent, 100
Building relationships, 45, 93, 95-96, 149, 185

Business personality, 74, 112-113
Buying behavior, 98, 173
Buying language, 85, 256, 268
Buzz and shares, 87, 97, 128, 140
By-product, 92, 103, 136, 175, 190-191, 193, 205-206, 208, 210, 217-218
Call to action (CTA), 3, 8-9, 10, 19, 29, 39-40, 57, 77, 110, 123, 140, 145, 146, 164, 185, 256, 259, 266, 274
CAN-SPAM, 89
Cart abandonment, 100, 168
Cash back/point shopping portal sites, 43
CCPA, 89
Challenges, 55, 67, 105, 140, 161, 165, 166, 168, 170, 194, 214
Chatbot(s), 81, 119, 247
Chroma key, 257
Circular process, 7, 9
Click-through attribution (CTA), 69
Click-through rate (CTR), 70, 173, 230, 257
Clone, 115, 149, 152, 260
Clubhouse, 43, 245
CLV (Customer lifetime value), 9, 32, 35, 149-152, 163, 171, 173, 185, 260, 264
Cognitive biases, 162, 196, 257
Collaborate/collaborating/collaboration/collaborative, 16, 43-44, 46, 47, 51, 64, 92, 98, 103, 124, 128, 135, 150, 159, 166-167, 169, 178, 188, 191, 193, 197, 199, 204-205, 207-208, 210, 213-214, 216-218,

224, 225, 226, 227, 228, 229, 231, 241, 248, 257, 269, 276

Color, 4, 14, 29, 42, 50, 84, 99, 101, 102, 110, 124, 144-145, 147, 153-155, 164, 171, 173, 204-205, 208-209, 217-218, 255, 257

Color palette, 144-145, 154-155, 171, 205, 257

Commitment, 176, 188, 206, 217-218, 257

Community-minded, 150-151, 161, 184

Compel/compelled/compelling, xi, xiii, xvi, xix, xx, 3, 8, 10-11, 14, 18, 19, 26, 27, 29, 33, 39-40, 42, 44-45, 47-48, 49, 52, 54, 57-58, 60, 61, 63, 71, 72, 76, 77, 84-87, 93, 98, 100, 101, 102-103, 104, 109, 122, 128, 133, 144, 147-148, 151, 156-157, 159, 172, 174, 179, 185, 202, 206, 209-211, 215, 236, 242, 243, 244, 255, 256, 257, 262, 263, 265, 266, 270, 273, 274, 280

Compel your prospects, 3, 10, 19, 42, 86, 144, 185, 256, 274

Competitive advantage(s), xx, 2, 42, 77, 128, 144, 193, 257, 273

Complacency, 258

Compliment, 116, 266

Complimentary, 58, 121, 257, 260

Confirmation bias, 187, 258

Connections and interacting, 258

Conscious/consciously, 12, 17, 38, 84, 112, 121, 182, 187, 273

Consistency, familiarity, and/or trust, xiv, xvii-xviii, xx-xxi, 3-4, 6, 11, 12, 22, 38, 51, 54, 66, 74, 84-90, 92, 96, 97, 103-104, 113, 134, 135, 144-145, 147-148, 153, 162, 167, 171, 176, 182, 184, 185, 192, 196, 202, 204, 205, 208-209, 211, 213-215, 217-218, 222, 227, 228, 229, 231, 233, 235, 239, 249, 256, 258, 259, 265, 270, 273, 279

Consumer behavior, 7, 12, 36, 77, 85, 109, 112, 115, 120, 122-123, 193

Consumer intentions, 7, 124-125

Consumer mindset, 7, 14, 36, 77, 101, 109, 112, 115, 120, 161, 196

Consumer packaged goods (CPG), 258, 273

Convenience, 123, 133, 134, 140, 145, 159, 165, 171, 174, 178, 204-205, 208, 210, 213-214, 237, 248, 258, 260

Convergent thinking, 189-190

Conversation preferences, 118

Conversation starter, 115-118

Conversation style, 118

Conversations, 64, 98, 115, 117, 118-120, 227, 241, 242

Conversion rate optimization (CRO), 35, 55, 62, 87, 259, 264

Conversions, 230, 239, 241, 259, 267, 272

Co-op funds, 259

Cookie-based attribution, 69

Copy generating platforms, 78

Cost-per-action (CPA), 34, 259, 264

Cost-per-click (CPC), 34, 230, 259, 264, 268

Cost-per-lead (CPL), 34, 259, 264

Cost-per-thousand (CPM), 34, 72, 230, 259, 264
Cost-per-view (CPV), 34, 259, 264
Coupons and coupon sites, 30, 43, 45, 232, 259
Courses, 15, 55, 102, 104, 198, 223, 250, 251
CPA (Cost-per-action), 34, 259, 264
CPC (Cost-per-click), 34, 230, 259, 264, 268
CPG (Consumer packaged goods), 258, 273
CPL (Cost-per-lead), 34, 259, 264
CPM (Cost-per-thousand), 34, 72, 230, 259, 264
CPV (Cost-per-view), 34, 259, 264
Creative thinking, 189
Creativity, xiv, xviii-xix, xxi, 2, 5, 10, 12, 27, 28, 38-39, 42, 43, 49, 63, 79, 80, 82, 101-102, 105, 108, 128, 133, 137, 144, 147, 157, 158, 178, 187, 189-190, 191, 202, 206, 204, 207-211, 213-214, 217-218, 225, 226, 233, 243, 244, 246, 263, 278
Credibility, 29, 45, 58, 72, 101, 104, 108, 145, 150, 171, 178, 213-214, 235, 259, 269
Critical thinking, 188-189
CRM (Customer relationship management), 8, 16, 32, 35, 57, 59, 60, 66-68, 79-80, 99, 112, 152, 154, 155, 164, 173, 175, 226, 230, 231, 233, 239, 241, 260
CRO (Conversion rate optimization), 35, 55, 62, 87, 259, 264
Cross-Promotion, 43-44, 146

Cross-Selling, 124, 132, 145, 159, 171, 204, 206, 208-209, 217-218, 260
Crowdfunding, 129, 138-139
Crowdsourcing, 105
Cryptocurrency, 137-138, 178
CTA (Call to action), 3, 8-9, 10, 19, 29, 39-40, 57, 77, 110, 123, 140, 145, 146, 164, 185, 256, 259, 266, 274
CTA (Click-through attribution), 69
CTR (Click-through rate), 70, 230, 257
Curious/curiosity, 184, 185, 190, 192, 193, 223, 267, 280
Customer avatar, 162
Customer lifetime value (CLV or LTV), 9, 32, 35, 149-152, 163, 171, 173, 185, 260, 264
Customer loyalty, 8, 86, 110, 129, 130, 131, 151, 165, 172, 204-205
Customer Relationship Management (CRM), 8, 16, 32, 35, 57, 59, 60, 66-68, 79-80, 99, 112, 152, 154, 155, 164, 173, 175, 226, 230, 231, 233, 239, 241, 260
Customers come first, 199-200
Cybersecurity, 15, 54, 70, 100, 249
Cycling, 136-137, 175, 208, 210
Data appending, 98-99, 173-174, 175, 260
Data security, 100
Deep learning, 81, 243, 244, 247, 261, 267
Delegate, 109, 254, 261

Delighted customers, 8, 22-23, 109, 165
Demographic(s), 7-9, 14, 36, 112, 149, 152, 164, 173, 193, 260, 261, 268, 270, 273
Demonstrations, 45, 47, 50, 52, 59, 80, 92, 130, 135, 150-151, 198
Detail(s), xix, 2, 15-16, 18-19, 39, 48, 60, 74, 81, 131, 144, 153, 155, 182-184, 185, 197, 208, 213, 216-217, 235, 263
Digital Account-Based Marketing, 36, 56, 70, 261
Directories/Directory, 42, 73, 235, 261
Directory and search engine listings, 42, 55, 235, 261
Discovery ads, 56, 85-87, 154, 261
Display advertising, 261
Display, search, and native advertising, 55, 72, 86
Disruption, 16, 54, 75, 178-179, 190
Domain name, 100, 242, 261
DOOH, 37-40, 48, 51, 81
Dots per inch (DPI), 261, 268
Ebook(s), 10, 19, 55, 57, 93, 103, 110, 146, 150, 175, 185, 256, 262, 265, 274
Effective marketing, 42, 114
Effectiveness of color, 154
Efficiency, 16, 74, 118, 145, 157, 171, 198-199, 217, 223, 262, 271
Email autoresponder platforms, 35, 55, 57, 59, 60, 66, 262
Email deliverability, 56, 237, 262
Email preferences, 89

Email split testing, 27, 33, 55, 57, 62, 123
Emotional, 12-13, 22, 110-111, 156-157, 268, 271, 272
Emotions, 12, 14, 20, 93, 102, 109-112, 113, 129-130, 172, 192
Employee promise, 176
Energy, xvi, xx-xxi, 6, 18-19, 47, 108, 121-122, 128, 144, 183, 185-186, 193, 195, 202, 217, 258, 263, 275-276, 282
Engagement, 19, 39, 57, 72, 73-74, 77, 82, 119, 166, 230, 232, 242, 245, 261, 262, 272
Engaging, 8, 42, 46, 49-51, 63, 74, 85, 92, 94-95, 99, 104, 108, 113, 115, 117, 136-137, 144, 149, 158, 198, 206, 207, 209, 214, 238, 246, 255, 256, 257, 260, 262, 263, 273, 274
ERP platforms, 99
Ethical bribes, 94, 262
Evaluate(s), 54, 94, 106, 139, 160, 162, 197, 199, 212, 243
Evaluating your business, 121
Events, conferences, and trade shows, 43, 49, 51
Evergreen content, 262
Exclusive experiences, 8, 110, 129-131, 134, 140, 147, 172, 213-214
Experiential marketing, 48-49, 140, 147, 178
Expertise, 29, 45, 52, 92, 101-102, 104, 108, 124, 128, 138, 150, 158, 161, 165, 169, 174, 178, 188-189, 199, 213-214, 226, 238, 243, 254

Index | 301

Explicit scoring, 175
Exterior signage, 42, 44, 49
Facebook, 29, 62, 65, 78, 83, 150, 230, 233, 235, 236, 241, 245, 246, 267
Familiarity, xiv, xx-xxi, 3-4, 11, 38, 54, 92, 144-145, 231, 258, 265, 270, 279
Feedback loop, 76, 78
Firmographic(s), 36, 173, 262
First touch, 33, 68-70
Five-star, 22, 48, 52, 109, 113, 117, 152, 171, 182
Focus groups, 27-28, 269
Focused, xvii-xviii, 3, 8, 10, 20, 26, 28, 30, 36, 40, 44, 51, 63, 71-72, 105, 114, 149, 150, 152, 160, 163, 171, 175, 183, 185, 186, 194-195, 209, 212-213, 218, 227, 240, 250, 255, 263, 266, 270, 276
Focused on success, 194-195
Follow-up, 4, 21, 59-60, 99, 145, 148, 149, 158, 240, 247, 262
Fonts, xx, 4, 144-145, 154-155, 171, 232
Free companion course, xv, xxi, 5, 277
Free trial(s), 52, 123, 129, 133-134, 164, 265
Friendly picketers, xix, 262
FTC, 15, 249
Fulfillment, 96, 157, 159, 168-170, 197
Fulfillment service, 169-170
Funnel(s), 33, 54, 56-60, 66, 67, 77, 83, 164, 236, 266

Fusion/Affiliate Marketing, 43, 46-47, 51, 92, 98, 103, 128, 135, 150, 152, 174, 178, 191, 193, 197, 204-205, 259, 262, 264, 265
GDPR, 89
Geofencing, 46, 55, 70, 87, 263
Geographic, 7-9, 46, 268
Getting to the "why", 137, 195
Gift/Gifted, 98, 119, 123, 128, 151-152, 206, 246, 270, 273
Gimmick(s), xx, 4
Giveaway(s) and/or sample/sampling, xix, 36, 39, 46, 47-48, 49, 51, 52, 55, 58, 105, 123, 129, 133, 140, 192, 238, 262, 273
Global ecommerce, 165
gMarketing.com/Club, xv, xxi, 5, 40, 222, 229, 236, 248-249, 263, 276, 278-279
Google, 18, 29, 33, 35, 55, 62, 69, 83, 85-87, 89-90, 152, 159, 223, 224, 225, 226, 231, 235, 236, 237, 238, 244, 255, 261, 263, 271
Google Ads, 33, 90
Google Alerts, 236
Google Analytics, 35, 152, 236, 237
Google Maps, 18, 263, 271
Google My Business/Google Business Profile, 18, 55, 87, 235, 237, 263
Guerrilla Company Attitudes, 5, 19, 23, 54, 63, 72, 105, 112-113, 122, 148, 177, 181-184, 185, 191, 197
Guerrilla Company Attributes, 5, 19, 23, 42, 54, 72, 105, 112-113, 143-145, 177, 191, 197

Guerrilla Creative and Advertising strategy, xiv, xxi, 3-6, 26, 42, 218-219, 263, 279

Guerrilla Creativity, xiv, xix, xxi, 2, 5, 10, 42, 43, 49, 63, 105, 133, 144, 157, 178, 189-190, 204, 206, 208-211, 213-214, 217-218, 263, 278

Guerrilla E-Media Marketing, 5, 23, 26, 53-56, 68, 135, 174

Guerrilla Human-Media Marketing, 5, 23, 107-109

Guerrilla Info-Media Marketing, 5, 8, 23, 91-93, 135

Guerrilla Marketing calendar, xxi, 4-6, 263

Guerrilla Marketing foundation, xv, xvii, 2, 4, 6, 277

Guerrilla Marketing plan, xiv, xxi, 3-6, 42, 128, 205, 208, 213, 217-218, 263, 279

Guerrilla Marketing ten-word profit challenge, xxi, 3, 6

Guerrilla Maximedia Marketing, 5, 7, 23, 25-27, 68

Guerrilla Minimedia Marketing, 5, 7, 23, 41-43

Guerrilla Non-Media Marketing, 5, 23, 127-129

Hard sell, 20, 63-64, 263, 272

Hierarchy of needs, 114

High definition, 264

High energy, 18, 183, 186, 193, 195

Honest interest in people, 63, 183, 190, 192, 205-206, 270

Hot lead(s), 175, 264, 265, 270

Ideal customers, 9, 31-33, 36, 120, 135-136, 149, 152, 162-165, 172, 175, 176-178, 196

Ideal employees, 172, 176-178

Identity, 15, 94-95, 145, 171, 202, 204-205, 208-210, 213-214, 217, 242, 264, 269

Images, 10-11, 12-13, 20, 29, 38-40, 56, 81, 82, 102, 104, 105, 147, 159, 164, 167, 189, 232, 234, 242, 243, 246, 248, 261, 267, 268, 272, 273, 274

Imagination, xvi, 185, 202, 216, 231, 258, 263

Impact of color, 153

Implement, xvii, xix, xxi, 7, 9, 17-19, 36-37, 89, 128, 197, 281

Implicit scoring, 175

Impressions, 80, 130, 230, 259, 264, 268

Indifference, 22, 122-123, 255

Influencer, 47, 55, 66, 74, 87, 103, 135, 162, 191, 264

Innovation, 3, 30, 123, 141, 144-145, 158-160, 171, 178, 189-190, 191, 193, 199, 204-205, 212-215, 250, 264

Innovative, 21, 52, 160, 163, 186, 211, 215, 227

Inside out, xx, 6, 17, 121-122

Inspect what you expect, 137, 146, 191, 194, 195, 199, 200

Inspire, 20, 54, 122, 156, 177, 184, 188, 203, 204, 224, 263, 264, 272, 281

Instagram, 62, 65, 233, 241, 245, 264, 267

Intelligent marketing, xiii, xiv, xvi-xvii, xx-xxi, 2, 6, 144, 202, 263, 264, 275, 278, 281, 282

Intelligent positioning, 110, 145, 171, 204, 213-214

Interaction(s), xvi, xviii, 3, 33, 50, 54, 60, 63, 66, 90, 98, 101, 108-109, 111, 113, 120, 121, 125, 128, 144, 148, 164, 177, 183, 214-215, 236, 260, 262, 272

Interior design and signage, 42, 49, 157

International, 165-170, 203, 216, 224, 251

IP-based targeting, 70

Irresistible, 14, 140-141, 210, 257

Jingle, 112, 144-145, 171, 264

Key performance indicator(s) (KPIs), 17, 34, 69, 149, 152, 166, 177, 260, 264, 267

Keyword(s), 55, 231, 233, 242, 248, 271

Know, like, and trust, 12, 66, 84, 214

Knowledge and action, 18

Knowledge base, 197-198, 229

KPI(s), 17, 34, 69, 149, 152, 166, 177, 260, 264, 267

Last touch, 33, 69-70

Lateral thinking, 161, 184, 186, 195, 199

Laws and regulations 132, 165, 251

Lead magnet, 58, 265

Lead scoring, 136, 164, 172, 174-175, 230

Leads, 35, 58-60, 68-69, 100, 173, 174-175, 240, 264, 265, 270

Learning style(s), 14, 101, 188

Left Brain, 12, 265

Lifetime value (LTV), 9, 32, 35, 149-152, 163, 171, 173, 185, 260, 264

Likes and shares, 98

Linear, 33, 69, 157, 189

LinkedIn, 29, 62, 64, 70-73, 81, 233, 235, 245

List Building, 55, 62, 265

Logo, 10-11, 20, 30, 112, 144-145, 154, 171, 205, 256, 265, 266, 274

Longevity, 32, 148, 170-172

Loyalty and reward program, 98

LTV, (Customer lifetime value), 9, 32, 35, 149-152, 163, 171, 173, 185, 260, 264

Machine learning, 30, 75-76, 77-79, 80-81, 82, 90, 125, 158-160, 178, 244, 247, 261, 265, 267

Magalogs, 103-104

Managing preferences, 89

Market research, 2, 265

Marketing and sales funnels, 33, 54, 56-60, 66, 67, 77, 83, 164, 236, 266

Marketing attribution, 30-34, 255

Marketing automation, 35, 57, 59-60, 66-67, 78, 79, 99, 173, 175, 230, 231, 260, 266

Measure/measuring, xviii, 2, 9, 17, 26-27, 32-33, 34-35, 37, 39, 55, 63, 72, 99, 149, 152, 162, 177, 196, 198, 236, 238, 259, 260, 264, 269, 273

Measurement, 9, 27, 32, 55, 152, 236, 269
Media contacts, 47, 92, 191, 193, 266, 270
Meet prospects and customers where they are, 60, 88, 101, 109, 110, 114, 137, 185, 208, 210, 213-214
Meetups, 70, 128, 130, 134, 150, 164, 193
Membership(s), 52, 55, 57, 102, 128, 132, 137, 150, 163, 238, 243, 250
Meme, 10-11, 63, 144-145, 171, 266
Memorable, 2-3, 21, 48, 49, 85, 128, 129, 134, 146-148, 151, 156-157, 172, 209
Mentor/mentoring, 130, 161, 184, 198, 250, 281
Message bot(s), 56, 76, 80, 115, 119-120, 158, 198, 266
Metacognition, 187-188
Mindset, 7, 13-14, 36, 77, 93, 96-97, 101, 109, 112, 115, 120, 161, 184, 195-196, 262, 281
Modality, 14, 93, 101, 188
Monadic design, 28, 266
Motivate(s)/motivating, 7, 9, 10-11, 12, 14, 17, 18, 19-20, 23, 27, 29, 33, 36, 37-39, 42, 44, 46, 48, 50-51, 54, 57-58, 60, 61, 71, 77, 84-86, 88, 94-97, 100, 101, 103, 104, 105, 110, 114-115, 116-117, 118, 122-124, 125, 130-131, 132, 133-134, 136, 140, 145, 146-147, 154, 156-157, 164, 176, 185, 198, 214-215, 242, 256, 257, 263, 264, 265, 266, 268, 270, 271, 272, 273, 274
Multivariate/multivariate testing, 28, 30, 241, 267
Mystery shopping, 195-197
Nanocast, 8-9
Narrowcast, 8-9, 256
National Cyber Security Alliance, 15, 249
National Federation of Independent Business (NFIB), 250
National Retail Federation, 250
Native advertising, 55, 72, 86, 103, 212, 267
Native and social outstream advertising, 267
Natural language processing (NLP), 76, 81, 178, 247, 267
Net promoter score (NPS), 35, 264, 267
Neural network, 233, 261, 267
Nextdoor, 235, 245
NFTs, 139, 178, 267
Nimble, xviii, 83-84, 255
NLP (Natural language processing), 76, 81, 178, 247, 267
NPS (Net promoter score), 35, 264, 267
OOH (Out of home), 37-40, 43, 48, 51, 81
Opinion polls, 27-28, 111, 269
Optimize/optimization/optimizing, 9, 17, 34-35, 55, 62, 71, 80, 87, 157-160, 178-179, 229, 234, 237, 238, 242, 248, 259, 268, 271

Opt-in, 22, 58, 60-62, 68, 73-74, 98, 265, 267, 272
Opt out, 88-89
Out-of-home (OOH) advertising, 37-40, 43, 48, 51, 81
Pain point(s), 8-9, 12, 42, 45, 58, 72, 77-78, 85, 101, 104, 111, 112, 116, 118-119, 120, 123, 140, 147, 164, 197, 211, 256, 264, 268
Pay-per-click (PPC), 35, 72, 264, 268
Payroll percentage, 35, 177
Perception, 30, 131, 161-162, 196
Perception and reality, 161-162, 196
Personality of your business, 112-113
Personalization, 8, 42, 67, 80, 98-101, 123, 125, 152, 158, 172, 240, 262, 266, 268
Personalized, 54, 56, 72, 79-80, 81, 97, 98-100, 102, 116-117, 119-120, 123-124, 125, 152, 166-167, 172-173, 179, 237, 239, 242, 265
Pixels per inch (PPI), 261, 268
Pleasure points, 8-9, 12, 45, 72, 85, 112, 116, 140, 164, 256, 268
Podcast, 27, 31, 47, 52, 55, 82, 92, 103, 150-151, 226, 243, 247, 250
Pop-ups, 46-47, 61, 115, 182
Positioning, 110, 145, 171, 204, 213-214, 268, 280
Power of color, 14, 102, 110, 147, 153-155, 164, 173, 204-205, 208-209, 217-218
Powerful colors, 153
PPC (Pay-per-click), 35, 72, 264, 268
PPI (Pixels per inch), 261, 268

PR (Public Relations), 44-45, 47, 103, 129, 135, 151, 229, 243, 254, 257, 266, 269
Print publications, 104
Privacy concerns, 68, 88
Private labeling, 268
Product displays/experiences, 205-206, 208-209, 217-218
Profit(s)/profitable, xi, xii, xiv-xv, xvi-xix, xxi, 3-4, 6, 14, 18-19, 26, 27-28, 32, 34, 42, 48, 60, 66, 74, 75-76, 79, 81, 84, 103, 106, 108, 110, 124, 128, 146, 149, 153, 155-156, 162-165, 178, 183, 185, 191, 202, 206, 210, 222, 229, 230, 236, 254, 258, 262, 263, 264, 270, 273, 278
Programmatic digital advertising buying, 80, 268
Psychographic(s), 7, 8-9, 14, 36, 112, 149, 152, 164, 173, 193, 260, 268, 270, 273
Public Relations (PR), 44-45, 47, 103, 129, 135, 151, 229, 243, 254, 257, 266, 269
Push notifications, 56, 88, 242, 269
QR codes, 30, 40, 48, 234, 269, 278
Qualitative and quantitative, 269
Quality, xviii, xx, 17, 20, 21-22, 34, 35, 44, 51, 63, 99, 102, 104, 111, 119, 122, 131, 134, 138-139, 144-145, 148, 159, 162, 163, 171, 173-174, 175, 176, 178, 188, 199, 222, 224, 229, 230, 241, 242, 243, 247, 250, 260, 269, 271

Radio, 26-27, 32, 79, 103, 117, 135, 222, 269, 274

Radio DJ or on-air personality endorsements, 269

Ratings and reviews, 52, 86, 140, 144, 148, 182, 211, 269

Reach, xx, 13, 37, 39, 48, 52, 54, 56, 64, 73, 80, 84, 85-86, 114, 119, 139, 141, 152, 214, 230, 235, 249, 261, 262, 266, 268, 269, 274

Reciprocity, 123

Recycling, 136

Referral(s), xiv, xxi, 3-4, 9, 10, 13, 19, 23, 31-32, 35-36, 38, 54, 56, 77, 86, 88, 92, 98, 104, 113, 117, 118, 122, 130-131, 132, 133-134, 136, 140, 145, 148, 149, 152, 163, 165, 167, 171, 172, 175, 178, 185, 192, 193, 202, 244, 258, 260, 264, 265, 267, 269, 270, 273, 274, 279

Referral program, 32, 86, 98, 113, 130, 140, 145, 148, 163, 171, 172, 264, 270

Referral sites, 56, 175, 264, 265, 270

Relatable content, 101

Relationship(s), xviii, 7-8, 13, 16-17, 22, 32, 35, 43-45, 54, 57, 59, 60, 62-65, 66-67, 72, 74, 79, 92, 93-96, 101, 102, 108, 110-111, 118-119, 121, 122, 125, 128, 131, 135-136, 148, 149-152, 155, 160, 164-165, 167, 174-175, 185-186, 191-192, 198, 200, 240, 242, 243, 245, 258, 260, 265, 266, 269, 270, 281

Relationship builder/building, xviii, 7, 22, 43, 59, 63, 65, 74, 93, 110, 118, 128, 148, 152, 160, 185, 191-192, 270

Relationship building skills, 63, 128, 191-192, 270

Relevant, 33, 46, 81, 88, 92, 96-97, 120, 163, 171, 173, 215, 247, 281

Repeat purchases, xiv, xxi, 3, 4-5, 8, 10, 13, 22, 38, 51, 54, 77, 88, 90, 92, 104, 115, 122, 131, 134, 145, 152, 185, 202, 236, 258, 260, 270, 274, 279

Repetition, xvii-xviii, 6, 11, 12, 69, 85-87, 96, 147, 171, 202, 204-205, 213-214, 264, 266, 270, 273

Replicate, xix, 59, 75

Research, xxi, 2, 4-5, 7-9, 19, 58, 65, 85-87, 89, 94, 96-97, 99, 102, 112, 125, 129, 131, 153-154, 173, 186-187, 231, 233, 235, 242, 250, 265, 270, 273

Research and knowing, xxi, 2, 5, 7, 58, 173

Responsive search ads, 80, 89-90

Retargeting, 36, 55, 70, 86-87, 100, 241, 271

Retargeting advertising, 55, 86-87, 100, 271

Return on ad spend (ROAS), 35, 69-70, 264, 271

Return on investment (ROI), 35, 60, 166, 245, 264, 271, 275

Reuse, 136, 238

Review(s), xix, 9, 13, 17, 22, 48, 52, 86, 104, 105, 113, 135, 140, 144-145, 148, 152, 161, 163, 171, 182, 186, 210-211, 262, 269

Reward program, 98
Right brain, 12, 271
Right people in the right places, 198-199
Roadblocks, 23, 49, 54, 66, 121-122, 131, 133
ROAS (Return on ad spend), 35, 69-70, 264, 271
Rock-solid Guerrilla Marketing foundation, xv, xvii, 2, 4, 6, 277
ROI (Return on investment), 35, 60, 166, 245, 264, 271, 275
Sales funnel, 33, 54, 56-60, 66, 77, 83, 164, 236, 266
Sample(s), xix, 36, 39, 46, 47-48, 49, 51, 52, 58, 123, 129, 133, 140, 192, 238, 262, 273
Satisfied and delighted customers, 8, 109
SBA (Small Business Administration), 15, 177, 251
Search engine(s), xix, 55, 87, 103, 231, 242, 271
Search engine keyword(s), 54-55, 231, 233, 242, 248, 271
Search engine optimization (SEO), 55, 71, 87, 92, 242, 271
Segmentation, 36, 98, 112, 136, 163, 172-174, 175, 240, 241, 242, 268
Self-actualization, 114
Self-justification, 13, 20, 272
Sellable content, 97, 101-103, 178, 213-214
Senses, 14, 102, 110, 113, 147, 155-157, 205-206, 208-209, 217-218
Sensory experience, 155, 218

SEO (Search engine optimization), 54-55, 71, 87, 92, 242, 271
Sequential monadic design, 28, 266
Seven learning styles, 188
Sharable, 14, 47, 63, 86, 93-97, 156-157, 213-214
Sharing, 13, 22, 47, 52, 63, 71-73, 85-86, 93-97, 104, 105-106, 120, 128, 130, 135, 151, 156, 215, 223, 224, 228, 229, 233, 241, 269
Sharing personality types, 94-95
Ship internationally, 169
Skilled debating, 190
Skilled thinking, 101, 178-179, 186-191, 194-195, 199
Small Business & Entrepreneurship Council, 250
Small Business Administration (SBA), 15, 177, 251
SMBs, xiv, xvi-xviii, 15, 44, 138-139, 177, 191, 248, 272, 275, 278
Social badges, 105
Social commerce, 64, 65-66, 103, 105
Social desire, 105-106
Social linking, 73-74
Social live broadcast, 8, 103, 146, 256
Social media monitoring, 56, 87, 272
Social outstream, 267
Social selling, 59, 62-65, 70-71, 73, 105
Social Selling Index, 64, 73
Soft sell/soft-selling, 20, 63-64, 104, 263, 272
Solopreneur(s), xiv, xvi, xviii, 272, 278
Solution(s), 39, 58, 60, 64, 76, 77, 101, 104, 108-109, 118, 125, 137-

139, 147, 150, 160-161, 178, 189-191, 197, 224, 226, 227, 228, 231, 237, 240, 247, 260, 268, 270, 272
Spin-off, 146, 208-210
Split test/split testing, 27-30, 33, 55, 57, 60, 62, 98, 123, 154, 240, 241, 267, 269, 272
Sponsorships, 272
Spotlight, 8, 134-136, 151, 156
Squeeze page, 60, 272
Stories that sell, 272
Strategy, xiii, xiv, xvi-xix, xxi, 3-6, 26, 42, 166, 168, 202, 207, 219, 261, 263, 272, 273, 274, 279
Street teams, xix, 43, 46, 51, 273
Strong foundation of Guerrilla Marketing success, xv, xvii, 2, 4, 6, 277
Subconscious/subconsciously, 12-13, 17, 38, 84, 117, 121, 182, 187, 273
Subliminal marketing, 146, 155, 273
Subscription(s), 57-58, 93, 102, 131-132, 134, 137, 163, 170, 210, 212-214, 228, 254, 271
Superb listener, 192-194
Supercharged details, xix, 18-19, 48, 60, 74, 153, 155, 183, 185
Survey(s), 9, 27-29, 37, 93, 98, 102, 105, 111, 123, 154, 164, 166, 173, 175, 186, 200, 225, 229, 237, 240, 241, 245, 246, 248, 265, 266, 267, 268, 269
Tactic(s), xi, xiii, xiv-xv, xvi-xxi, 4-5, 8, 17-19, 26, 31-33, 34, 54, 59, 68-69, 70-73, 85-86, 92, 99, 103-104, 108, 122, 124, 128, 133, 141, 144, 146, 148, 164, 170-172, 174,

175, 178, 202, 204-205, 208, 210, 213, 217, 236, 249, 255, 257, 262, 263, 264, 265, 266, 271, 273, 275, 277, 278-279, 282-283
Tagline, 11, 112, 144-145, 171, 256, 273
Take action, 7, 11, 18, 37, 38, 101, 133, 140, 183, 186, 193, 195, 257
Target audience, 4-5, 29, 263, 265, 273
Target market, 2, 4, 268, 270, 273
Technographics, 36, 173, 273
Television, 27, 31-32, 47, 52, 103, 135, 254
Testimonials, 13, 52, 86, 93, 97, 104, 113, 135, 140, 145, 148, 151, 171, 273
Testing, 27-30, 33, 34, 36-37, 55, 57, 60, 62, 77, 80, 84, 98, 123-124, 154-155, 190, 240, 241, 267, 269, 272
The International Association of Privacy Professionals (IAPP), 251
Third-party selling platforms, 103, 167-168, 169
Thirst for knowledge, 197
TikTok, 62, 65, 83, 245
Timing, 37, 60, 61-62, 68-69, 84-85, 87, 116, 141, 280
Top-of-mind, 11, 29, 47, 87, 130, 146, 148, 150, 209, 273
Touch point(s), 109
Tracking, 4, 9, 34, 60, 69-70, 90, 120, 137, 149, 152, 168-169, 202, 226, 228, 229, 239, 256, 259, 260, 262, 271, 273

Transparency, 137-138
Trust, xiv, xxi, 4, 12, 38, 51, 66, 74, 84, 90, 92, 97, 103-104, 113, 134, 135, 145, 147-148, 153, 167, 176, 192, 222, 228, 233, 235, 249, 256, 258, 259, 265, 270, 279
Twitter, 56, 62, 230, 233, 234, 236, 240, 242, 245, 246, 264, 267
Two-faced business, 121
Typeface, 144-145, 154-155, 171
Unconscious, 12-13, 162, 182-183, 196, 257, 273
Unconventional, xi, xiii, xiv, xvi, 42, 46, 52, 157, 184-186, 202, 208-210, 263, 274, 279
Understand their needs, 114
Unexpected, 15, 46, 48, 84, 116, 133-134, 147, 156, 194
Uniforms, 3, 11, 21, 48, 108, 113, 204-205
Unique Selling Proposition (USP), xxi, 2-3, 5, 42, 48, 64, 72, 75, 77-78, 86, 92, 102, 104, 113, 128, 130, 140, 144, 147, 171, 197, 202, 264, 266, 273, 274
Unlimited, 131-132, 225, 226, 234, 241, 246, 248
Unsubscribe, 88-89, 228
Upcycling, 136
Upgrade opportunities, 124, 145, 171, 274
URL(s), 29-30, 71, 100, 243, 246, 269, 274
USP (Unique selling proposition), xxi, 2-3, 5, 42, 48, 64, 72, 75, 77-78, 86, 92, 102, 104, 113, 128, 130, 140, 144, 147, 171, 197, 202, 264, 266, 273, 274
Validation, 13, 94-96, 117, 135, 187
Valuable content, 72, 73, 97, 151
Video, xv, xxi, 8, 10-11, 29-30, 38-39, 52, 55, 73, 79-80, 81, 82, 87, 92-93, 100, 102-103, 139, 152, 158-159, 182, 224, 226, 227, 229, 236, 241, 243, 244, 247, 254, 259, 261, 262, 264, 267, 274, 277, 280
Viral, 54-55, 87, 243, 274
Virtual reality (VR), 49-50, 178
Visual, 82, 112, 153, 155-156, 188, 218, 225, 226, 233, 242, 246, 248, 256, 266
Warranties, guarantees, and service programs, 52, 129, 132
Webinar(s), 45, 55, 102, 150, 229, 250, 274
What makes this volume of books unique?, xiv-xv
What you stand for, 148
WhatsApp, 56, 65
White labeling, 102, 274
Why people share, 93-94
Win-win, 47, 135, 191
Your ideal customers, 9, 31-33, 36, 135-136, 149, 152, 162-165, 172, 175, 176-178, 196
Your podcast, 27, 31, 47, 52, 55, 82, 92, 103, 150-151, 226, 243, 247, 250
YouTube, 33, 56, 65, 233, 264

www.ingramcontent.com/pod-product-compliance
Lightning Source LLC
Chambersburg PA
CBHW020854180526
45163CB00007B/2499